Eric MacLeod was born in Dingwall in the Highla... early career was in accountancy, but he made a life change at the age of thirty to become a crofter and self-employed in a variety of ways. Since leaving the croft he has worked as a business adviser across the Highlands, and now runs his own business in horse feed supplements. He lives in the area of his birth with his wife Ruth.

Very Best Wishes

EMacLeod

THE KERRACHER MAN

Eric MacLeod

SANDSTONEPRESS
HIGHLAND | SCOTLAND

THE KERRACHER MAN

First published in Great Britain by Sandstone Press Ltd
PO Box 5725, 1 High Street, Dingwall, Ross-shire,
IV15 9WJ, Scotland

Printed 2008 (four times), 2009, 2010

Copyright © Eric MacLeod 2007

The moral right of Eric MacLeod to be identified as the
author of this work has been asserted in accordance with
the Copyright, Design and Patents Act, 1988

Editor: Moira Forsyth
Maps by Ruthie MacLeod

ISBN-10: 1-905207-15-8
ISBN-13: 978-1-905207-15-2

Designed and typeset in ITC Giovanni by River Design, Edinburgh

Scottish **Arts** Council

The publisher acknowledges subsidy from the Scottish Arts
Council towards the publication of this volume

Printed and bound by J F Print, Yeovil, Somerset

SANDSTONEPRESS
CONTEMPORARY QUALITY READING

www.sandstonepress.com

For Ruth, who made it all possible.

THE KERRACHER MAN

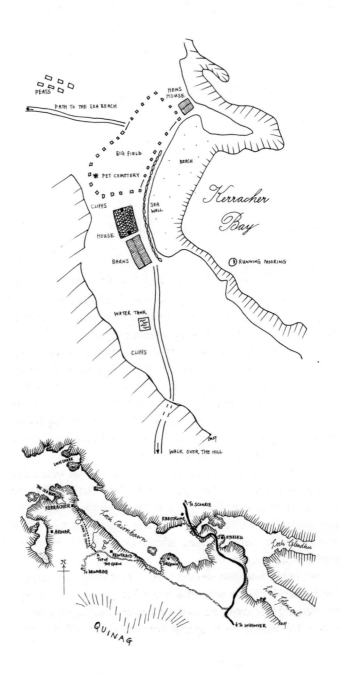

PEATS

PATH TO THE SEA BEACH

HENS HOUSE

BIG FIELD

BEACH

PET CEMETERY

Kerracher
Bay

CLIFFS

SEA WALL

HOUSE

BARNS

① RUNNING MOORING

WATER TANK

CLIFFS

WALK OVER THE HILL

LOCH SHARK

THE SEA BEACH

KERRACHER

TO SCOURIE

KERRATRAID

TO KYLESKU

Loch Cairnbawn

ARDVAR

RENTRAID

Loch Glendhu

TOP OF THE GLEN

KERGOWN

TO DRUMBEG

Loch Glencoul

TO LOCHINVER

QUINAG

THE CROFT IN THE BAY

'How would you like to live there?' I asked Ruth as the motor launch chugged out of the bay. Gradually we pulled away and the derelict house sitting on the shore receded, mysterious in the grey of a damp November day.

The house was on the croft where my father had been brought up, in a remote corner of north-west Sutherland. Sitting close to the water's edge, it was tucked into a bay backed by a 200-foot rise of cliff and hill. To its right a flat area of semi-arable land ran alongside the beach for about 200 yards until it came to a rocky outcrop that disappeared into the loch. There was no other dwelling for miles.

I had visited this place as a child. That was when my grandfather, grandmother and Uncle Jim had lived there with their cows, hens, collie dog and fishing boats. Now they were all gone and my father was visiting to take stock of his former family home, which he had just inherited from his brother Jim.

My father had just resumed his career after a retirement that lasted all of one week. He was taking a day off to check the state of the croft, so that he could decide what to do with it. My sister Jean, pregnant with her first child, was also with us, sharing my nostalgia. The fifth person in the boat was its owner, the proprietor of the inn at Kylesku, Willie Moffat. Willie was a few years younger than my father, and had known him as a boy. The boat was necessary because there was no road. To get to the croft you faced a walk over the hill of a mile and a half, or a journey by boat from nearby Kylesku.

The house had been neglected over recent years, a result of my uncle's age and ill health. My father lived eighty miles away in Dingwall, so he was going to find it difficult to give the house the attention it needed. The owner of the estate surrounding the property had made him an offer, but that was not an option any of us wanted to consider.

So the question I asked my wife – *how would you like to live there* – was meant just to start a family discussion, now we had seen the place. Of course it didn't make sense for *us* to live there. I was a management accountant with a rising career in an international company, and we had two young daughters, Clare and Ruthie, aged three and five. Besides, Ruth had always been a town dweller. She was brought up in Fife, then during our marriage had lived in London, Chester, Johannesburg and Reading. The nearest shop to Kerracher was six miles away over a hill and a twisting single-track road, and then it was only a single village shop and post office. We were even further from the primary school.

And yet the idea which had begun to creep into my mind must have taken root in hers too. And perhaps my father had caught a glimmer of it already. As soon as she answered, he broke into a broad grin, as he began to light his pipe to warm him on the damp journey back down the loch to Kylesku.

Ruth gazed at the now receding croft house.
'I would love to,' she said.

———

Later, relaxing in the warmth of the Kylesku Hotel bar, we started to discuss the possibility of living at Kerracher. My father was a mild-mannered man who kept his own counsel, but he did agree that he was content to let Ruth and me have Kerracher if we wanted to make it our permanent home. My sister Jean egged us on. We were still enthusiastic about it when we got back to Dingwall.

My mother was horrified, and so was Ruth's. Indeed we soon discovered this was the reaction we would get from most people. Neither of our mothers could understand why we would give up such a comfortable and secure life for something akin to living in a cave.

It was some time before I realised where this attitude came from. Both had been brought up between the World Wars when there weren't many opportunities for ordinary folk, especially in the Highlands. Their generation had worked hard to give their children an education that would lead to professional jobs and comfortable lives. They were bewildered when we chose to give that up and go back to the disadvantages of the past.

Somehow, as we went on talking about it, we found we had made a decision. We were going to live at Kerracher. The first person we had to inform was Lord Buxton, the owner of Ardvar Estate on which the croft stood. He lived in rural Norfolk and we in Berkshire, but as soon as our letter reached him he got in touch, wanting to visit. Kerracher was the only croft left on the estate and we thought he must be keen to meet his tenants.

We arranged for him to visit one evening after the girls were in bed, and it all started well.

'What a lovely home you have here,' he said, then, seeing a photograph of the girls, 'and what lovely children.'

But he didn't take long to get to his point.

'You're seriously thinking of exchanging this beautiful house for the house at Kerracher?'

We assured him that was exactly what we planned.

'And how are you going to earn a living there?' he asked. 'What is it that you do at the moment, Eric?'

I explained that although I had a good job with excellent prospects, our present life wasn't what we really wanted. We both saw Kerracher as an opportunity to change the way we lived.

'But there aren't any opportunities at Kerracher for someone with *your* skills,' he pointed out. 'How are you going to earn a living?'

'I'll have to learn new skills. Until I do we'll live off our savings.'

He gave me up for the moment, and turned to Ruth. 'How will you cope with no running water or toilet facilities? How are you going to manage washing clothes? I expect you have a washing machine here. And what will you do without electricity or heating?'

'I'm sure I'll cope,' Ruth said, 'just like Eric's uncle did and his family before him.'

Then came his clinching argument. From the mantelpiece he picked up the girls' photograph. Two angelic faces smiled out at him.

'Are you willing to risk the lives of these two beautiful children?'

'We don't see it as risking their lives,' I told him firmly.

'Well, you will be if something goes wrong. There's no road to the place. If you had an emergency with one of the girls I hate to think of the consequences.'

'Eric's grandparents brought up a young family at Kerracher, and they all survived,' Ruth retorted.

'But that was in days when it was *normal* to live in such circumstances.'

'Are you saying it isn't normal to live at a place like Kerracher?'

'Well, the house is certainly not equipped for normal living.'

We reminded him again that people had lived there before – why should it be any different now?

'They were equipped for it. You're a modern family and you haven't had their upbringing. You know, it would be irresponsible of me to let you take these two young and vulnerable children to such a place.' Frowning, apparently full of anxiety, he looked down at us. 'It would be on my conscience if anything went wrong. I don't want to see you both making the biggest mistake of your lives.'

I stood up and took the photograph from him.

'Thank you for your concern, but we've made our decision. We've given it a great deal of thought, and we're going to take our chances.' I replaced the photograph on the mantelpiece. 'We look forward to being your neighbours when you visit your Highland estate.'

He could see there was no point in going on, but he left us amicably enough, confirming his willingness to advise us. He even wished us success. But when he had gone, Ruth and I were even more resolved to go through with the move and to make it work.

Later, we suspected Lord Buxton's reasons may not have been wholly altruistic. He had offered my father £1000 for the house, which no doubt would have ended up as a holiday home to complement his lodge about a mile distant.

Over the next few months we began to make preparations for the move, researching the area through every means we could, though we were 700 miles away. There were no web sites to visit in those days, so the process was quite laborious and we had to write a great many letters. However, after about six months' investigation and reflection, we felt we were ready.

Up to that point it was all speculative – no more than talking and planning. Giving up my secure job was the first irrevocable step. I wrote my resignation letter to the chief accountant. As word rapidly went round the office, I was met with astonishment and disbelief, even with some resentment from the finance director, who felt I was throwing away the considerable investment the company had made in me.

In the middle of my final interview with him, I suddenly recalled a conversation a couple of years earlier when I was the company's branch accountant in Johannesburg. On a visit there the director had said, 'No doubt one day you'll be looking to fill my shoes.' I agreed at the time but in fact those very words planted a seed of doubt in my mind. Now I knew that the answer was actually *No*.

Only one voice said, 'Go for it, lad. There's plenty here that would like the idea of doing what you're planning – except they'd be too scared.'

Peter was the only person at work who actively encouraged me. He even took to bringing in information about machinery which we might make use of. He reckoned that a small tracked Kubota digger would be the ideal machine. He was right, but unfortunately the cost was prohibitive. Ahead of his time, he also suggested wind power for generating electricity. I did follow up on that while still working in Reading, as the University was researching it even then, but, again, the cost was out of our league.

The last day at work came very quickly. I was given a Reader's Digest DIY manual, a wad of cash and a 'Best of Luck' card from all my colleagues. I made my farewells, then emerged into the sunshine of Reading and the outside world.

It felt unreal. I was no longer an employee. I had no job to go to. As I stood still for a moment in the street, just outside the office, a crowd of conflicting emotions enveloped me – sadness at leaving good friends, a sense of freedom in casting off shackles. But also a feeling of being lost, adrift from the system that had sustained me since leaving University.

Then the heavy burden of responsibility hit me. My family were now wholly dependent on what I could achieve at Kerracher. It was like the first step off the cliff when you abseil. Was I brave or foolhardy to take such a risk?

I wandered for a while through the centre of Reading with the sun glittering on the windows of the tall buildings and the mid-week morning shoppers hurrying past. But they were all oblivious.

Ruth and I had to get on with our lives on the basis of the decision we had made and all the planning that had gone into it. Time to test the strength of my own convictions. There was nothing else for it.

For a few panic-stricken moments that was all that stopped me from running down the High Street and back to the tower-block sanctuary of the organisation which had looked after me for the past eight years.

WE PLAN TRANSPORTATION

After selling our house and saying goodbye to our many friends in the south, we packed our belongings into a hired truck and headed for the far north of Scotland. It was the hot summer of 1976.

The journey in itself was an adventure, especially for our cat, Penny, who sat on the children's knees the whole way. Then, in Dingwall, Penny was dispatched to a cattery and the furniture to a local removals company. Leaving my family with relatives in Fife, I drove the truck back to Reading and returned with a second-hand Land Rover suitable for travelling on remote single-track roads.

An aunt and uncle of mine who lived in Argyll had kindly offered a caravan for us to live in while we renovated the house at Kerracher. Though in good condition it was far from new and had been parked for some time. With a bit of manoeuvring we hitched it to the Land Rover and soon we were on the road north to Fort William and along the shores of Loch Ness. We reached Inverness, then turned west and north to Ullapool and eventually Kylesku, all at a snail's pace. As the front wheel bearings and track rods on the Land Rover had almost gone, it was a journey of agonising slowness, like dragging an army tank along a main road.

By the time we reached Ullapool the traffic had thinned, which made driving easier. The day was hot and sunny and north of the town we began to notice a difference in the landscape. The hills became rockier, higher and more barren. They weren't as green as further south and there were few signs of population. The odd house or two was placed near the roadside but they were so far apart it was clear that this was an area of few people, unlike anywhere we had lived in our previous life.

The girls brightened up, and began to absorb this new landscape. At the brow of each hill came the same questions –

'Are we there yet?'

'Is it Kerracher over the *next* hill?'

We breasted a good many hills before eventually reaching Kylesku, where we parked in a roadside clearing. We got out of the car and headed up a grassy rise. It was a steep climb but when we reached the top the scene was breathtaking.

A very blue Loch Cairnbawn stretched out in front of us, sunshine dancing and sparkling across its surface. The hills climbed from the edges of the loch, rolling back on the right into the Duke of Westminster's estates and on the left becoming the blue-black shape of Quinag, the hill whose shape was to become so familiar.

'There it is.' I pointed towards the horizon where the loch met the sea and merged into the skyline.

'I can't see anything,' said Ruthie, squinting in the sunlight.

'Nor me,' Clare chimed.

Ruth kneeled down beside the girls and pulled them close. With her arm outstretched she guided their gaze to a small white dot in the distance.

'Look where my finger is pointing. Can you see a little white house at the end of the loch?'

Ruthie peered again. 'Yes I can see it!'

'Well, that's where we're going to live.'

'Yes. Yes, I can see it too!' Clare didn't want to be left out, whether she was seeing it or not.

I got down in the grass beside them and the four of us sat in the warmth of the sun, gazing out to where we were going to make our home.

'Where is the road we go on to get there?' Ruthie asked after a moment.

'Well, that's the problem.' I said. 'There is no road to get there.'

'Do we go on a big ferry?'

'I don't know yet. But we'll get there, don't worry.'

Kylesku was the last staging post on our way to the house. We now had a three-mile stretch of water between us and Kerracher.

We knew the house would be uninhabitable. It had been built in that curious old Victorian-Highland way of tucking the dwelling into a wall of rock and facing north so that it was not exposed to the prevailing west winds and rain but also, as a result, didn't get much sun. This made the house dank inside with that fusty smell houses acquire when they haven't been lived in for a while. It had stood empty for over a year at the mercy of the West Highland climate. The remains of a sheep lay waiting for us in the floorless living room.

All that was ahead of us: our first task was not to make the house habitable, but to find a way of transporting the caravan to Kerracher along Loch Cairnbawn from Kylesku. We spoke to the head ferryman for the Kylesku to Kylestrome crossing. He thought it might be possible to hire the ferry after hours and take it up to Kerracher. That was nipped in the bud when I applied to the council in Inverness. The words *risk*, *safety* and *insurance* all rang in my ears. There was no point in protesting, so I sat down to reconsider.

Perhaps the army or navy could helicopter it in if they were up on manoeuvres? As they weren't planning to be in the area in the immediate future, that one was ruled out too. After discussion with some of the local fishermen we decided it might also be too problematic to try to load it across the decks of a creel boat.

In the end the best and simplest way was to build a raft, load the caravan on from the ferry slipway and tow it.

My only tools were a bush saw, hammer, rule and a varied assortment of screwdrivers. But first to the drawing board. The design was simple – a cage of two-by-two lengths of wood, decked with four-by-two planks, containing six-teen empty forty-gallon drums. These were all materials we could re-use in the renovation of Kerracher.

It didn't take long for the local population to take us into their small community, not so much because of our wacky idea of towing a caravan to Kerracher, but because I was the nephew of Jim Kerracher and even better the grand-son of the 'Kerracher Man'. Many of the locals remembered my grandfather even though he had passed on some twenty years earlier. So I was almost instantly accepted, especially as I was planning to live there and introduce a young family to the area.

We collected wood for the raft from one of the many suppliers in Inverness and loaded it onto the now repaired and fully functioning Land Rover. Bouncing along a rough road, though, with a load of timber that extended over the cab of the vehicle, did give the roof some additional contours.

After making enquiries in Inverness about the supply of second-hand forty-gallon drums I realised it wasn't going to be easy to lay my hands on them. Then I discovered the local council roads team had some in their yard. One late afternoon we stopped off at the foreman's house. This was another Mr MacLeod, known as Ian Strathcroy, the name referring to the place where he and his family had always lived.

The door was opened by a rugged individual with a very serious expression. 'Yes. Can I help you?'

I'd barely introduced myself when his face broke into a broad smile. He grabbed my hand, shaking it firmly and announcing to someone behind him in the house, 'It's the new young Kerracher man.'

A smiling woman, Ian's wife Katie, joined us at the door. She shook my hand in welcome, then peering over my shoulder, she spotted Ruth and the girls. Beckoning them in, she said, 'You'll come in for a cup of tea – and I'm sure the girls would like some juice.'

She wouldn't take no for an answer, so all six of us were soon seated in a cosy room in front of a tremendous spread of home baking. I explained that I was building a raft to take our caravan down the loch to Kerracher, and that I was looking for sixteen used forty-gallon drums. Alistair wanted to know what we planned to do at Kerracher, so I explained that we would renovate the house, then work the croft as much as possible.

'Are you planning to get animals? How many sheep are you allowed on Kerracher?'

So the conversation moved away from the forty-gallon drums and it was nearly two hours before we eventually managed to excuse ourselves. At the door, Alistair suddenly said, 'I'll get the men to drop off the drums by the caravan next week.'

He wouldn't hear of any payment. 'Just leave them in the same spot when you've finished with them,' he said.

As we drove away I said to Ruth, 'He knew I was going to ask for them.'

'I doubt if you can do anything here without people knowing about it!'

As we were building the raft on the foreshore at the Kylesku Fishermen's pier, we attracted a great deal of interest from the creel fishermen who tied up there. To begin with there was some amusement and head tapping when the fishermen discovered an ex-city slicker with accountant's hands, who hadn't done a day's DIY in his life, attempting to build a raft from old oil drums, wood and a box of six-inch nails. Many times during that unusually long hot summer I was asked if I knew something that everybody else didn't. Was there going to be a lot of rain coming?

This was how we met Roddy MacLeod and his wife Joan, who were to become lifelong friends. Roddy hailed from Scalpay, one of the smaller of the Outer Hebridean islands. He had previously worked as a lighthouse-man at Stoer where he met Joan. After Roddy left the lighthouse service they moved to Kylesku where they built their own house and purchased a creel boat to catch prawns and lobsters. It wasn't long before we were invited to tea and scones in their bungalow high above the harbour.

The talk as always came round to how we were going to *get* to Kerracher, never mind how we were going to survive there. I had just bought a sixteen-foot open clinker boat with an eight-horsepower outboard engine. Roddy pointed out, kindly enough, that there was no way it would pull a raft decked with a twenty-foot caravan. He persuaded me to accept his offer to tow the raft and caravan to Kerracher on his way out to sea. I also accepted a good deal of advice and help with building the raft and preparing for the sea journey.

At the same time as building the raft, we plied between Kylesku and Kerracher in our small boat as often as we could. When I felt I'd got the hang of steering this craft through the straits at Kylesku and down the open Loch Cairnbawn, I began to see how quickly I could make the journey. We grew tanned and healthy that summer with our open boat journeys. The girls loved the adventure and soon became seafarers, but Ruth was different: she found it hard to remain calm even when the loch was a sheet of glass.

On these journeys we got to know the character of the hillsides rising around the loch, and the changing colours of the heather and trees. The aspects and contours of the rocky shoreline were becoming familiar. We had begun to learn the land we were to live in.

On one of these forays we witnessed an odd occurrence that led to the second of our lifelong friendships along the loch side. As I was approaching the bay at Kerracher I noticed some activity on the hillside to the west of the loch.

Going up the path from the house was a small group of youngsters struggling up the hill with what looked like creels on their backs. I recognised the creels – old-fashioned home-made ones, which had belonged to my Uncle Jim and were stacked in the barns. I cut the engine of the boat to listen to what they were saying: I had discovered that sound carries very well across water. I couldn't quite make out the words, but the voices were distinctively English. My first instinct was to get to shore and confront them but I was too far away and would have had to find a place to moor the boat before I could make chase.

On return to Kylesku I discovered that the culprits were more than likely a family who had a holiday home at Reintraid, situated on the same side of the loch as Kerracher, but nearer Kylesku by a couple of miles.

We happened to have a visit from Lord Buxton's factor that evening. Stan Roy was an ex-policeman who had retired to the area with his wife Moira. In his quiet manner, he assured us we had nothing to worry about. The rowdy bunch of thieves belonged to the family of Lord Jellicoe who owned the house at Reintraid. They came up regularly and were well known. I agreed not to pursue the matter further as long as they returned the creels. Time they realised that Kerracher was not a derelict property that anyone could 'plunder'. The MacLeods were once more in residence.

The following evening was hot and muggy and we were imprisoned in the caravan because of the midges, which were to spoil many summer evenings. There was nothing else for it but to retreat into the caravan and get a board game out. We were engrossed in our game when there was a knock at the door and Ruth, rather reluctantly, went to open it.

'Good evening.' The speaker accompanied his words with several slaps to his own face. 'I'm George Jellicoe. I'd be most grateful if I could have a few words with you.' There followed even more frenzied slaps.

Ruth hurriedly invited him in, to prevent the whole caravan being invaded by swarms of midges heading for another four warm-blooded victims.

'I do apologise for interrupting your evening.' *Slap, slap, slap*. A portly man in a loose-fitting cardigan and slippers extended his hand as I stood up to welcome him.

The resulting handshakes developed into something like a bizarre jungle ritual when two tribes meet. Our free hands went flying back and forth in a series of seemingly well co-ordinated self-inflicted slaps.

'Please have a seat,' I said and beckoned our visitor to a space on our seating. (*Slap – rub – slap*).

'Thank you' – *slap* – 'but I am expected down at the inn for dinner – *rub* – 'and won't take your time up' – *slap* – 'I've come to apologise to you for the' – *slap* – *swish* – 'misbehaviour of our young gang' – *swish* – *slap* – *rub*. 'They'll put your creels back tomorrow' – *slap* – 'and as we are now neighbours, my wife Phillipa and I would love you to come and have supper with us some evening.' (*Slap – slap – slap*).

'That would be lovely,' answered Ruth, flailing her arms about her head in a mad frenzy.

'Phillipa will pop down tomorrow' – *slap* – 'and arrange a day with you' – *slap* – *rub* – said George, desperately trying to find enough space in the now claustrophobic caravan to ward off the invaders.

The girls were beginning to groan quietly in the background, rubbing their heads in desperation. The caravan was definitely over-populated with five manic human bodies competing with a hundred thousand midges, apparently breeding fast.

'I must fly' – *swish* – *slap* – *swish* – said George, straining at the door handle in an attempt to make a quick exit. The door didn't respond – there was a knack to opening it. There was almost a cry of anguish from him as Ruth, in getting to the jammed door, performed a weird dance around him, each flapping their arms like drunken windmills.

The door opened and shut as our visitor exited so quickly it seemed like a disappearing trick accompanied by a puff of smoke. Unfortunately the puff of smoke was another cloud of incoming midges.

However, it wasn't as large as the cloud that engulfed Lord Jellicoe as he ran down the road towards the Kylesku Hotel.

A CARAVAN ON A RAFT

Within a couple of weeks the raft was complete. Roddy explained it would be best to launch it on a high tide, and fortunately there was a spring tide coming up. We scarcely realised then how vital a part of our lives the state of the tide was to become.

The plan was to position the raft at the top of the ferry slipway in the evening and then run the caravan onto it and secure it. At the top of the tide next morning we could tow it off and along the loch.

The evening was thick with midges, but that didn't deter the whole population of Kylesku coming out to help. I found myself relegated to a minor role as the task took on a life of its own. People I hardly knew were securing the caravan, and telling everyone else what to do. If I'd disappeared into the hotel bar I don't think I'd have been missed. It was tempting.

The caravan was eventually secured on the raft and we left it at the top of the slipway, looking high and precarious. I heard a few mutterings about how it would all end in disaster if the wind got up and the raft was caught in the vicious tidal flow through the narrows.

There is a little part of the Highlander, and indeed most of us, that almost wishes for the worst to happen. Perhaps that's why we had been invited to call into the BBC radio office in Inverness once the journey was done to tell the tale.

The following morning was as still as you can get in that part of the world. The loch was like glass and there was not a breath of wind – perfect conditions for launching and towing a raft. However, they were the worst possible conditions for human kind. An early West Highland morning, warm and muggy with absolutely no air movement, means midges by the millions.

Roddy, with Don, his crew, came round to the slipway with his creel boat and tied a rope between the boat and the raft. As the tide came to its peak the water inched its way up the side of the raft. Inch by inch it came off the slipway and began to float. The first critical moment was over. I was no engineer, but with advice and a few sums, I had calculated the number of drums needed on the basis of the weight and size of the caravan. Too heavy and water would lap over the deck. Too light and the drums would sit too far out of the water, risking it tipping over.

It had worked: the whole unit was sitting pretty in the water with the raft taking the weight of the caravan very evenly. It looked quite majestic in the early morning haze. The water shimmered as Roddy took the strain on the towrope and gently pulled the raft away from the slipway. The whole village stood watching and waving us away.

Roddy was a careful man who understood his sea and its ways. Because flow turns to ebb at a slow and deliberate pace, he kept both boat and raft near the slipway, watching and waiting until he could catch the tide's turn. Only then did he move the boat out into the main stream and catch the rip going out to sea. He caught it perfectly and what could have been a difficult and hazardous stretch of water through the narrows was managed smoothly. He turned into the expanse of Loch Cairnbawn and headed for Kerracher.

Ruth and the girls waited at Kylesku with Roddy's wife Joan while I trailed Roddy's *Fortitude*, in our own boat. The journey took an uneventful hour, giving me plenty of time to reflect on the larger journey we were now embarking upon. I really hadn't a clue what was ahead, other than that we were going to try to live where no modern family had survived. I was beginning to realise how much we had to learn, especially about the sea – living on it and indeed from it.

We had planned to get to work on the house first, to make it habitable. In the meantime we had only a cramped caravan to live in. That was a real challenge, but the girls saw it as a huge adventure and that, more than anything, lifted our spirits when it looked a bit too daunting.

There was no going back. We had to rise to the challenges ahead.

When we reached Kerracher the tide was still high enough to float the raft up onto the beach. However, that was not high enough for future tides. So the *Fortitude* was moored in the bay and Roddy and Don transferred to my small boat. Don was an ex-naval man and extremely practical. With the raft placed at the bow of my boat we pushed it up to the edge of the tide, far enough to have its front end sitting on the beach. Don and Roddy then created a complicated system of ropes and pulleys, which they anchored to a stanchion, already secured in the earth high above the beach. My grandfather had no doubt inserted it there many years before for that specific purpose.

I got the ramps for the caravan into place and then all three of us pulled on a rope, tug-of-war style, to ease the caravan off the raft and up onto the higher area of the beach. With hard work, sweat, and much cursing of midges we eventually secured the caravan where we had planned it to sit, tucked nicely into a corner. There it was sheltered from west winds by a small cliff at the back and from east winds by a promontory on that side. Mission accomplished!

Roddy and Don then set sail for the waters of the Minch and I for the calm of Kylesku. That afternoon we called in at the BBC radio studio in Inverness, as agreed. The trip also gave us the opportunity to visit my parents in Dingwall.

The interview at the radio station was something of an anticlimax.

'What problems did you encounter taking your caravan on a raft out to sea on Loch Cairnbawn?'

'None.'

'Did any ropes come undone?'

'No.'

'Did the wind get up?'

'No.'

'Did any sea water get into the caravan?'

'No, it's as dry as a bone.'

The interviewer was not really interested in finding out how a young family intended to meet the challenge of surviving in such a place. He just wanted to know what had gone wrong!

The next stage was to organise the delivery of our furniture to Kylesku and this time Roddy decided his boat would suffice to ferry it to Kerracher. The removals company which had stored our belongings duly deposited all of them at the top of the ferry slipway at Kylesku and left them there for the world to view. The world included many interested tourists. Fortunately, that Saturday afternoon was another glorious summer's day as we needed two trips to finish the job.

Loading the boat at Kylesku wasn't difficult as there were willing extra hands to help, and the furniture was on the flat slipway with an easy walk to the boat. At Kerracher it was a different matter, with new problems we would have to get used to.

To begin with, the furnishings and boxes had to be transferred from Roddy's boat to our small open boat and taken ashore. The tide of course does not keep still, so it wasn't long before we had a tough walk up the sloping beach. It was a long hot afternoon and we worked well into the evening. But Highland summer evenings are long and full of light. To the seagulls circling above we must have seemed like a colony of ants scurrying back and forth between the shoreline and the house.

Eventually we cleared Roddy's boat and at the end of a beautiful and eventful day we waved a very grateful good bye to him, Joan and their daughter Donella as they steamed off back down the loch towards Kylesku. With the house now jam packed with our belongings and Ruthie and Clare tucked into their beds in the caravan, Ruth and I lingered on the doorstep. The night was still with only the sound of the water lapping the shore. In the peace and solitude I whispered my original question to Ruth,

'How would you like to live here?'

'I'm going to love it,' she answered.

THE BARE NECESSITIES

'Where have you been?'

'I was getting the water.'

'How long does it take you to get a kettle-full of water?'

'As long as it takes for the kettle to fill up.'

'But it's only along the path.'

'Yes, but I had to wait ages for the kettle to fill.'

What Ruth didn't realise was that with the glorious summer came a problem we hadn't anticipated – a water shortage. She has always enjoyed her first cup of tea of the day and on this particular morning I was eager to get going early. The water container was empty so this meant a twenty-metre walk along a narrow path built many years earlier by my grandfather, no doubt with help from his sons. The path continued as a faint track, meandering up the hill and away from Kerracher for a mile and a half, towards the Kylesku/Drumbeg road. Where the hill began a stream of water cascaded down a rocky promontory and along a narrow channel to the beach and eventually to the sea.

The water for Kerracher had always been taken from this rock, but today it was down to a mere trickle that was very difficult to capture as it slid over the moss on the rock face.

'There must be a blockage,' suggested Ruth, 'or maybe the stream's got so overgrown it's restricting the amount coming down.'

'That will be my first job after breakfast,' I decided as I finally poured boiling water into the teapot.

Ruthie and Clare came with me as we traced the stream uphill. We found that it stretched for only another twenty or so metres before, to the girls' delight, it sprang from under the ground. I began to dig back from the water source but gave up after an exhausting attempt to cut into a hillside that had lain undisturbed for many years. It was pointless to try to find the source of this stream. The task now was to clear the passageway from the spring to the rock at the bottom of the stream. This provided a morning of activity for the children, as they had the fun of pulling out the small stones that had accumulated over the years.

'I've made my own path to walk up the hill,' declared Ruthie, indicating the stones she had extracted and carefully placed next to the stream.

'So have I.' Clare had a smaller array of pebbles that she had arranged in a circle with some scattered inside.

'You're just playing at making a field for horses.'

'Well it can be my path as well,' Clare said. 'Anyway, I can't lift big stones like you.'

'You've both done very well,' I said. 'The main thing is to clear the stream. That should let the water come down easier.'

The result was not as successful as we had hoped because it had been a very hot dry summer and there was, naturally, a shortage of water on the hill. This meant we had to look to another water source for the rest of the summer until the rain came. There were two other sources of water nearby in the form of fresh water lochs but, as each was quite a walk in opposite directions from the house, we opted out of using them that summer. Instead we bought a couple of five-gallon water containers and filled them up when passing the pier at Kylesku. Water was used very economically from then on.

We found one way of saving a lot of water – at bath time. Ruth still had the baby bath she had used for the girls and it came back into service. But before the water was thrown out she used it herself, then with some contortions I too would attempt to bathe. It was impossible to get all of me in the bath at the same time, and indeed even to wash without getting a good deal of water on the floor of the caravan.

———

To begin with, living in a caravan away from any amenities was like a camping holiday and we tackled it in a spirit of fun and adventure. The hot summer weather lasted well into the autumn and the feeling of being on holiday lasted with it.

During that time we had a number of early visitors at Kerracher, mainly family and friends. Ruthie's sixth birthday fell on a Saturday and we had a family party. My parents, sister Jean, her husband Steve, and their baby daughter all came to visit.

I collected the women folk by boat from Kylesku and my father and brother-in-law drove to the top of the glen and walked over from there. My father wanted to trace the path over the hill and mark it with a number of cairns. He still remembered the original track and, though it had long since become overgrown, the use made of it in latter years by Esther, the postie from Kylesku, meant there was still a discernable path. After this walk, we had a route with markers strategically placed to help us where the path took a turn or crossed a stream or boggy area.

Ruth took the catering for the birthday party in her stride – no mean feat since her 'kitchen' consisted of two rings and a grill, fired from a bottle of gas, and a small sink supplied from a plastic water container. The table was hinged to an end wall of the caravan and propped up by one leg. Extended for use it stretched between the two single beds. It was a precarious arrangement and we did have a number of spills until we learned to be careful.

That summer Ruth produced an amazing array of meals on this table. At the birthday party we started with prawns that had been left on the doorstep the previous day by an anonymous creel boat donor. Boiled and shelled, they were mixed with mayonnaise and lettuce. This was followed by pot-roasted brisket with crispy roast potatoes done in a pan of hot oil, accompanied by peas (tinned) and carrots (fresh from my father's garden in Dingwall). It was all rounded off with the girls' favourite dessert, Angel Delight, along with a fresh fruit salad made up from the provisions carried in by our guests. The birthday cake with its six candles had been baked by my mother. All this was washed down with lemonade and, in the case of my father, Steve and I, a few beers nicely cooled in the chilly water of the loch.

Using the lavatory in the caravan was another new experience – and pretty uncomfortable for any visitor caught short. The chemical loo (a large bucket with a toilet seat lid on top), which was housed in a cupboard of the caravan, had to be kept fresh with the right level of water and a dash of a dark blue chemical. This meant it had to be emptied as often as possible – a costly affair in terms of the chemical.

Needless to say it had to be emptied and ready for service whenever we were expecting visitors. The instructions recommended that the contents be buried. To begin with I tramped along to the area where my forebears had grown their vegetables to dig a hole and empty the contents into it. That meant a lot of digging, so that the garden area soon resembled the graveyard of some species of small animal with raised bumps of earth set between clumps of bulrushes. This went on until a visiting local saved me a future of constant digging by suggesting that the sea was large enough to take our family's waste without any real harm to the environment. 'There's a lot worse dumped at sea than a little diluted chemical and some shit,' he told me.

The sea became our repository for household waste we weren't able to burn. Tins were squashed flat so that they would sink to the bottom of the loch. The girls loved the task of dumping the rubbish, as we had to ensure that everything would sink and sometimes objects had to be kept submerged until they headed downwards. Ruthie was old enough to help and Clare kept a watch out for anything that bobbed up again.

The sea was also a source of food. Early in that first summer my father decided he would take the boat out for the day to catch some fish. When he was a young man he'd often caught enough fish to fill a frying pan. He took great delight in telling the girls about a time when he took in a couple of large fish, and, as it was lunch-time, the family decided to eat them there and then.

'My mother, your great-granny, gutted the fish and cleaned them out,' he told them. 'Then she put them straight in the frying pan. They were that big, they filled it right up.' He went on, 'We were all sitting waiting for our dinner, when there was a terrible scream from the kitchen. What do you think had happened?'

Ruthie and Clare shook their heads, absorbed in the story.

'Well, I rushed in to find my mother with one hand over her mouth and the other over her heart and the two fish – guess what – lying on the floor. They had both jumped out of the pan at the same time, they were that fresh!'

As Dad pushed the boat out that morning his last words to Ruth were, 'Don't worry about cooking tonight. Just have the frying pan ready.'

During the day we watched the boat slowly mapping Loch Cairnbawn, end to end and side to side. We were surely going to have a feast tonight, with enough over to share with our neighbours and friends. It would be good to be able to return some of the generous hospitality given to us. We'd often been grateful for fresh sea fare left at the door of the caravan.

When Dad returned, he was greeted eagerly by the girls.

'How many fish have you got, Grandad?'

The disappointment showed on all our faces when he reluctantly admitted that the bucket contained only the remnants of the lures he had taken with him. Changed days.

———

Most of the first month at Kerracher was spent clearing out the house. Up the very narrow stairs were two bedrooms with a box room in the middle, which acted as a third. Downstairs were two rooms with a small pantry between.

Some old bed clothing and mattresses from upstairs had to be thrown out and we cleared the rooms enough to put in our own beds and a number of boxes from the flitting. Downstairs, however, was not in quite the same condition.

My Uncle Jim had become a recluse after my grandparents died. He hadn't the woodworking or practical talents of my Uncle Bob or my father, and the house hadn't been looked after. There was much rotten wood and a pervasive smell of damp. Almost all the remaining furniture had traces of woodworm and had to be burnt. Worst of all was the 'best' room that, when I was a young visitor, had been used only on the staunchly kept Presbyterian Sabbath. Every other day it was out of bounds. I remember it always smelling of mothballs. My younger sister Ann once kindly offered Jean and me a 'mint sweet' each – she had found them in the room. We should have cottoned on – it wasn't like her to be so generous. Jean and I have had an aversion to mothballs ever since.

The room had now lost all its peaceful dignity. The walls had a powdery sheen of mould, and there was a gaping hole in the middle of the floor where Uncle Jim had taken up several floorboards, exposing the damp earth underneath. The sparse furniture in the room had the same covering as the walls. There was no other remedy than to destroy the remaining furnishings and pull up what was left of the rotten floor. It was in this room earlier in the summer that we had found the carcass of a sheep. So it was quite cathartic to gut the room and prepare it for renovation.

The remainder of the house needed airing and with the coming of winter there was little chance we'd get rid of the dampness right away. During a visit from the Jellicoes the conversation got round to what it would be like here during the winter.

'You surely can't live in this caravan,' said George.

'George, I think that Ruth and Eric should stay at Reintraid for the winter, don't you?' Phillipa suggested.

Ruth and I looked at each other with mixed emotions.

'You would be doing us a favour living in it,' Phillipa went on.

We realised this did make sense. Reintraid was just over a mile nearer to Kylesku at the end of a half-mile track off the Kylesku to Drumbeg road. A croft dwelling similar to Kerracher, it had a large kitchen extension and an upstairs lounge at the sea end with picture views of the loch. It even had electricity, supplied by a generator and, having been lived in most of the summer, would give us a warmer, more comfortable existence during the winter.

George wouldn't take no for an answer, so we agreed we would carry out some maintenance work in exchange and gratefully accepted his kind offer.

The house had significance for me. It was at Reintraid that my mother had first met my father, thirty-three years earlier.

I GO FISHING BUT RUTH EARNS
THE MONEY

I was keen to learn about the sea and in particular if I could make a living from it. Roddy at Kylesku suggested I join him on his creel boat.

'I'm short of a crew next week.'

'What's happened to Don?'

'He's going into hospital for a few days. What are you doing?'

'Nothing important – but I've never worked on a creel boat before.'

'It's not exactly rocket science. You'll have no problems. Being the Kerracher Man you've already got the sea in your blood.'

He seemed quite confident.

The following Monday morning I was knocking at Roddy's door at seven o'clock with my flask and piece box under my arm, all togged out for a day at sea. It was a glorious morning and as I accompanied him from his house down to the pier I began to whistle a favourite tune. All was well with the world.

'Stop that,' he said abruptly.

'What?'

'Whistling.'

'I didn't think I was that bad,' I said, taken aback.

'There must be no whistling today at all,' he instructed.

'Why not?' I asked.

'You'll whistle up the wind.'

'That's just superstition,' I said surprised, for Roddy was a church-going man who took his religion seriously.

'Maybe, but I'm not taking any chances.'

'Anything else I shouldn't do?' I checked.

'No. As long as we don't meet any of the women we'll be OK.'

'What do you mean?'

'It would be bad to go to sea if we met a woman before getting aboard,' he said. He was quite serious.

I was learning the ways of the sea – or perhaps the ways of a fisherman.

We quickened our steps to the pier and the safety of the boat.

Loch Cairnbawn was calm as we glided towards Kerracher. Roddy blew his foghorn when we passed the bay and I waved to the unseen Ruth and the girls who were watching through the binoculars from an upstairs window.

As we reached the open sea Roddy explained the onboard procedures and the operation of catching the buoy, lifting the fleet of prawn creels, emptying and re-baiting them, then stacking them at the back of the boat ready to go into the sea at another point. All I had to do was pick the buoy out of the water, re-bait the empty creels and then stack them. Roddy would see to the rest.

His first fleet was marked by a buoy bobbing about in what was now a significant – and rapidly increasing – swell.

I grabbed the buoy. Roddy quickly put the engine out of gear, stepped out of the wheelhouse, took the buoy from me, and secured the attached rope over the hauler. The boat rose to the top of the waves with a grandstand view of Stoer Point but then slid into the deep trough between each one where all we could see were two walls of water.

I found it exhilarating at first and quickly got into the motion of the boat heaving to and fro. We were almost at the last few creels of the first fleet when I felt the first twinge.

'Are you all right?' Roddy shouted.

'I think so. Why?'

'The look on your face,' he said, concerned.

'Just a niggle in my stomach,' I said. 'Nothing to worry about.'

I managed a few more creels but the niggle became more of an ache. The ache then turned into a pain. Beginning to panic, I stopped in the middle of fixing a piece of salted mackerel to the bait holder and stepped back from the edge of the boat, doubling up.

'I don't know what's wrong. It must have been something I ate for breakfast,' I gasped.

Roddy just smirked. My brow was moist with cold sweat.

A terrific abdominal convulsion seized me and I began to retch. I just reached the other side of the boat and leaned over the gunwale before the contents of my very early morning breakfast came up and into the heaving sea. I hung on there grimly, apparently bringing up my complete innards. Eventually the spasms subsided. Roddy had completed baiting and stacking the last few creels of the fleet and pulled the boat round into the waves. This seemed to help.

'The egg I had must have been bad.'

'You think so?' he said, with what was now a broad grin.

I gulped in fresh air, still feeling very queasy, but I managed to throw the creels back into the sea as Roddy took the boat along his plotted course.

'I'm OK now. Let's go for the next fleet.' I paced the deck, and by the time we reached the marker buoy for fleet number two, I felt more settled.

By the third creel I succumbed again. This time the grip in my stomach was even fiercer but as I retched over the side of the boat nothing was coming up. I wished the sea would swallow me, but I didn't even have the strength to fall overboard. That was the only moment in my life when I didn't mind if I died.

Roddy eventually finished the fleet and again pulled the boat round into the waves. That forward motion as opposed to the side rolling motion did help.

'I've never been seasick before!' I protested.

'We'll stop for a cuppa and see how you get on.'

Roddy busied himself in the galley below as I stood in the wheelhouse above, clutching at the wheel, struggling to keep the boat headed into the waves.

'Here, have a swill of this. It will help put a lining on your stomach.' He handed me a mug of strong brown tea laced with Carnation milk.

I tried but after one sip I was bent over the side of the boat once more. This time I couldn't stop retching. My whole body heaved as the stomach muscles went into spasm. In a few moments I was prostrate on the deck. I tried not to think. I concentrated on breathing. I watched the clouds pass across the sky, which was marginally better than having my eyes closed. I just wanted it all to end.

'There's only one cure for seasickness,' Roddy eventually offered.

'What's that?' I moaned.

'To stand under a tree!'

It was a humbled and delicate Eric who surprised Ruth by returning from his first day crewing a creel boat at 11a.m. It seemed that this particular Kerracher Man didn't have the requisite amount of sea in his blood!

Ruth found her niche in the community when local people discovered that she had trained as a hairdresser before she married. Before she could protest that she hadn't seriously done anyone's hair for the past six years, she was hi-jacked. Joan, Roddy's wife, and Esther, the post lady at Kylesku, arranged for her to visit them one Saturday afternoon to give them hairdos in Joan's kitchen. That was the start. Before long everyone knew they had a hairdresser in their midst.

Ruth's skills had not abandoned her and as a result of being in such demand she bought a portable hairdryer. It was ironic that we now owned something we could use only in other people's homes. We had ditched most of our electrical appliances before coming to Kerracher, keeping only a Habitat standard lamp and a Black and Decker drill.

Ruth got to know many of the women around the area of Kylesku and Drumbeg as a result of her visits, which were fitted in with the girls going to and from school. She also trimmed some of the men folk's hair but they generally seemed reluctant to have a female barber.

If it hadn't been for the hairdressing, Ruth would have been a prisoner at Kerracher as she couldn't drive.

The other contact Ruth had with the outside world was the mobile library that stopped at the top of the glen each Tuesday. Both the librarians we got to know over the years were exceptionally helpful people. There was no book that, if we asked for it, wouldn't be sitting on a shelf when they next arrived. For all of us it was a lifeline with the outside world and the evening of the library visit was always a quiet one in the Kerracher household. The girls made use of the service when the library visited the school in Drumbeg. After dinner they would be eager to get their heads into their new books and as a treat they were allowed extra time to read before going to bed.

We were by now well integrated into the communities of both Kylesku and Drumbeg – perhaps more so with Drumbeg as it had a small shop run by Jack and Rita Gregory, who willingly tried to get us any item we asked for.

We did much of our food shopping at Drumbeg but we also discovered the small variety of shops in Lochinver, about twenty miles from the top of the glen. The village had petrol pumps, a couple of grocery stores, a newsagent, garage, butcher, baker, ship's chandler and a bank. The doctor was also based there. It became our main shopping stop. Occasionally we would venture as far as Ullapool, our nearest small town, but only when Ruth needed things like birthday gifts.

Our more numerous trips to Lochinver made us better known in the area and, like our comings and goings in Drumbeg and Kylesku, they established us as part of the larger community.

THE WINTER AT REINTRAID

We moved into Reintraid early in October and soon established the routines of daily living without the more severe disadvantages that Kerracher presented. It also gave us the opportunity to have a more social existence: Reintraid was much more accessible to visitors.

However, it wasn't long before we met another of the problems of using a homemade water system that comes directly from nature. The first frosts came early that year, and one November morning I was wakened by Ruth shaking me vigorously.

'We've got no water!'

'What?' I struggled to consciousness.

'I can't get any water out of the tap.'

For a moment I thought it must have dried up as it had at Kerracher but the shock of the cold when I sat up dispatched that idea. It was so cold there was frost on the inside of the window panes.

There was water coming through the hot water tap in the kitchen but not the cold tap. So at least we managed breakfast.

'What do you think has happened?' Ruth asked me as

she got Ruthie ready for school. 'Is it frozen somewhere?'

'I think so,' I said. 'After I've taken Ruthie to school, I'll start with the tank, if I can find it.'

The tank wasn't difficult to find as all I had to do was follow the black plastic pipe that ran for most of its length very near to or on top of the ground. Ruth was right; the water was frozen. Later in the day it was restored by the rise in temperature. Thankfully, it was early in the winter and the frost was not severe. But we would always have to keep a reserve supply of water. We became dedicated weather watchers.

Spending our first winter at Reintraid was well worth while. We had a good introduction to living remotely, without the harshness of managing without a road, running water or electricity. Surviving that first winter was crucial, and getting through it in a house that was designed for summer use only, and which needed a lot of work, was no easy option. It wasn't long before we learned about another essential of life – power, in this case a temperamental generator.

One very wet and windy evening when Ruth and I were sitting quietly reading in front of the open wood burner in the kitchen, the lights dimmed for a moment.

'It must be the wind,' I said, looking up from my book. It was blowing a gale. A few moments later we were plunged into darkness.

'Better see if I can find those candles we brought,' I said, feeling my way to the front door, where we kept a powerful torch. There was an abundance of candles under the sink and it wasn't long before we were sitting down again in front of the log fire in the candlelight.

'It's quite romantic,' Ruth said, snuggling up to me as we waited for the power to come on again.

As we sat cosily on the old sofa contemplating the changing pictures in the fire while the logs burned, a slow realisation dawned. Our electricity supply was fed from the generator by a thick cable that ran from the shed to the house just under the surface of the ground. The wind had nothing to do with our loss of power.

I pulled on a coat, grabbed a torch and left the cocoon of the warm room to brave the elements and trudge the short distance to the generator shed. I didn't realise it but that winter I was to become well acquainted with this path. Fighting my way through wild gusts of wind, I tugged open the shed door to find a completely silent generator. I shone the torch all around the brute, but I had suddenly reverted from Kerracher Man to Management Accountant. I didn't have a clue about machinery and certainly knew nothing about generators. Securing the shed door, I admitted defeat. We'd have to wait until the following day when I could ask Stan Roy for his advice.

Stan and Moira had taken us under their wing from the very start, and although they were concerned about how we would survive at Kerracher, they were also delighted that a young couple with children was coming into the area. It was a rare occurrence in those days when most of the young people were leaving to find their fortunes elsewhere. The Roys lived at Glenleraig, almost four miles along the road towards Drumbeg. There was always a welcoming cup of tea and a chat when we put the world to rights in their large, comfortable kitchen. Later that morning Stan returned with me to the generator shed at Reintraid.

'Well, that's easily solved,' he told me after a quick look. 'You're out of fuel.' He saw my expression, and laughed. 'Easy when you know how,' he added. 'Never mind, I can give you enough to keep you going until you get a new supply.'

That winter I learned quite a bit about generators and their peculiar workings.

—

The house at Reintraid was situated a hundred yards above the seashore, cosily tucked into the side of a hill with its face taking full view of any sunshine from the south. To get to the road you had to climb a rough track snaking up a steep incline for a good half mile. The Jellicoes owned an old Land Rover that was used for ferrying people and goods. So when the diesel arrived it had to be filled into a bowser at the top of the track, carefully towed down the track by the Land Rover and then pumped into the diesel tank along from the generator shed. This was a whole morning's work, since we had to hand pump 250 gallons of diesel. It certainly helped keep me warm that winter.

We were learning what was truly important in our new life – running water, fuel and working machinery for heat and light. We learned to supplement the heating by foraging in the nearby woods for recently fallen trees. There never seemed to be any shortage of these. We chopped them into lengths which could be carried back on my shoulders to the house, where we would cut them to size with the trusty bush saw. Another lesson we learned was to buy more than one blade at a time.

We were learning about the boat too. The jetty at Reintraid was a leftover from the Second World War when Loch Cairnbawn was used for developing mini submarines, which would later attack the Norwegian fiords. Reintraid was the base for the operation, and all along the rocks between Reintraid and Kerracher were the remains of huge anchorage points for the ships that had visited the loch thirty-five years previously. The mooring that sat off the jetty was certainly not a leftover from these bygone years, as I found out to my cost.

Our system for mooring was a relatively simple one: we left the boat on a running mooring that sat out in the water a safe distance from the shore. A rope ran from the shore out to the buoy and through a ring to return to the shore where it went through another ring with the two ends spliced together to form a loop. The boat was tied to a point on the loop and then the rope was run out to the mooring buoy or in to the shore depending on where you wanted the boat to be.

One morning after an easterly wind I found our boat high and dry on the rocks. Loch Cairnbawn runs east to west and both Reintraid and Kerracher are situated on the west side and so always exposed when an easterly wind gets up. I realised that the mooring had to be heavy enough to hold the boat that was tied to it. Unfortunately, the Jellicoes had not installed a mooring for an old heavy wooden clinker boat but for their much lighter inflatable.

Before I could rescue my boat, I had to wait for the tide to return to the high water mark where the boat was perched, tightly wedged between two rocks. I could then replace the mooring weight at the bottom of the sea. Of course, the tide reaches its high point only twice in twenty-four hours, so I had a twelve-hour wait before I could get the boat back in the water. Because the last high tide was early morning, this meant the water would only be reaching the boat in the evening when it would already be dark. Moreover, when the wind got up it took the water a little higher up the shore. It was calm now though, so next time the tide wouldn't come in quite so high. I was learning the vagaries of the sea.

At first sight it looked as if all was lost as the boat was not only high and dry but the way the stern was wedged between two rocks meant the bow was sticking out into mid air with water dripping from its underside. I checked the outboard engine first to find that it was almost off its position on the stern but at least intact with only some scratches and dents. In addition, there was water in the bottom of the boat that was putting pressure on the front half, as it was all congregated in the bow.

The first task was to find some wood to prop up the front end to ease the strain on the keel. Next job was to take out the heavy bottom boards and then empty the water from the boat. As there was obviously some damage, the concern now was how to repair it in time for the next high tide later in the day. The boat was heavy and wet and not in a position that made it easy to get at the parts that needed attention. I couldn't even tell yet what attention was actually needed. Inside the boat there were no obvious holes or gaps, so I thought it could probably be repaired without too much difficulty.

I had to leave it as it was in any case, for now. Later that day when I collected Ruthie from school at Kylesku, I managed to speak to Roddy.

'Get it along to Kerracher, that's the best way,' he advised. 'You can beach it there to do the repairs.'

'What do you think it's likely to need?' I asked.

'From the way you describe it,' he said, 'I think all you'll need to do is seal it with some cold tar round the bottom.'

I decided to take his advice. It wasn't absolutely necessary for the boat to remain at Reintraid.

That evening, in bright moonlight, I managed to lever the back end of the boat out of its clamp of two rocks and down a small but efficient ramp of sticks, old fence posts and lengths of tree trunks, to slide it towards the water's edge. Thankfully, that night, there was no east wind to contend with, otherwise it would have been an impossible task. I jumped into the boat as it hit the water and salvaged the wood I had used before starting the engine. I'd spent the afternoon checking and preparing it, but it did take a few more pulls than normal to fire it into action. The sweet sound of it bursting into life was followed by a sustained *putt-putt-putt*.

The journey to Kerracher in the dark was not as difficult as I had anticipated. Ruth had made me take our most powerful torch but I found I hardly needed it. The moon lit up the whole loch, framing it in a landscape of silhouetted greys and blacks. The boat glided as if on a shiny mirror through this shadowed darkness and for a few moments I let myself drift, caught by a sudden peace after an anxious day. Then, with one hand on the engine handle, I turned to the crucial task of using the other to scoop out the bottom of the boat where water was relentlessly gathering, and I threw it in an upward and outward motion over my right shoulder, sending it splashing back into the sea.

Setting the boat as high up the beach as I could, I tucked it into the sheltered end below where the caravan stood. I secured the bow with a rope to the shoreline and to the stern with two more, one tied to rocks on the shore side and the other to a large stone that I threw into the water. At least it would be moored securely and safely when the tide rose during the early hours of the morning.

Kerracher was bathed in moonlight. I turned to face the house, and stood quite still. The bay arching away in the distance, the water gently lapping the shore, the house standing quiet and empty, tucked into the face of the hill behind – I breathed it all in, and the peace, the utter peace of the place. We have done the right thing, I thought. We were right to come here.

After a moment I stirred myself, and set off over the hill towards Reintraid. I had never walked it before in the dark, but it wasn't long before I was picking my way across the now familiar route, stepping confidently with the moon as a shining light to guide me. I walked almost the whole distance without using the torch and when I arrived at the top of the track at Reintraid half an hour later, I was exhilarated.

'Come out,' I said to Ruth, bursting into the house. 'It's wonderful out there – I didn't even need the torch.' Wondering, she followed me outside and we stood quietly together, in the stillness of the moonlit loch and hills.

—·—

We spent the winter and a good part of the spring settling into our new life with lots of visitors, some announced but many who were not. It was getting to be like an extended holiday where our visitors would expect to talk, walk, eat and sleep all day. As a result we didn't do as much on the house as we had planned. The speed of life went into first gear and remained there. We adapted to this new regime very easily. Ruth, however, kept her routines with the children and did gently remind me from time to time that we had a lot to do. Otherwise my Highland genes might have put everything off indefinitely.

One of our biggest concerns was how we were going to make a living. I had been successful in my tender for the school run, taking the children from Kylesku (with Ruthie of course), to and from the school twice a day. This helped, but it was not enough. I also gathered stones and painted them to sell to a few local craft shops, but they didn't open their doors until after Easter.

Next I turned to cutting and gathering seaweed with a man who was based at Kylesku. It was a task that was possible only when the tide was at its lowest point. It was back-breaking work, but because of the moving tide, it didn't last for more than a few hours. This meant it also didn't earn me much.

Then, one late winter's evening, coming home by boat, I decided it was definitely not for me. We had ringed the cut seaweed together ready for collection by the boat that would come from Lewis. It was a raw wintry night but I was well wrapped up as I set off for home. The putt-putt of the small outboard engine and the gentle splash of the bow of the boat into the oncoming waves created a rhythm that lulled me into what turned out to be a false sense of comfort.

I was musing about how much one could see on the water even when it was dark when I suddenly realised there was something else on the loch ahead of me. It was large and black, but it had no lights. All the boats I had ever seen on the loch at night were easily and early identified because of their lights. Now it was difficult to make out how big and how far away this vessel was. I didn't know how much time I had before it would bear down on me and I had no way of telling what direction it was taking other than towards the mouth of the Kyle, out of which I was slowly emerging. Then I heard the chugging noise from its engine and I realised it was nearer than I thought.

There was no option but to turn and head for the nearest bit of land, the rocks that edged the opening to the loch. At least if the skipper of the boat knew where he was going, it wouldn't be towards the rocks. I could only trust him on that.

Within a matter of minutes I was passed in the dark by a towering hunk of steel so close I could hear the voices of the men aboard. Now I could see dim lights muffled against the dark hull and upper structure of the boat. Its bulk swept past, leaving me rocking in its wash.

It was a rusty old tub that plied the Minch for many years collecting seaweed from all corners of the Hebrides. When I saw it in daylight the following day I realised why I couldn't see the navigation lights. The boat was filthy, every part of it coated with a grimy mixture of oil, salt and brown extract of seaweed.

We had our savings to live on of course, but they were for renovating Kerracher and wouldn't last long if we used them for day-to-day living. So we had a frugal existence that winter, dependent on catching fish as well as charitable assistance from locals who would occasionally drop in with something freshly caught at sea or off the hill.

'Off the hill' was the term used for the venison which occasionally appeared on our table. At that time of year a few of the local men would drive out in the evening to scour the deserted road edges for any deer coming down from the bare exposure of the hills. A flash of light would be followed by a shot and then someone would be dispatched to gralloch it (bleed it and clean out its intestines) before carrying the carcass back to a waiting van.

It wasn't long before I was invited by some friends,

who'd better remain nameless, to accompany them on such a foray.

When I arrived at the door I was ushered into the kitchen and asked immediately, 'Do you have a knife?'

'No. But I can hold the torch,' I offered.

'Ok, you can help with lifting as well.'

'Now, Eric, if we're stopped by the police,' the other man instructed me, 'we're taking you home after a night down at the Kylesku Hotel.'

'Why would the police stop us?'

Naively, I hadn't yet realised this was (and still is) a criminal offence. From the way these guys talked I had the vague idea that it was an old tradition of 'one for the pot', and their birthright. One local worthy recalled being out on the hill when he was a young lad with my grandfather, a law-abiding, religious man who would never have countenanced breaking the law.

'Better get going before it's too late.'

Soon three of us, squashed into the cab of a small pick-up, were parked in a passing place, scouring the hillside, following a pinprick of light at the end of the torch beam.

'I thought I saw something to the right there!' I exclaimed.

'Shisht!' was the reply. 'Keep it quiet. You'll frighten them away.'

I shut up and waited for the action, but there was nothing happening at that spot. We moved further along the single-track road but there was nothing happening anywhere on the road that night. After an hour of stopping, sweeping the hillside with the torchlight, moving on and stopping again it was decided we should give up and go home.

Back in my friend's kitchen the whisky came out. As we

were about to down the first dram the usual toast of 'Slainte' was offered, then our companion, a veteran of many campaigns on the hillside, put up his glass and exclaimed, 'Here's to blood in the heather!'

I went home that evening to a wife fully expecting her hunter man to return with a trophy. I was to disappoint her. However, two nights later our friend called in with a large piece of venison wrapped in newspaper. They had popped out the evening following our expedition and had been successful. I never received another invitation to join them, I suspect because they believed I put the 'bushnak' (the mark of bad luck) on them. They decided it would be best not to tempt fate and have me bring further bad luck.

By the time winter turned into spring we had adapted to our new life. We had also got to know and become friends with almost everyone in the hamlets of Kylesku and Drumbeg. When we returned to Kerracher during the spring we felt that we had settled in to the community and become part of it. All we had to do now was settle into Kerracher.

HALLOWE'EN COMES AND GOES, AND SO DOES THE SHEEPDOG

It was the girls who first helped us become part of the community we had chosen to live in, through our contact with the primary school, and all the village activities associated with it.

When we arrived at Kerracher our assumption was that they would go to the school at Kylesku as it was nearer, and Kylesku was central to much of our coming and going. So Ruthie became a pupil at Unapool Primary School, which was based along the road from Kylesku.

It was this school run I had successfully tendered for. It meant transporting Ruthie and two children from Kylestrome, which was across the water from Kylesku. This brought in a small income, which contributed to our survival at Kerracher, and for a year the arrangement worked very well.

However, during the following summer, when the school run contracts came up for renewal, I was surprised to be told by the Education Authority that my tender had not been accepted. They cited the canvas back on the Land Rover, saying it was unsafe to carry children. I pointed out that we'd been using it for a whole year, and no one had objected till now, but they were adamant. Since I was not in a position to change my vehicle I had to give up the contract just as Clare was about to start school too.

Then the bombshell came: the new contractor would not be collecting our children. We would have to transport them ourselves. To rub salt in the wound, I would not even be paid a mileage allowance as I would be transporting my own children.

The only alternative was for our girls to go to the school at Drumbeg, taken to and from there by Hughie Matheson, the school teacher's husband, as he had the contract for Drumbeg. We weren't too pleased as Ruthie had been very happy and settled in Unapool. An even greater concern was that the Drumbeg journey was much longer and on a more dangerous road. From the Education Authority's point of view, there could not really be any change in their position. In the long term, it was planned to close the Kylesku school and keep Drumbeg open, so there was a push to increase the numbers at Drumbeg. In the end we decided to keep the girls at home, and teach them ourselves.

As the new term approached both girls began to get excited, especially Clare who longed to go to school with her big sister. Towards the end of the last term at Kylesku, Ruthie had been coming home to find Clare eager to know what she had learned that day. Ruthie got her toy blackboard out and demonstrated to Clare, who sat at her own small desk.

'I have some news for you girls,' I announced one evening.

'Oh good. Are we going to Inverness?'

'No. We aren't going anywhere. From Monday you'll have a new teacher who'll be coming here to Kerracher.'

There was a surprised silence.

'But I want to go back to school at Kylesku,' Ruthie said, adding quietly, 'I'll miss seeing all my friends there.'

'Is Mrs MacQuillan coming here?' Clare asked, puzzled.

'No, but your new teacher will be lots of fun.' I reassured them. 'Guess who it might be.'

There followed some hilarious proposals of unlikely candidates. Sensing the girls' disappointment, Ruth tried to tone this down. But I was charging on oblivious. 'No it's not the man on the moon. He's much closer to you than that!'

Perhaps it was the 'he' that changed the mood. The smiles disappeared, replaced by puzzlement.

'Are we going to have a man teacher?' Ruthie said.

'What's wrong with that?'

'Well …' There was a pause. 'You don't get men teachers,' she decided.

'Will he stay with us?' was the next question.

'Yes, and he'll be sleeping with Mummy,' I said with a wink.

'That's enough.' Ruth thought I was going too far now. 'It's going to be Daddy.'

The girls went to bed that night in a state of confusion. They were disappointed to be missing out on school at Kylesku but on the other hand they were full of questions about where we would have the school room, when they would start and finish and have their playtimes, and if anyone else was going to join them. What they did not see, nor could they understand, was my annoyance at the Education Authority's decision and Ruth's uncertainty about the plan.

We began the following Monday promptly at 9.30a.m., which is when the girls would have been starting at Drumbeg Primary School. I set up Ruthie's blackboard in the caravan and placed the girls on either side of the table. The first few days went well and we had lots of fun with excursions outside to draw sea creatures on the beach or wild plants in the hill behind us. Ruth would come to the caravan with drinks and biscuits at playtime, then in the afternoon she would take over to let me get on with the renovation work on the house.

As time went on, some flaws in this plan began to appear. The distinction between the required discipline of school and the relationship of father and daughter began to blur. The happy relationship I'd had with my daughters began to disintegrate. I was turning into an ogre – strict and grumpy. Ruthie was also making it obvious she hankered for the more sociable life she had known at Kylesku and I could not replicate that. My plan was not working.

There was also a sustained campaign from our families and some local friends to get me to change my mind and allow the girls to attend Drumbeg Primary School. Apart from what I saw as the illogical reasons for the change of school, my main concern was with the treacherous road to Drumbeg and perhaps even the fact that someone else would be doing the driving. After further discussion between Ruth and me, I finally relented.

I broke the good news to the girls as they sat at the caravan table on their last Friday morning of schooling at Kerracher.

'I have some very sad news this morning,' I announced.

There was a puzzled look from Ruthie and Clare pursed her eyebrows together in a serious frown.

'This is your last day at school. Well, at least at Kerracher school.'

'Does that mean we don't have to be at school ever again?' asked Clare, bewildered.

'Are we going back to school at Kylesku then?' asked Ruthie.

'No. But you will be going to a new school – at Drumbeg.'

———

There was great excitement on the bright sunny day we took the girls to their new primary school. Although pleased at the prospect, both of them were anxious, so when we arrived in the school playground Ruth and I watched with some apprehension their first meeting with the other nine children, only two of whom they had met before. The teacher, Mrs Matheson, introduced us to everyone, including some of the other children's parents. In some ways it was a relief to watch Ruthie and Clare, hand in hand, walking with the group of other children towards the door of the school to become a part of the daily life of Drumbeg.

As a result of the girls being back at school our links with local people increased and so too did our involvement with Drumbeg. The school at Drumbeg was also used as the village hall, so almost everything in the village involved the children in some way, from sales of work to the Christmas concert.

Soon it was Hallowe'en, which was celebrated principally by the children in the community. In the last week of October, the children made masks and 'guiser' costumes at school and at home.

When the big evening came round we were invited to stay over with Moira and Stan at Glenleraig. The girls could hardly contain their excitement, as it was the first time they were to perform publicly with the other children. The children's performances formed the main part of the celebration. They would sing (sometimes in Gaelic), recite poetry, play the recorder or tell jokes as they went round all the houses in the area. Hughie organised transport for them to visit each house, cramming into what were often small living rooms to perform in front of the appreciative occupants. It was the first time our girls had sung for their supper and in return for their efforts they collected lots of goodies in their plastic carrier bags: home baking, crisps, fruit, sweets, more sweets, nuts and money.

When Hughie eventually offloaded Ruthie and Clare at the door of the Roys' house, very late in the evening, two exhausted but still excited girls came rushing in with bags bulging. For a few minutes it was mayhem but eventually they settled down with mugs of hot chocolate. They had sung in almost every home but in some they told a joke or recited poems. A couple of the older children had played tunes on their recorders. They began to describe the houses they'd visited and the people – and animals – they had met there. We heard what each family had given them: the one household that had presented them with a crisp £1 note each especially impressed them.

'It was so new it could be a forgery!'

'They must be very rich.'

'You should have seen the huge house the Munro sisters live in.'

'We had to sing two songs for really old people in Nedd, one in English and one in Gaelic, and they wanted us to play the recorders too.'

'Clare tripped in the dark and scratched her knee when we went up to Non's and she got an extra cake.'

'It's still a bit sore, but I can't wait for next Hallowe'en,' Clare reassured us.

It was late when we got them to bed, still chattering non-stop as we tucked them in, but they weren't due in school until ten o'clock the next morning and they wouldn't have any walk over the hill. They were soon asleep, dreaming no doubt of their wonderful evening.

———

One other factor which helped us integrate was the fact that I was an able-bodied young man willing to follow in the traditions of my predecessors, and establish Kerracher as a working croft.

Many crofters retained a quota of sheep. This was determined by the amount of grazing available to their croft. Kerracher had a quota of ten sheep and two cows. My grandfather had owned two cows and my grandmother allowed me to help milk them when I was on holiday. Then she took the enamelled pail brimming with warm creamy milk back to the house and set it on the kitchen table, giving my sisters and me instructions to guard over it, to stop my grandfather from scooping out a cupful. In the pantry she would later turn it into the richest butter I have ever tasted. My sisters and I helped by rotating the churn.

I could also remember the smell of the huge heap of manure next to the barns where the cows were housed, so we decided not to go for cows. We were allowed to substitute five sheep for each cow, which meant we could keep up to twenty sheep on an area that extended to 4,000 acres. A number of local crofters convinced me that it would make sense in our position at least to take advantage of our quota. Since there were sheep already on the ground and hefted to the area, the advantage was already with me: I wouldn't need to introduce new sheep with the problems that could entail.

The sheep were there because a tenant shepherd on the Ardvar Estate had cleared them to give up shepherding. We witnessed the clearance during our first summer when we were living in the caravan at Kylesku. As we sailed to Kerracher one day we could see several men walking across the hillside, a few scattered sheep running madly ahead of them. Occasionally a couple of barking black dogs appeared and disappeared in the heather, chasing the sheep as they fled. We duly reported the scene to Stan Roy, concerned that some holidaymakers were allowing their dogs to worry the sheep. Stan smiled: 'That was the sheep owner gathering them!'

After the clearance we counted at least eighteen sheep roaming on our land, so we made an offer for them, which the owner accepted. The next step was for me to become a shepherd.

Acquiring a dog was essential. Hughie, collecting the girls for school one morning, told me about an old man in Drumbeg who was being admitted to hospital for a long stay. Apparently he had a canny old sheepdog we could take and see how we all got on. The following day as he unloaded the girls, Hughie also unloaded a huge collie, which accompanied us home. Bobby reminded me of Glen, the dog my grandfather had when I was a boy, and it seemed right that Kerracher once again had a collie in residence. The girls made a great fuss of him as we walked over the hill, and fed him as soon as we got home. That evening we lodged him in the shed at the end of the barns in a fish box padded up with an old blanket.

The poor dog howled all night, but when we walked over to the school car next morning, he came with us and returned quite obediently with me when the girls went off with Hughie. I had him accompany me during the day, including a walk through to the sea beach where I had last seen the sheep grazing. They became nervy and ran for the hill, but he didn't bat an eyelid, just went on walking alongside me. I took that as a good sign.

On the second day I had to take the boat to Kylesku, drop the girls off at Reintraid and walk them up to the school car from there. We left Bobby at home with Ruth. When I got back to Kerracher I found Ruth frantic. She couldn't find Bobby anywhere, despite scouring all round the croft shouting his name, and even walking to the top of the cliff above Kerracher to scan the walk across the hill.

The day went by and Bobby was still missing. I walked across the hill that afternoon to collect the girls wondering what I was going to say to Hughie, and how the girls would react, but when I told them, all Hughie said was, 'Och, I wouldn't worry. He'll be back at Kerracher when it comes round to dinner time.'

'We'll have a search party for him when we get home,' the girls suggested.

As we walked home the hills reverberated to shouts of 'Bobby', but he was neither seen nor heard – we had definitely lost him. What a start to shepherding!

When we arrived at the school car the following morning, we were welcomed by Hughie, and, alongside him, an apologetic-looking Bobby.

'He arrived at his home in Drumbeg last night,' Hughie explained. 'Take him home again and have another go. Maybe worth locking him up for a few days so he doesn't have the chance to take off.'

Bobby walked back to Kerracher with me as if he had always done it, and he greeted Ruth warmly when she welcomed him with a bowl of water. Then he settled down in the sunshine on the front doorstep.

All was well for a few days until I again had to leave him at Kerracher with Ruth. We had decided that he had to stay of his own accord and not as a prisoner, so we left him free to roam, but when the girls and I returned that afternoon it was to find him gone again. We all agreed that if Bobby walked back to Drumbeg then it was because he was missing home and he should stay there. The next morning Bobby reappeared with Hughie once more, but this time he didn't have to do any more walking. He returned to Drumbeg for good.

Our search for a sheepdog started again, and soon the mother of one of the girls' school friends said her brother had a working dog he wanted rid of. The following Saturday morning we all drove across country to Golspie to fetch it. This was only a journey of some sixty-five miles but the road was single track and new to us, so it took almost two hours. We did our shopping first and loaded up the back of the Land Rover with supplies for another month's survival. Then it was off to the car park to collect our dog.

The owner was there as arranged, but there was no sign of the dog.

'Did you not take the dog with you then?' I asked.

'Oh yes.' He walked round to the back of his car and opened the boot to reveal a bewildered and terrified sheepdog blinking at the light. 'He doesn't like travelling so I have to lock him in the boot.'

Now here we were with a Land Rover with no boot, just a back filled with provisions, and a two-hour journey ahead of us accompanied by a terrified dog.

'What's his name?' Clare enquired.

'Glen.'

'Glen,' we chorused, attempting to coax the dog out.

'Does he bite?' Ruth asked warily.

'No.' The man tugged the shaking animal from the boot by a length of string tied around his neck. Then he pocketed his cheque, got back into his car and drove away.

'Where are we going to put him?' Ruth asked.

'We'll take him in the back with us,' the girls offered hopefully.

'Not among the food,' Ruth objected. 'Anyway he might jump out.' The Land Rover had a canvas-covered back, with a rear flap that a desperate animal could easily squeeze through.

'He'll just have to sit in the front beside me,' Ruth decided, 'and you will both have to sit in the back.'

We secured the girls in the rear and Ruth got in the front. I followed and led Glen to the passenger door, Ruth urging him in with a 'Come Glen. Come Glen.'

He looked up, still shaking. He seemed unsure what to do, and kept glancing nervously around the deserted car park, tail between his legs.

It was a few minutes before we eventually encouraged him in. I quickly shut the door and ran round and jumped into the driver's seat. Gently, we both tried to reassure the terrified animal that he was going to be all right and I switched on the engine. He glanced down to where the floor was now reverberating, then looked up quizzically at Ruth as I edged the Land Rover out of the car park and onto Golspie High Street.

By the time we left the village, the old dog seemed more settled. However, we had to get the girls to stop shouting out questions about how he was doing as it was unnerving him. We agreed that we'd all have to be as quiet and calm as possible. The only problem to deal with now was the overpowering smell. Even with the front vents and both our windows wide open, it didn't do much to rid the Land Rover cab of the aroma of a dog that had been cooped up in a locked kennel for the past six months. He was sweating now, which didn't help. The return journey was a long sixty-five miles.

We all hastily disembarked at the top of the glen. The poor dog immediately relieved himself and after that was much more at ease. He stood patiently by Ruth as the girls and I packed the various items of our shopping trip into knapsacks and bags. The remainder that we couldn't carry we stuffed into what we called our Snoopy box. This was a customised post box resembling the kennel belonging to Snoopy in the Peanuts cartoon. The postman was the only other person with a key. Then it was off over the hill towards Kerracher with the dog accompanying us as if he had known us all his life. As soon as we got home the girls fed him a tin of dog food, which he promptly threw up, mainly because he'd wolfed it down so quickly. Undaunted, he hoovered up the ejected food, leaving no trace. We then dispatched him to his bed in the corner of the shed and left him for the night.

The following Sunday morning the girls were quicker than usual to get up and out after breakfast, eager to set him free. Glen was ecstatic and as we undid the string around his neck he wagged his tail, unable to keep still. The girls took him for a walk along the seashore and in no time he was running and jumping high in the air for the sticks they threw for him. Glen was free and he knew it.

After that he settled into our family life, always keen to walk with us wherever we went and even tolerated by Penny the cat. There was a collie named Glen in residence at Kerracher once again – albeit with a question mark over his head about his prowess as a sheepdog.

———————

Hughie invited me to some of the shepherds' gatherings, which took place in Nedd and Drumbeg. He described it as my 'apprenticeship' but I was quite aware the other shepherds saw it as an opportunity to benefit from the help of a younger pair of hands, however inexperienced.

I learned to gather, dip, dose and clip sheep all in one summer. These gatherings brought together many of the crofters who had sheep on that area of common grazing and it was an excellent way of getting to know people.

Nothing was done in a rush. There were always the obligatory stops for tea and sandwiches or home-baked pancakes and scones. The tea was frequently laced with a drop of whisky and in some cases more than a few drops. Sometimes at the end of the day there was a meal, with a final dram to help us on our weary way home.

The gathering often took a whole day and indeed sometimes several days, depending on the terrain and the skills of the gatherers. Most of the men were not trained shepherds but crofters to whom crofting was a way of adding a little more to a meagre income. This was brought home to me one day when I was on the hill, gathering with Danny McCrimmond.

Until then my previous experience of shepherding had been of watching dogs struggling to control the sheep. Tongues hanging out, they ran back and forth, trying to make sense of shouted, more often screamed, instructions from a beetroot-faced crofter, his arms waving like a frenzied windmill. I never had the sense that there was any kind of order to this exercise, until I observed Danny, a small lean man who had been a shepherd all his working days. He didn't have much to say and what he did say was succinct and to the point. He never seemed to be in a hurry, and his dogs ignored everything except him and his few muttered words.

'Come by.'

'Heel.'

'Good dog.'

His dogs wove an invisible pattern around the sheep but also seemed to spend much of their time behind him. On the hill he found a vantage spot and leaned on his crook with a couple of fingers in his mouth. All he did was whistle and his dogs responded. There was an order and efficiency about the operation that I had never seen before. No exasperation. No frustration venting itself on the poor dogs. He was a professional doing his job.

THE HILLSIDE GOES UP IN FLAMES AND
WE DEAL WITH THE ROOF

During our first winter we regularly walked over from
Reintraid to Kerracher to work on the house. It was dank
and depressing at first, but when we lit a fire in the old
range the place soon warmed. Because we were limited in
what we could do over the winter, we decided to start the
renovation proper in the spring when the weather would be
better and allow us to open up the roof. We raised the
skylights and the downstairs windows as much as possible
to try to air the house, but it was only a token attempt in the
battle against damp. We did manage to gut the living room
and strip the walls of their lath and plaster, exposing the old
stone and leaving the room an empty shell.

We also spent some time making the barn next to the
house a safe area. When I was a child this long low building
housed the cows at the far end, stored hay in the middle
and was a work shed at the end adjoining the house. Now it
was dilapidated: the felt roof was falling in and parts of the
thick stone walls were dangerously close to collapse. We
took most of this down, leaving only the work shed intact.
Though dark, it would give us shelter to work on a wet day.

It still contained an assortment of old tools and crofting implements, many riddled with woodworm. There was also a good deal of seafaring tackle, such as rope, shackles, brass bits off boats and an assortment of buoys. Ruth rescued the buoys, each about the size of a baby's head. When she cleaned them up their green glass sparkled, so she kept them as ornaments.

When spring arrived we returned to Kerracher and living in the caravan. With the weather improving, we could start the real renovation work.

Because the house still had no running water and therefore no sanitation, our main priority was to address these difficulties. First, we had to get the water to run out of the underground stream, further up the hill behind the house, into a holding tank. That simply meant a few days' digging away a channel to divert the water to a flattish area a little below where it came out from under the ground. It didn't take long to clear a piece of solid rock and, with turfs and earth, build an area to take the holding tank.

Unfortunately it had to be large enough to take two tanks. The local council's Environmental Health office had to approve any water taken off the hill as fit to drink. Although a family had lived there for well over a hundred years safely drinking water that came from the underground stream, the council sent a man from Inverness to take away a number of samples for testing. The first sample showed that bacteria of all sorts contaminated our water. So the man from Inverness returned for more samples. After enjoying Ruth's home baking and absorbing the tranquillity of Kerracher for a few hours, he took further samples and waved us goodbye.

This time the levels of bacteria were not so high but the water was still considered unfit to drink. As these bugs were clearly not affecting us, we were allowed to proceed if we installed a filtration system.

After checking out a number of systems which would all be very costly, we decided we would have to build our own. This involved filling a tank with stones, graduating from large ones on the bottom to rough sand on the top. We installed this and the water-holding tank up on the hill. We had no shortage of materials for filtering as the beach provided them, but it was fifty metres from the water filter tank – a steep fifty metres.

Installing and connecting the tanks was quick and easy but filling the water filter tank seemed to take forever. The only way was to put as many stones as I could carry into two bags and with one in each hand walk up the hill for the fifty metres and place them in the tank. I eventually took to hanging the full bags on the ends of a long pole and then settling the pole across my shoulders – primitive but effective.

The girls sometimes helped, and on the day when the final layer of rough sand was spread over the tank-full of stones, they were keen to be there to ensure it all worked.

'I'm putting my sand over the end where the water will come out, so you put yours over the other end of the tank,' Ruthie directed Clare. I had set up two standing platforms of large stones at opposite ends of the tank to enable them to spread the final layer of sand.

'I think we have enough sand in now,' I said.

'But it's not full up yet,' Clare pointed out.

'We don't want it to be right to the top otherwise the sand will wash into the water tank,' I explained.

'Of course, silly,' Ruthie scoffed.

'Ok, when I give the signal you both pull away your turfs.'

I had blocked the channel from the main stream with large sods of earth but now we had to pull them out to let the water run into our tank system.

'Pull turfs out!' I shouted. The girls heaved their turfs out and, clinging onto them, both fell backwards into the heather. Quickly they pulled themselves up and rushed to the tank to watch the water rise up from the inlet at the bottom.

'But nothing's happening.'

'Where's the water going?'

'It's going to take a bit of time for it to fill,' I explained.

The three of us leaned over the edge of the tank, absorbed in the sound of water trickling from the stream and patiently waiting for it to appear through the thick layer of sand. For some time we watched while the sun shone on our backs and birds sang in the trees further up the cliff behind us. Life slowed to the tranquil pace of the water trickling into the tank.

'There's some water!' Ruthie was leaning over the lower edge of the filter tank.

'I can see it too,' said Clare, not to be outdone.

We watched a small but ever growing reservoir of water cover the sand, inch its way up the sides of the tank, and eventually trickle through the outlet pipe to the larger water tank. I lifted Clare up so that she could see better.

'We've done it!' Ruthie exclaimed, peering over the edge of the tank with us.

'Let's go and tell Mummy,' said Clare.

Water supply dealt with, I turned to the house itself. During the winter, using the architect's plans, I had compiled a list of materials and tools we would need to replace the wood and windows for the roof. The suppliers delivered the windows to Kylesku but I collected the other materials from Inverness myself, carrying the lengths of timber strapped on top of the Land Rover and deepening the dents made by the raft wood. Roddy obliged by transporting everything on to Kerracher.

Ruth's father, Bill, a joiner by trade, was booked to make a start on the dormer windows. I had prepared the roof by stripping the thick Ballachulish slates from the front and stacking them carefully in order in the garden area in front of the house. Bill helped to open up the space where the windows were to go and together we inserted the first of the long supporting beams of the dormer windows through into the roof space. That was a defining moment for us all: we felt that at last we were on our way to making the house habitable. It didn't take long before we had the whole stretch of roof trusses in place both front and back of the house.

Our next step was to lower the front wall of the house to give enough space to take the windows. For that we were joined by my brother-in-law Steve. Steve is a big fellow and he saw himself as chief of demolitions. That was fine with us: we stood back as he lifted the sledgehammer to reduce the height of the front retaining wall.

'Everyone clear below?' he called as he looked through the gap in the roof to Ruth, Jean and the children who stood watching from below. 'Stand back!' He swung the sledgehammer, giving it his considerable strength. He followed this blow with another – and another. After four he stopped in bewilderment to investigate. The wall, which had been put together about a hundred years before, was stubbornly intact.

'What's happening?' Ruth asked.

'Nothing much,' Bill and I chorused. Exasperated, Steve prepared to have another go. But this further pounding had just as little effect.

'Double porridge for you at breakfast tomorrow, Steve,' was the best we could suggest.

Eventually, as the next youngest man available, I had a go, to give Steve a break. In less time than he had, I too gave up. Attacking the wall in this way was going to take forever and waste us all in the process. Jean, Ruth and the children gave up in disappointment and headed back to the caravan to make a cup of tea for the failed workers.

Over a brew we discussed the matter. We decided to try dislodging the wall stones by removing what was holding them together. Steve was disappointed; this wasn't nearly as dramatic as wielding a sledgehammer. But it worked, and it wasn't long before we eventually dug out the first top stone by using a hammer and cold chisel to chip away, little by little, first the plaster facing then the dry fill bonding it to the other stones.

At least the house was solidly built. But we were coming to realise that our renovation work would be a series of slow painstaking steps. Perhaps it was just as well we didn't know at the time just *how* painstaking.

Spring and summer were taken up with getting the dormer windows built into the roof, three at the front and one at the back. I acquired a short but definitive book from Stan Roy, *Mitchell's Guide to Construction*, which gave detailed instructions on how to build a house. I had amassed a collection of DIY books but that one explained it all so well and clearly that it became my builder's bible, though it was more than forty years old.

After the demolition work was complete we got on pretty well, but there was one heart-stopping moment. We were about to start work on the timber framing to take the windows.

'There is one very important rule about joinery,' announced Bill, as we were about to lay the first length of timber on top of the wall of the house to provide a wall plate for the window frames.

'What's that?'

'When you measure for a length of wood, before you cut the wood, measure it again. That way you have less chance of wasting wood.'

'I'll try and remember that – measure twice, cut once,' I confirmed. Unfortunately there was many a time after that when working away on my own and sometimes with my mind on other things, I forgot this advice and indeed wasted wood.

We laid the wall plate without any mishap and then began the process of measuring the uprights for cutting. I measured the space between the wall plate and the beam that was extended from the rafters of the roof to give us the lengths to cut.

'Best check that size with the height of your window frames,' said Bill.

I quickly nipped down the ladder and went off to the barns where the frames were sitting awaiting installation. I measured and re-measured the height of two of them, just in case.

'Height is fifty-four inches,' I shouted up to Bill.

'What did you say?'

I got to the top of the ladder where he was standing inside the house and squinting at the end of his measuring rule.

'Fifty-four inches,' I confirmed.

'Are you sure?' he said.

'Yes. I measured two of them, and twice, as you told me. Why? What's the matter?' I began to wonder if he was winding me up.

'The space we have between the wall plate and the beam is only fifty inches,' he answered, so precisely that I knew there was no kid-on here.

'Can we do anything to change the height of our space?'

'I wouldn't want to put the beams in any higher. Anyway, I wouldn't want to *un*install them. We can't make the wall any lower without taking out a layer of huge stones and we'd only to have to build it up again,' he said.

'So what you're saying is we need to replace the window frames.'

'Looks like the only solution.'

'How could that have happened?' I tried to defend myself. 'I definitely ordered the right sized frames according to the plans.'

'I'm sure you did. But you can't always believe what an architect has stipulated.'

We had seven frames altogether. The whole lot had to be returned by boat to Kylesku then by road to Inverness. The replacements, the right size this time, made the same laborious journey in reverse shortly after.

———

In the middle of this complicated roofing business, we were also making a start at being crofters. One man took upon himself the duty of ensuring we would survive, and that was Lal MacLeod. Lal remembered my grandfather well and recalled how he had helped his own father with cutting the family peats. According to Lal, my grandfather had been a great storyteller, but he seemed to suspect many of the tales were embellished. He also told me that my grandfather would never give away how well or not so well he was doing with the lobster fishing.

Lal decided we ought to be cutting peat, as a number of crofters still did at that time. My parents both remembered well how the peat was cut in their youth. So one warm and pleasant day late in April I brought Lal to Kerracher to survey our peat bogs and give me advice on where to cut, and also how to use the implements we'd discovered in the work shed. They were all intact, though a couple required new handles because of woodworm.

The peat bogs were a short walk from the house to the north edge of the croft. It was clear where they had been cut before, but it had been many years ago and the heather was now growing up to two feet high over the peat. Lal first showed us how to slice the top turf off. Unfortunately, the flaughter, which was the tool for the job, was far too cumbersome and certainly not sharp enough. I had a long-handled spade that seemed to do the work more easily so we used that instead.

What made reopening the banks that first year even more difficult was that the face was overgrown and had first of all to be cleaned up by taking off a slice of turf. We found a spot where the heather was not so thick and high and that was where we started, taking off a bit of turf at the edge. We had to abandon the tool for this too, the rutter, and again make use of my spade.

We did manage to use the tusker, the implement for cutting out the peat. When we took samples we found that underneath some of the banks the peat was black and dense, ideal for long-burning peats. Taking stock at this point, Lal announced we would have to burn the heather on top of the banks we selected.

'Are you sure?' We were doubtful about such a drastic step.

'Aye, laddie, that's the way it's done. I've done a lot of heather burning in my time.'

We were concerned about any birds nesting in the area but after a thorough inspection we decided it would be all right, so Lal and I began setting the heather alight. Ruth, with Clare in tow, watched us from the edge of the peat field apprehensively, but also with excitement.

'I'm going to tell Ruthie when she gets home from school that I watched Lal burning the heather,' said Clare.

The brushy heather soon took light and began to burn very well. A warm breeze off the sea fanned the flames as they reached into the bright blue sky. It was all going so well that we decided to adjourn to the caravan for some lunch.

Both Ruth and I were anxious about the fire getting out of control. When we said as much to Lal we were met with his confident assurance that there was no need to worry, as he had done this all his life and he knew what he was doing. The area we were burning backed onto the sea on the north and west sides and was edged with a wide ditch of peat before it met with the flat arable area of our croft. The south side, which led high into the hillside to the back of our croft, and beyond into the depths of the Assynt Estate, was separated from it by a narrow gap running from our croft westwards to the sea. A bare stony path with no heather growth, built many years before by my grandfather, ran through this gap. It would act as a natural barrier to the fire if it went that far.

As we sat enjoying our lunch, we became aware that the

pall of smoke rising from the peat banks was growing thicker and higher. What was more worrying was the spread of the flames. Eventually the whole hillside beyond the peat banks seemed to be ablaze and spreading rapidly.

Unable to contain myself any longer, I pointed this out to Lal.

'It'll be fine, laddie. No need to worry.' Calmly, he went on munching his sandwich.

I couldn't take my eyes off the hillside. 'I think we ought to finish lunch and get over there,' I said, getting to my feet.

'The hill needs a good burning. It hasn't been burned for years,' replied Lal, impervious to my rising panic. He was reluctant to come away from his meal. 'There's nothing quite like a good fire. It'll burn itself out by the time we finish eating, laddie.'

I gave it a few moments, but then I just couldn't wait any longer. 'I'm finished, so I'll go over and check it out.'

I hurried off, leaving a half-eaten sandwich on the plate. Lal and Ruth, with Clare attached, followed me a few minutes later to find that not only was the hillside behind the peat bogs ablaze, but the fire was spreading over the south hillside that led further inland, heading towards the 4,000-acre Assynt Estate.

The enormity of the situation suddenly hit Ruth and me. Here was a fire beginning to consume the thick dry heather, untouched for years, which could engulf the whole area. The consequences were potentially disastrous. What were we to do? There were only three of us plus a small child, one an old man in his seventies and two of us lacking any experience of heather burning. But we had to start beating out the fire. Ruth ran back to the house leaving Clare sitting with enormous glee on a high boulder out of harm's way, while Lal and I picked up the spades we had used earlier.

The breeze off the sea now seemed like a gale and was fanning the flames across the whole hillside. The main task was to stop the fire spreading on the south side. I ran from fire patch to fire patch frantically beating out the sparking heather. Ruth reappeared with a number of hessian sacks she had found as well as another spade. She joined me in a desperate bid to prevent complete disaster. Lal, however, was not at all put out, and seemed in no hurry. It suddenly dawned on me that he was actually enjoying the spectacle. Was Lal a secret arsonist?

All afternoon we went on running, beating and stamping out the individual fires catching on the south hillside. By the time I had to return by boat to Kylesku to collect Ruthie from school and return Lal, we had thankfully succeeded in keeping the blaze to our side of the gap dividing us from the Assynt Estate. The breeze had died down and there was less chance of sparks flying across to the south hillside. I had to leave it, hoping the wind wouldn't get up again and that the fire would burn itself out.

As I returned in the boat with Ruthie the whole shoreline at Kerracher was a bright glow, even in the sunlight, and the smoke cloud was drifting upwards and away to the north. That was a good omen for it meant that there was less chance of the fire heading south and to calamity. The sparks that were carried up into the pall of smoke would extinguish themselves over the loch and wouldn't be a threat to the forestry on the other side.

I spent a long evening going from spot to spot beating out anything that was burning and eventually gave up when exhaustion overtook me. Ruth and I slept uneasily that night after praying that the wind would not rise again.

Thankfully our prayer was answered. We woke to a still morning with all the smaller fires extinguished, leaving a blackened hillside and a peat bog area scalped of heather. It was ready for cutting peat, or it would be when it cooled down.

The bank that divided the croft from the peat cutting area was still glowing fiercely. It ran for a length of about 50 metres alongside the edge of the arable land. It burned like that, glowing hot and bright, for almost a week after the fire. I had occasion to come home along the loch late one night and there was a bright glow directing me all the way to Kerracher.

Lal thought it was a triumph and seemed to have no sense of the enormity of the potential damage. He was focused on the task we now had ahead of us: getting peat cut so that we would have fuel for the next winter

The hardest part of peat cutting was skimming off the top layer of turf. Once that task was complete, cutting the rectangular slices of wet black peat had a certain satisfaction to it. It wasn't easy to cut each peat with the tusker to a regular size and shape. It was even more difficult to throw each cut slice up onto the bank and pile them between six and eight deep. The first few were easy to get in line but to stretch out the last few to a distance of about three metres took some practice to perfect. This was all new to me and I found muscles in my back and arms I hadn't realised existed. However, the sight of a complete stretch of cut peat bank covered with a layer of shiny black slabs – like tiny gravestones toppled over – was always to be a most fulfilling sight.

My job became the cutting and it fell to Ruth to be the 'lifter', a job I have to admit I hated. Once the peats had been lying in the sun long enough to be dry on their top surface, the next task was to lift and stack them vertically in groups of three, leaning in on each other for support. A fourth peat was then placed across the top and they were left to dry out completely. By this time, the peat bank looked like a crowded Stonehenge in miniature. I found that part of the job back breaking but Ruth enjoyed the urgency of it, for if they weren't lifted in time they would never dry. Instead they would erode with time, eventually merging back into the peat bank. The girls helped her with this task and as they grew older became very adept at it. We were a good team when it came to peat production.

Once they were completely dry they had to be stacked. As we had never done that before, my mother and father, both brought up on crofts, came to show us how to complete the job. Because it was a job that was done towards the end of the summer, that gave them the excuse to come and stay with us then. My mother, who had been less than delighted at the prospect of our living the kind of life she had had as a young girl, now found she enjoyed taking part in an activity from her youth. Better still, it was wonderful to see the joy in my father every time he returned to his family home.

We all liked stacking the peat – even Ruthie and Clare, who carried peats in their small barrows. The stack at base was about two metres long and one metre wide and it was built to a height of about two metres tapering in at the top like a mini-pyramid. This was made up of hard briquettes that bore no resemblance to the slices of cold wet peat cut out of the bank all these months before.

The realisation that we were indeed crofters came on the completion of our first peat stack. We had a deep sense of satisfaction that we had taken our first step towards self-sufficiency and could survive in this remote part of the Highlands.

I COME VERY CLOSE TO GIVING UP

By the beginning of the autumn I had managed to replace the defective sarking on the roof, mainly around the ridge and the chimney stacks, and had the whole roof now covered with felt, ready for the slates to go back on.

The renovation of the house was a slow process but we were keen to get the slates on before winter set in. The interior had to wait and that meant putting up with a state of disrepair. The main living room was still unfloored, so we lived mostly in the dark, cramped kitchen. From then on the caravan was occupied by the succession of relatives and friends who were visiting us, keen to experience our new way of living – temporarily at any rate.

Getting through the everyday household tasks took up a lot of time, especially for Ruth. She had to carry all the water from the 'well', cook with only four small gas rings and wash clothes after heating pots of water in an aluminium bath tub my father had acquired at the Auction Rooms in Dingwall.

When the darker evenings set in we used tilley lamps. Lighting these was a delicate art.

To begin with, the brass-covered chamber at the base,

which looked like an upturned bowl, had to have enough paraffin. There was a pump on the bowl that was primed until enough pressure was established. Then a small wad of wick, soaked in methylated spirits and placed just underneath the mantle at the top of the stem, was set alight. The clip holding the soaked material was clamped to the long stem that protruded upwards from the bowl at the base of the lamp to just underneath the bulb at the top of the stem, which produced the light.

The bulb was a flimsy globe of silky material like a deflated balloon. Once the burning meths had heated it a valve at the top of the stem was unscrewed to allow the pressurised paraffin from the bowl to move up the stem and into the bulb. The bulb then inflated to a small ball filling with light – if we'd got it right. All the lamp needed then was a small pump from time to time to keep the pressure up.

The tilley lamp hissed away for hours on end and a bowl full of paraffin would last the evening. After it was first lit the bulb would last for as long as it wasn't damaged – something that was all too easy to do, as it was made of a fragile material that became ash-like when fired and liable to disintegrate at the least movement or touch. Perhaps it was not all that environmentally friendly, but in the utter darkness of a West Highland night, with no electric light, the glow of the hissing tilley was a comforting friend to have next to us as we sat reading. Not great for the eyesight either, but better than candlelight.

These routines were laborious but Ruth carried them through with a fortitude that helped keep us all going. We were becoming used to this way of living and learning to deal better with our frustration at not progressing as quickly as we'd have liked. Patience was a virtue we all began to develop.

———

Then came one terrible night when I nearly gave it all up.

Ruth had just spent a week in the hospital in Golspie after a minor operation to remove a cyst, the first of several she had to deal with down the years. While she was in hospital I looked after the girls, and thus found out the hard way what it was like to keep up with household chores.

Because both girls were attending school at Drumbeg by now, I was able to visit Ruth the day after her operation. Then, at the end of the week, we arranged for the girls to be dropped off at Stan and Moira's on the way home from school, so that I could bring Ruth home. She and I joined them at Glenleraig and stayed overnight before going on to Kerracher the following day. Fiercely independent, Ruth was keen to be home to get on with her life. Both our mothers were concerned about her going back to the conditions at Kerracher so soon, but Ruth was adamant she would cope.

It was late September. The gales had set in again and the tides were very high. A week after Ruth had come home, we'd settled down to read one evening with the wind howling and the sound of the waves thumping on the sea wall outside. The girls hadn't long been put to bed when the kitchen door creaked open and Clare's small head popped round.

'I can't get to sleep for all the noises, Daddy.'

I carried her upstairs to their bedroom where Ruthie was fast asleep, oblivious to the storm. I tucked her in, persuading her that we were all safe and she had nothing to worry about. I waited outside the bedroom door for a moment to make sure she had settled. As I listened I heard not just the wind and the sea but also some very disturbing flapping sounds from the roof above.

I bounded downstairs and grabbed our searchlight. Then, calling to Ruth that I was 'just checking something', I wrapped up warmly and hurried out into the storm. There was a good vantage point at the back of the house as the land rose steeply above the level of the roof, and here I used my searchlight to find out what was making the thumping noise. My heart sank. All the roofing felt I had almost finished tacking on to the bare sarking, ready to take the slates back on, was coming undone before my eyes. The roof had turned to a sea of waving pieces of felt, lapped up by the battering wind.

I sprinted to the work shed and grabbed my hammer, nail bag and ladder. As I reached the house again, I shouted to Ruth what was happening. Positioning the ladder at the point which seemed the worst damaged, I climbed up. But holding a searchlight and a hammer at the same time as pinning down the felt to knock in nails was going to be impossible. I went back down the ladder to fetch Ruth, but all she could do was point the searchlight at the lengths of felt being ripped up by the wind, as I tried to catch hold of them. Frantically I tried to tack down as many pieces as I could, but it was a losing battle. As I was knocking in a nail on one flapping piece, another would tear up again an arm's length away.

Eventually it dawned on me that nailing a number of lengths of wood to the roof would help to hold it down better. Using some of my supply of two-by-ones I began to pin down as many as I could, zigzagging them over the back roof. Ruth couldn't do anything other than continue to hold the searchlight in place to help me see where I was going. By now of course both girls were awake, so she went back into the house to reassure them. After what felt like a whole night, but in reality was perhaps only an hour or two, I managed to pin down most of the felt and keep it on the roof both back and front. It was now looking battle scarred and weary – much the way I felt myself. I persuaded Ruth to go to bed, while I cleared up.

The wind was falling and the rain had almost stopped but the swell of the sea continued to batter the sea wall and send up spumes of spray. When I returned the tools to the shed I realised the true height of the tide. The water was lapping onto the shed floor. As the outbuildings were on a slightly higher level than the caravan I ran along to check it, to find the water rising over its doorstep. However, it was secure and I could deal with any internal water damage in the morning.

It was when I turned back that my torch revealed a scene which was enough to defeat me altogether. Our stack of peat, which we had built at the end of the barns for use over the winter, was being completely washed away. The peats were getting sucked out to sea by what was now a receding tide. Worse, our stack of wood for the house renovation was also floating, broken up and likely to be carried out to sea. The peats I let go – there was nothing else for it. But I rescued the wood there and then by wading into the sea and pulling the planks one by one back to the shore.

It was the early hours of the morning when I eventually collapsed into bed. Ruth was still awake.

'I couldn't get to sleep for worrying that you would be ok,' she whispered as I settled in beside her.

'Just be thankful there's no road out of here,' I said.

'What do you mean?'

'You and the girls wouldn't be in bed now, you'd be in the Land Rover with me – heading south.'

I don't know whether she answered or not. I fell asleep at once, exhausted.

The next morning we rose to perfect calm, but also to find the whole high water mark of the bay strewn with debris, including many of our peats. The caravan floor was damp. The shed floor was all right as it was concreted, and nothing was damaged. But the house roof looked as if it had barely survived a face lift carried out by a plastic surgeon wearing boxing gloves. At least most of the felt was still on, with only a few bare patches that could easily be covered again.

There is always relief after a storm, and the horrors of the previous night paled into memory when viewed in the very different conditions of the morning. So we stayed at Kerracher and got on with the extra work the storm had left us.

It was now imperative to get the slates back on as soon as possible before we had any further storms and repeats of the previous night. I had been dreading this but I'd bought an adze for the purpose, so with that in one hand and the Mitchell book in the other I set to.

We had been very organised in stacking all the slates in the garden space in front of the house. The rows of piled slates graduated from the smaller ones at the back to the larger ones at the front, as these would be used in the first rows on the roof. Of course, they had now been thoroughly pre-washed by the waves. Miraculously, the storm hadn't damaged them.

The first morning started slowly as I got everything ready. I measured the line of the first row of slates and eventually nailed in the first of them to follow with a double line on top. It was when I started to go onto the second row of single slates that my troubles began. Because many of the slates had been damaged where the nail-hole was, I had to knock a new hole into many of them as near to the top as possible. This had to be on an area of the heavy Ballachulish slate that was thick enough to take the impact of the adze without shattering into pieces.

The adze was not an easy tool to use. It was something like a butcher's meat cleaver with the addition of a vicious spike on the top edge of the blade. The spike was sharp and slightly curved. It was a heavy tool that was used like a hammer: to produce a hole, the spike was brought down on the slate as if hitting a nail in.

This turned into a nightmare as a small pile of smashed slates began to appear beside me. Slate after slate was being thrown to the side after fruitless attempts at punching new holes. By lunchtime all I had managed was one line of slates along the bottom edge of the front roof of the house, and a good pile of abandoned slates by my bench. It was all right to discard a few because we now had the dormers, so fewer slates were needed. However, I couldn't afford to carry on like this. Soon I wouldn't have enough slates to reach the dormer windows, far less cover the roof.

In the end, I spent that first afternoon practising making holes in the shattered remnants lying at my feet. I did manage, eventually, to master (in my own fashion) the skill of holing the slates. Well, the majority of them. Finally, I managed to get on with the actual re-slating. I had just enough to finish the job some weeks later, but there was a good pile of broken slates left over. No doubt they would come in handy for something later on.

The external covering of the house was of prime importance so we fixed the lead flashings, pointed the chimney stacks, sat the chimney pots on, topped the roof ridge with ridge tiles and covered the dormers with three layers of felt. That work went on for many painstaking months. This was how it was going to be with all of the renovation – a step at a time, spread over a long but educational seven years of Do it Yourself.

We were resigned by now to every job having a hitch of some sort, but there were times when that didn't make the frustration any easier to bear.

To install the septic tank I had to dig a hole to take a bulb-like container, which was over three metres in height and width. The hole had to be a certain distance away from the house and deep enough to allow sufficient pipe descent. We couldn't hire a digger as it would have to be ferried to us. Our raft had long gone, used up for the materials needed in the house. So we had to resort to hand tools. In this case a spade, to dig the hole.

Because the hole was close to the sea wall I was effectively digging into the beach, so it was extremely stony. After a couple of days' solid digging I reached a stone which got bigger and bigger as I cleared the debris around it. Eventually the 'stone' covered the whole floor area of the hole, which by this time was about twenty five centimetres from the required depth. Only it wasn't a stone – I had hit solid bedrock.

As I was now deep enough to need a ladder to get in and out I was beginning to feel as if I'd been in there for an eternity chipping through pebbles and stones. I had thrown spadeful after spadeful over my shoulder and above my head to create a huge mound outside. Now this would all have to be thrown back into the hole. Then I'd have to start digging another one only a couple of metres away. Thankfully the bedrock slanted down and away from the house as I probed it. So I didn't have to dig an entire new hole: only half a new one. There was no alternative: the tank had to reach a certain depth, otherwise it wouldn't connect with the waste pipe from the house.

In normal circumstances, many of the errors and obstacles which hindered us would have been a matter of a few hours' delay. Our remoteness meant we were often held up for days, especially when we had to return items which turned out not to be fit for purpose after we got them to Kerracher. As well as the new windows all having to go back down the loch I also had to return 600 quarry tiles that could only be moved a box at a time. I had put sixty boxes altogether into a vehicle at the builders' yard in Inverness. I then took them out at the pier at Kylesku and lifted them into the boat; then lifted them out of the boat at Kerracher and carried them up to the house. Then when I opened the boxes I discovered that none of them had been properly glazed. They then had to be lifted back onto the boat at Kerracher ... This time, needless to say, I checked the replacement tiles before they were loaded into the vehicle at the builders' yard in Inverness. I was a very happy man when I eventually finished laying them on the kitchen floor.

Although I had bought the bulk of the materials we would need at the outset, I did have to keep ordering more, and there were many times when I had to carry heavy bags of cement in and out of the boat. Then there were the kitchen cupboards. They came in flat packs and arrived at Kylesku during a spell of easterly winds, which put the boat out of commission for most of a week. As I wanted to get on with the job, I decided to carry them over the hill. It meant several journeys, but by carrying a few at a time on my back, I got them over to Kerracher and eventually put them together to form our kitchen. I must have looked an odd sight to anyone passing on the road, half bent with a couple of flat packs strapped across my back. The lengths of worktop were the most difficult pieces to carry, but I was well used by now to carrying things over the hill.

These things were all necessary for our renovation. It was a different matter when visitors were going home. We often had to walk them over the hill rather than take them by boat. They would have left their cars at the top of the glen, and, besides, they weren't all 'boat people'. They arrived with luggage topped up with food and gifts, so you'd think their bags would be nice and light for the return trip. But people seem to feel they should never return from holiday with less than they brought. Many a collection of stones from our beach was carried over the hill from Kerracher for display in suburban gardens. I was often tempted to make a 'customs' inspection of visitors' suitcases before they left, but perhaps that wouldn't have been too well received.

The heaviest and hardest things I ever carried I took only once. My parents were with us one Christmas when we ran out of bottled gas. I got through some nasty weather to Lochinver and collected two canisters. As the weather was so foul I had left the boat at home and was planning to walk over the hill. However, I didn't relish the thought of having to make two walks over the festive period carrying a 25kg canister each time. So I decided to carry both at once.

I picked up a canister in each hand and walked what I thought would be a distance I could manage without dropping them. I counted fifty paces and then let them down. I counted to fifty in my head and then picked them up and walked another fifty paces. I continued like that for the full mile and a half, apart from going up the incline from the small loch to the cliff above Kerracher. There it had to be twenty paces and a count to fifty between each carry. I did make it to the house – but for about an hour after I had almost no feeling in my arms.

LAL IS INGENIOUS, AND SO ARE WE

I soon realised we weren't the only ones who had to devise roundabout ways of getting jobs done. Indeed, my ingenuity was nothing compared to Lal's.

A couple of weeks after the heather burning incident I called in to see him on my way to Inverness. I found him with a brand new Lister generator sitting on wooden blocks at the mouth of his Dutch barn.

'Where are you putting that?' I asked.

'The new shed is ready for it now.'

I walked into the small block-built shed he had built himself, to find a concrete plinth rising about half a metre from the floor. A number of bolts, which had been embedded in the concrete, were sticking out of the top.

'Who's going to help you get the gennie across here and up onto that?' I asked.

'No one. I'll manage it myself.' He was as matter of fact as usual.

'But it's a good distance from the barn, never mind getting it up high enough to get it onto the plinth.'

Did he realise what he was taking on? The generator probably weighed more than a ton and Lal was a wiry but diminutive old man.

'Have you got some pulley system?' I suggested, since I could see only a few blocks of wood scattered around the base of the generator.

'I've got everything I need. But I have a list of a few things you could get me if you're going to Inverness.'

He hobbled off to the house, leaving me bewildered. How on earth was he going to manage this?

He soon reappeared with his shopping list scrawled in a shaky hand. I checked everything on it with him, then I lingered as he got his tools together, including a long crow bar and a hammer.

'Are you not getting going?' he asked.

'I'm waiting to see if you need a hand.'

'No need, laddie.' He placed a block of wood next to the generator and wedged the lip at the end of the crow bar just under the base of the machine. Then he levered the crow bar on the wood so that the edge of the generator rose very slightly. Immediately he wedged a small block of wood neatly into the space under the generator so that it was now tilted.

Gradually, as I watched him, it dawned on me how he was going to tackle the job.

'See you when I get back,' I said, thinking as I climbed into the Land Rover, 'That's going to take *forever.*'

When I returned from Inverness late that evening his generator was sitting next to the plinth in the generator shed.

'I'll leave it to tomorrow to get it in place,' Lal said.

'That will need a lot of blocks,' I ventured, still not seeing the solution.

'Aye, a wee bit more,' he answered looking up to the open rafters of the shed.

I followed his gaze to see a pulley system with block and tackle hanging from the apex of the roof ready for action.

———

Later in the summer of that year we learned our own lesson in patience and ingenuity.

After the boat had been left high and dry on the rocks at Reintraid the previous year, it began to leak. Roddy confirmed my own view that it needed new internal ribs to help pull the planks together, and that if we managed this, we could also take the opportunity to replace some of the rotting wood on the gunwale.

I bought wood for the replacement ribs at a boat builders' yard in Inverness and we picked a week when the weather forecast was promising. We would take the boat in at the highest point of the tide, so that we could prop it up on land which would remain dry for nearly a fortnight. It was extremely heavy and needed at least two strong men to manoeuvre it. However, we didn't have two strong men available, so Ruth had to step into the breach. As always she was up to the task.

Getting the boat high and dry at the top of the beach wasn't too much of a problem but propping it up off the ground so that we could access and work on the underside seemed at first impossible as we had no lifting gear and couldn't hire a crane. We had to resort to Lal's tactics with the generator. With several blocks and a good strong length of wood to act as a lever we slowly and patiently raised the boat about half a metre off the ground, propped up by a small scaffolding. That took us almost a whole day but by the end of it the sight of the boat nicely balanced and stable enough for us to work on gave us great satisfaction.

That was the easy part. Now we had to strip the boat down to bare wood. There was layer upon layer of old paint to remove with painstaking slowness. It took us several long days, but we were helped by a spell of ideally hot dry weather.

Next came the technical challenge of nailing pieces of wood into the floor of the boat and in the process bending them enough, without breaking them, to take the shape of the boat. For this the ribs needed to be steamed so that the wood would become pliable.

'How are you going to manage that?' Ruth asked, when she realised what we'd have to do.

I was quite confident about this – having spent some time deep in a book on boat building I'd got from the mobile library. 'All we need is a kettle with a long tube attached that will house the rib,' I explained, showing Ruth the page illustrating this. 'It's all in here.'

'Well, we've got the kettle,' she conceded, 'but where are you going to get the tube? And how on earth can we heat a kettle down on the shore?'

'Don't worry, I've thought it all out,' I assured her.

What I planned to do was use the down-pipe at the end of the house, which was made of cast iron. We were planning to replace it with a plastic one in any case. I'd feed that through the caravan window so that the end inside was next to the kettle on the gas ring, and attach the kettle spout to the end of the down-pipe. I'd put the first piece of boat rib into the pipe, and stuff the other end with cloth to keep the heat in. The steam from the boiling kettle wood would heat the wood enough so that it became pliable. At least, that was the theory.

Ruth considered this. 'That wood was expensive so you can't afford any mistakes,' she pointed out. But I'd thought of that – I had bought three extra lengths of rib, just in case.

The following day I detached the down-pipe from the front of the house. It was ideal as it was slightly longer than the ribs. I then cut a small piece of the tough piping that was coiled ready for our future water supply. I taped that to the spout of the kettle. Next I propped the down-pipe through the side window of the caravan and arranged it so that one end was sitting next to the kettle. Then all I had to do was insert the end of the water pipe into the end of the down-pipe and secure it with cloth wadding and tape. I eased the first rib along the down-pipe and stuffed the open-air end with a rag while Ruth filled the kettle and when I was ready, lit the gas.

The kettle soon boiled and we left it till it was almost dry. Ruth filled it again and we let it boil away a second time.

'It's surely ready now?'

Wearing industrial gloves, I gingerly pulled out the hot rag and extracted a length of warm wood. I immediately replaced the rag to prevent any escape of steam or heat. Carefully, I tried to bend the end of the rib but it refused to yield.

'It's not been in long enough,' I decided, replacing it in the down-pipe.

We boiled the kettle twice more and drew out the rib again: it was hot and steaming. I charged over to the boat with it. With Ruth holding the other end we slowly pressed it into the bottom of the boat. It was bending well, almost taking the shape of the boat when there was a sudden 'crack' and the rib splintered, a piece in the middle sprung up like a jagged bone from a broken leg. It felt that way – just as painful. We had been doing so well too.

Ruth sighed. 'What do we do now?'

'Start another one,' I shrugged. 'This one's only fit for firewood.'

We started the process all over again but this time we boiled the kettle five times over. The rib felt very hot this time and again we rushed over to press it into place in the hull.

'Gently, gently,' we encouraged each other.

Eventually we couldn't press it any further so I grabbed the hammer I'd left on the floor of the boat along with the copper nails. I inserted the first nail through the small copper washer which would hold it in place, then hammered it through the rib and into the bottom of the boat. Working fast, I hammered in the rest of the nails, securing the rib to the boat. Then I crawled underneath the boat to place the washers over the end of each protruding nail and hammer the end flat. Ruth, above me, had to hammer down on the head of the nail in time with me hammering underneath. Needless to say we didn't master this synchronisation at the first attempt.

Eventually, though, we had the first new rib in place. It was a small step towards making the boat seaworthy again, but it felt like a huge step in learning the ancient craft of boat building.

It took us almost a week, but by the end of it we had twelve new ribs alongside the old ones. The replacing of the gunwale wood was relatively easy after that. Finally, we tarred the internal floor of the boat. We melted down a block of tar in an old cast iron pan on top of a fire on the beach. The hot tar was then poured into the bottom of the boat, covering the planks and ribs.

Our last jobs were to reinstall the seats, then paint every

piece of bare wood, internally and externally, first with a primer, then an undercoat and finally a skin of top quality marine paint. By the end of a month the boat was ready to go back in the water.

We launched it with a bottle of Babycham – Ruth's favourite tipple. We felt as if we had a new boat: it looked magnificent sitting high in the water, shining white with a dark blue gunwale and white seats, its black-tarred innards glistening.

Our pride in bidding it 'goodnight' as it bobbed in the sea that evening was completely dashed when we woke next morning to find it taking in water – up to the gunwale. We were very downcast – what had gone wrong?

When I bumped into Roddy later that day I told him what had happened.

'We were so careful.'

'Aye, but you have to give her the chance to expand again after drying out so much,' he said, smiling and matter of fact. 'Leave it as it is for a few days, then empty it and it'll be more watertight than ever before.'

We did, and he was right.

Another lesson learned – but another achievement too.

LOBSTERS AND WINKLES MAKE US A LIVING

After more than a year at Kerracher we had still made very little progress on the house, but it was at least watertight and weather proof. My system of starting any job with a book in one hand and a non-electric hand tool in the other meant we were never going to renovate the house in the timescale we had hoped. Our savings began to dwindle and we were forced to look for a way of earning a more substantial income than Ruth brought in with her hairdressing.

We started as near to home as possible. My Uncle Jim had made a good living in his time from catching lobsters, so we decided to try that. There were some old wooden creels, of the kind preserved in village museums, lying in the barn, about half a dozen of which were still in reasonable condition. I bought a coil of rope from the Lochinver Chandlery and bartered one of Ruth's hair dos for a fish box of dried salted mackerel. The girls helped gather up some of the metal buoys we'd found near the house, and painted them with a big blue 'K'. We attached each to one end of a length of rope long enough to sink six fathoms deep, with the other end fixed to a baited creel.

Primed with advice from both my father and Roddy, I ventured out at low tide to the point in the loch where it seemed I was most likely to find lobsters. There I carefully laid each creel amongst large fronds of seaweed close to the shore.

I had some idea of what I was doing. A year before we left the south I read a book by a diver called McKee who was promoting the sea-farming of lobsters. He described in his book how lobsters preferred the nooks and crannies of rocky parts of the seabed because it gave them shelter. As we were preparing to come north, I went along to the Reading Sub Aqua Club, intending to learn how to dive. On my first night there the instructor explained the admission tests, which included being able to swim a length of the pool fully dressed. I knew at once I was not going to be a diver.

As I placed the creels, I often wished I *could* be under the water to see exactly where the best spot would be. Our lobster catching was a hit and miss occupation to begin with, but things improved as I became better acquainted with the relationship between the weather, the tides and the seasonal life underwater.

It was a Saturday morning when the first creels were put in place, but as it was frowned upon locally to lift creels on the Sabbath, I waited until Monday before checking them. I took the boat out and headed for the first of the six grey buoys marking the creels, bobbing gently with its distinctive shiny blue 'K'. As I reached it I put the Seagull into neutral gear, then, with the engine idling, I hauled on the rope, getting water and loose seaweed all over the front of my legs in the process. I could see the creel slowly emerging through fronds of seaweed. There was definitely something in the bottom.

I pulled the creel free from the seaweed and into the boat with a flush of extra water and sea debris. And yes, there it was on the floor of the creel, exactly where it was originally secured with string – the large stone that weighted it. I was dismayed. What, no lobster? Not even bait.

Pulling myself together, I re-baited the creel, put the engine back into motion and found a new spot. I carefully replaced the creel on the floor of the seabed. And then went on to the next bobbing buoy.

It was the same there.

Eventually, after replacing all six empty creels, I made for home dejected and damp, clearing the boat as I went.

Ruth was waiting for me at the mooring. 'Well, how many did you catch?'

'Not a one,' I confessed.

'You'll never be a millionaire at this length,' she laughed.

I could hardly wait to get out the following day. But again the creels came out of the water in the same messy way with not a lobster in sight. Every day that week the creels were stubbornly empty. I almost went back to my book to check what a lobster looked like.

On the Saturday, the girls persuaded us to let them come with me. It was a still morning, so we togged them out with their wet weather gear and life jackets, then chugged across the loch towards the first forlorn-looking buoy. I had explained what we were going to do, and they knew that if they didn't follow my instructions and remain seated they wouldn't be allowed out again.

I hauled up the rope and the girls squealed with delight at the various sea creatures pouring into the boat with seaweed and debris.

'Look at that spidery thing!'

'There's a starfish!'

'And *huge* winkles.'

'Look at that seaweed, it's pink and flowery.'

They didn't spot the dark blue lump in the bottom of the creel when it tumbled over the gunwale into the boat. But I did. At last we had caught a lobster.

As they exclaimed over the sea treasures splashing about the bottom of the boat I tried to divert their attention to the lobster. With its tail curled up, it huddled in a corner of the creel, draped in a frond of dark brown seaweed. As soon as the girls saw it, they let out whoops of glee.

'Dad! Dad! You've caught a lobster.'

'It's huge.'

'Is it asleep?'

'No, silly. It's scared and trying to hide itself.'

'Ruthie, get me two bands please,' I instructed.

Clare handed her a polythene bag full of rubber bands and Ruthie extracted a couple.

'Hold them until I'm ready.'

I undid the string at the top of the creel and gingerly stretched my arm into it. I grabbed at the back of the creature and gripped it tightly, removing it back end first out of the creel.

'Quickly – give me a band,' I instructed Ruthie.

'Watch out Dad,' Clare shouted as the lobster immediately sprang into an aggressive stance, front legs held up high and spread apart, claws wide open ready to defend itself – or attack.

I held on tightly, keeping it facing well away from me as I reached across and caught the bands from Ruthie.

Now – how could I insert a rubber band on each claw so as to keep it closed? I had seen Roddy manage this deftly when I helped him.

The lobster has one very cumbersome club-like claw,

which it uses to hold its victim. The other claw is more scissor-like with serrated edges, for tearing the victim to pieces. I didn't want my fingers to end up shredded. Deciding to go for the smaller serrated claw I put the rubber band around my fingers and opened them up ready to fix the band. Fortunately lobsters don't have very fast reactions so I managed to catch the leg with the serrated claw and secure it before it could attack me with its bigger claw. Then it was easy to tie that with the second rubber band, efficiently handed over by Ruthie.

We placed the now limp lobster into a plastic bucket full of sea water so that I could clean out the boat. Then we headed confidently for the next creel. It scarcely mattered that the rest of the creels didn't produce a single lobster, for we had our prize. We were keen to show it off to Ruth.

The girls' shouts when we reached the home shore brought Ruth running out of the house and down the beach.

'We've caught a lobster, we've caught a lobster!'

'How big is it?' shouted Ruth.

I picked it up. 'I don't know. Get the kitchen scales and we'll find out.'

Ruth ran up the beach for the scales as I eased the boat onto the shore, jumping out and securing it before heading for the keep. I had made this from a wooden fish box with a lid nailed on the top and a couple of heavy stones secured to the bottom. A rope went from one handle to a small buoy.

We set the scales on top of the keep and as no one wanted to touch the lobster it was left to me to be brave enough to pick it up. It weighed all of two pounds four ounces.

'That's not very heavy,' Ruth said. 'We may as well have it

for dinner.'

'We could do – but we can have four dinners for what we'll get for it.'

Clare helped make the decision. 'I don't think I would like lobster.'

With the now limp creature inside, we headed the boat out to our running mooring where I sank the keep.

It was a pivotal day in our living at Kerracher, the start of making a living for ourselves from the environment. The girls thought we were going to be millionaires when I told them what we would get for the lobster.

We soon discovered that we also had an ideal beach to harvest winkles. At low tide the beach was littered with these black molluscs clinging to exposed seaweed. There were even easier pickings when we came across them congregated in rock pools. At certain tides and times they were even strewn out in patches on the wet beach, waiting to be scooped up.

They could only be picked when the tide was almost out. However, at some times of the year we found we had longer spells of time to collect them, especially when there were spring tides. Unfortunately, these times coincided with the worst of the weather. Many a wet and windy day was spent scouring the beach at Kerracher, bent almost double as we picked up these tiny creatures, collecting them in our buckets.

Ruth became our winkle-picking champion – she could fill two or three buckets to my one. But for me it was a miserable job, whatever the weather. The operation was simple – we pulled on our wellies, grabbed a bucket and headed for the beach – but uncomfortable, even in hot weather, because of the chafing of welly boots on bare legs. When the wellies were occasionally abandoned in summer, light footwear gave no protection to feet made numb by the cold water.

The majority of our winkles were not conveniently gathered together in rock pools but individually strewn across the beach, mostly hidden in seaweed. This meant picking one at a time and popping it into the bucket. After a while you learned to gather two or even three at a time in your hand, and eventually you could do this with two hands working simultaneously. Ruth mastered the art almost immediately: I never did.

At first the girls mostly played, but when they grew a little older the winkles they picked were allocated to them as pocket money, so they soon became skilled. It was back breaking work as you were bent over nearly all the time. Our hands suffered too. Ruth and the girls wore rubber gloves but I found them restrictive and so picked even fewer winkles. At the end of a day's picking, I'd go to bed with nail-less fingers and an aching back. Then when I closed my eyes, I saw nothing but winkles, and very often the noise of the wind was still howling in my ears.

Ruth and the girls spent the money they earned on clothes they would not otherwise have been able to afford. One of Ruth's first aims was to pick enough winkles to buy what was then a new type of coat – a waxed cotton jacket. The girls were full of joy when the post brought a parcel earned from picking winkles.

Each person's winkles were weighed and noted and then collectively put into hessian sacks, weighing about nine stone when full. Placed at the side of the rocks at the south edge of the beach they were kept at as low a point of the tide as possible, so that they would still be alive when the day came to take them by boat to Kylesku to meet the 'winkle man'. Every fortnight a van arrived at the jetty at

Kylesku to be met by a gathering of half a dozen people with an assortment of bags full of winkles and fish boxes packed with lobsters, crabs and, occasionally, prawns.

We all tried to hide what we had from the others, and certainly the weighing and handing over of payments were always done away from prying eyes. I suspect that the earnings were also kept away from the 'prying eyes' of the Chancellor of the Exchequer. When asked their names, many winkle sellers would answer 'Mr D. Duck' or 'Mr E. Presley' or often MacLeod, Mackenzie or Ross, all surnames well represented in the local phone book.

THE MERRY TILLERS' MARKET GARDEN

One of our early ventures was a plan to establish a market garden at Kerracher. We had already dug up a small patch of ground and found it fertile enough to grow vegetables. These were a great success: the family and friends we shared them with said they would love to be able to buy locally grown produce as good as this. We could see the reason why when we visited the local shops – the vegetables invariably looked tired.

To plan for this we went back to our well-used copy of the wonderful *The Complete Book of Self-Sufficiency*, by John Seymour. First we had to prepare the ground, which meant clearing a bed of thick rushes in the corner of the croft land adjacent to the house. There was only one way to get rid of them and that was to dig out each individual clump. My method was to plunge the spade deep into the ground around each clump and extract a large ball of roots and earth. I then chucked three or four clumps onto the barrow, and wheeled it to the top of the tide mark where I stacked them ready to load onto the boat. When I had enough I took them out to the middle of the bay and dumped them. There was great satisfaction in seeing them slowly disappear, knowing that each left a small space of rich soil waiting to be cultivated.

I had almost cleared the whole area when I had an odd conversation with one of the scallop divers who frequented the loch from time to time.

'I came across something really peculiar in your bay the other day.'

'Oh yes, what was that?'

'Bulrushes all growing nicely together on the seabed. Are you trying some new cultivation programme?' he asked, puzzled.

'Yes. I'm starting a market garden.'

Now he was really perplexed. 'On the seabed?'

'No, we're aiming to produce turnips, carrots, potatoes, cabbage – that sort of thing.'

'By growing bulrushes at the bottom of the sea?'

'If they're at the bottom of the sea I can grow my vegetables in the spaces they've left on land.'

'But why dump them on the seabed?'

'Why not?'

'Well, they get in the road of my finding scallops for a start.'

I reassured him that I'd got rid of the last, so he wouldn't be bothered with any more. The only conclusion I came to about that conversation is that two people can be making a living in similar ways, but operating in entirely different universes.

Digging a larger area of ground was becoming a real struggle, but if we were planning a market garden, we would have to cultivate the land on a commercial basis. We ordered a small cultivator by the quaint name of 'Merry Tiller'. When the shiny red machine with its four stainless steel tines arrived we thought that was the end of our labours with the spade.

Everyone wanted to have a go, even Clare who could hardly grasp both handles at once. Watched by Ruth and the girls I pulled the rope to start the engine. It fired into life and began to chug away. Now to engage the gear and let it dig up all this virgin ground.

I slowly pulled up the gear lever. The machine leapt into action, propelling itself forward with such force it was all I could do to hang on. It set off at speed towards the edge of the sea wall, jumping and jerking over the grass as if to the tune of some invisible pied piper. I managed to release the gear lever just as it was about to hit the top of the sea wall and topple over onto the beach six feet below. The girls tore after me, shrieking with delight. Only Ruth stood steadfast and with a shout of 'Switch it off!' brought the girls, the machine and me to our senses.

'Stop fooling about. That could have been dangerous,' she scolded.

'I wasn't fooling. The stupid thing just took off,' I protested. 'It's more powerful than it looks.'

'Can I have a shot, Daddy?' asked Ruthie.

'I'm afraid not. It's going to take *me* all my strength to control it.'

I slowly manoeuvred it back to the spot where we were planning to dig and set it ready to start up again.

'Stand well back now,' I advised everyone.

I pulled the rope and the engine again spurted into life, the whole machine vibrating wildly, about to take off on another mad journey. But this time I held on with all my strength. I managed to keep it in the same spot – I had tamed it.

'But it's not digging,' observed Ruth.

'Give me a chance. It's taking me all my time to keep hold.'

As the tines spun round I forced them with difficulty into the ground. At last they began to churn into the grass and small patches of earth started to appear. After a few arm wrenching minutes I put the machine out of gear for a rest.

'Are you sure you're doing this right?' asked Ruth, who had been watching me, arms folded.

'Do you want to have a go and see how it feels?'

'No, I'll leave it to you. But it might be quicker with a spade.'

'It's going to take a bit of time and effort,' I admitted, 'till I get used to it.'

'Perhaps it should be named a Merry Dancer rather than a Merry Tiller,' she remarked and headed off for the house.

After that I began to make some headway, and before too long had cultivated a small patch of ground. What had been covered with grass was now brown with good rich soil, even if it was peppered with divots of turf. The girls had long since lost interest and drifted away to play. Some time later Ruth appeared with a mug of tea to survey progress.

'You're right,' she said, 'it's going to take time.'

'Yes, but like everything else, it'll get easier and quicker with practice.'

We had set out on our enterprise to become market gardeners.

The land required a lot of preparation, but it was done during a very weather-kind spring. Eventually we had it ready for sowing and planting and after much consultation of horticultural books and seed catalogues we were ready to begin growing vegetables. We calculated we would be at least a fortnight behind the dates the books suggested, or even more because of our northerly location. Nevertheless, we sowed and planted and tended and weeded, and all four of us thoroughly enjoyed the experience. Soon the results of our labours became visible.

The summer came and our vegetable patch was lush and green. The time was right to harvest. We had tested the potatoes, turnips and carrots for ourselves and they were all ready. The peas and cabbage still had to do some more growing.

It was early August, not long after the date of our second anniversary of arriving at Kerracher, when we dug up, cleaned, weighed and bagged 54lbs of potatoes, 22lbs of turnips and 5lbs of carrots. We loaded them onto the boat and set off to Kylesku and Kylestrome where we sold the lot. That evening we were richer by the grand sum of £7.20. It didn't seem much but when we took into account the cost of the seed potatoes at £15 and a predicted yield of at least twelve times the weight in those alone, we felt confident we were on the right track. We might not become millionaires but at least we could survive through our own efforts. During the remainder of that summer and into the autumn we also sold cabbage, lettuce, peas, beans and cauliflower.

Although, overall, it was a success, I did learn an invaluable lesson in marketing. We had bought a seed potato called Foremost as it seemed to fit our requirements, but after only a few weekly sales the take up on the potatoes began to diminish. When I enquired why people weren't so keen on buying my potatoes I was gently told they were too wet. I hadn't taken into account what the potential customers' tastes and habits were, and indeed we hadn't taken our market research further than finding out that people wanted fresh vegetables. So the following year we planted Kerr's Pink, a dry fluffy potato, which sold well.

In the second year we were a bit more ambitious, and

added to our range with onions, spring onions, Brussels sprouts, leeks, beetroot and, in addition to our snowball turnips, swedes. We had expanded the area of cultivation and fertilised it with seaweed. Late in autumn after most of the first year's harvest was complete, we barrowed up as much seaweed as we could from the beach and dug it into the area where we were planning our potatoes for the following season. Apparently this was a local tradition.

Our second season of vegetable growing was a success in that we produced good wholesome products in yields that were satisfactory according to our books on the subject. It became clear though that the financial return for the effort did not make sense. We persevered for a few more years until we woke up one morning to find row upon row of our young plants stripped bare to the stems. It didn't take long to discover the culprits – our hens. I had not shut them up in their hen house the night before and first thing that morning they had wandered over to the house looking for food. They must have thought they'd discovered Shangri-la – row upon row of succulent young plants. By the time we got up and out the damage had been done.

A week later we woke to a fierce easterly wind blowing up the loch from the Kylesku direction. The easterlies didn't come often but when they did they were strong, and by the time the wind reached Kerracher it had risen to gale force because of the long bite of loch. This particular wind remained with us longer than any before, and day after day for almost a whole week it sprayed the house and croft with lashings of sea water. The shortest walk along the shoreline meant a drenching from sea spray.

It was only after the wind finally dropped that we discovered the damage. Our crops had turned black and many of the young shoots were being eaten away by the salt deposit from the sea spray.

Ruth and I found it very hard to take in such devastation. Our hard work was all for nothing. Yes, we could replant and sow more seeds but that meant spending more money as well as losing out on the yields. The growing season was short because of our location and any setback was almost irrecoverable. We did a little to recoup our situation, but it was not enough. At the end of that season it was clear that we couldn't afford to rely on the market garden to sustain us at Kerracher. We never stopped growing our own vegetables, but we cut back on the amount we produced for others. Our dream of supplying the north-west corner of Scotland with fresh vegetables was at an end.

THE GOOD SHEPHERD AND HIS DOG

The other natural source of income from the land at Kerracher was sheep. By now I had acquired Glen, and also the eighteen or so sheep left on the ground around Kerracher. I had also got a bit of tuition from helping out with some of the local crofters and their sheep activities. So what else was there to do but shepherd my own flock?

When I took Glen out on the hill with me I found him biddable enough. He would walk alongside me, tongue lolling out of the side of his mouth and seemingly keen to anticipate my commands. The first time we came across four of my sheep Glen looked up eagerly, waiting for instruction.

'Heel,' I commanded and obediently he held back.

One of the sheep also heard me – her head shot up from grazing, startling her companions. Immediately all four sprang into life and began to run. Although heavy with wool they were agile enough to bound away across the hillside. After a short burst they stopped to gather their wits and turned round to check out the danger. As soon as they saw I had a dog with me, they set off again.

'Go by.' I pointed towards the receding group. Glen

made off at once, but ran past them, so that they changed direction, but heading off to the right of me, higher up the hill.

'Stay!' I shouted.

Glen either didn't hear me or didn't understand because he continued running above the sheep. Suddenly he homed in on one, forcing it apart from the other three, which ran away to freedom. Glen lowered down on his haunches, his gaze fixed on this lone sheep, which stood stock-still, eyes bulging with fear. Each time it made a move to run, Glen kept it in check.

I slowly moved up the hill towards dog and sheep uncertain what to do next. The sheep seemed healthy and well enough, so I gave the command, 'Come in by, Glen.'

The dog looked quizzically at me but I repeated, 'Come into heel.'

He moved around the sheep towards me. Instantly the animal headed off towards the horizon after her companions. Glen turned to go after her but I snapped 'Stay' and he obeyed.

'Good dog.'

He jumped up, welcoming the praise, but I didn't want to encourage that.

'Down.'

As we set off home, I had a feeling Glen realised his new master was not an experienced dog owner.

When I spoke to Lal about the state of the sheep he recommended clipping. If I managed to gather them he would come up to Kerracher and help me. This was some time after I had attended the gatherings, and he clearly thought I needed more detailed instruction – and practice.

Ruth and I constructed a pen system over at the north end of the croft where there were some remnants of a previously built dry stone dyke. Then for about a week before we planned to shear the sheep, Glen and I scoured the area around Kerracher in the evenings, driving the sheep towards the croft. The good thing about this was that Kerracher was at the edge of the sea so they couldn't go past it. Or so I thought.

We had managed to get most of the sheep into one large group of fifteen. Three we could not find anywhere. I still had difficulty stopping Glen focusing on one individual sheep and holding it. He was a champion at that but not so good at keeping the group together as a unit and driving them. Despite that, we had slowly manoeuvred the fifteen animals in the general direction of Kerracher.

I struck lucky on the evening before we intended to get them all into the pen on the croft. We came across the three missing sheep just a short distance on the south side of Kerracher along the coastline towards Reintraid. I carefully took Glen away from the sheep and well behind them so that we could drive them towards Kerracher.

Of course, when they saw us they took fright and ran off in the general direction of the croft, but this was ideal. They would eventually join up with the others now grouped together near the house.

Sheep, however, are not rational beings. For no apparent reason, they suddenly veered towards the loch side, leaping down the incline through the thick heather towards the sea. As they reached the rocks at the edge of the loch one suddenly broke away, coming straight for us. Before the dog and I could make any movement, it bolted past us, eyes bulging with fear and a determination not to be caught. Glen made some attempt at running alongside it but the sheep carried on, ploughing through the rough heather.

I eventually called Glen back as I could see we'd never persuade this single mad sheep to rejoin its companions, which had by now stopped at the top of a rock face above the water. I decided to abandon this one and go for the two, which now looked a little calmer. Glen returned, tongue lolling and an eager gleam in his eyes, as if saying 'What's next boss?'.

'Heel,' I ordered. I was keen to get the other two back on track towards Kerracher, so we approached them cautiously.

One started making off towards Kerracher but changed its mind when the other remained where it was. I could see that this second one was looking for an alternative. Then it found one. Slowly it began to pick its way down the rocks towards the sea. There was a short drop of about of about twenty feet of rock face to the water level.

'Stay.' Glen squatted down where he was, eyes fixed on the solitary sheep now standing still but undecided above the rocks. I followed the other animal hoping I would be able to persuade it to change direction and rejoin its companion. It danced nimbly from rock to rock and ledge to ledge like a mountain goat of the Andes, sure footed and ignoring my gesticulations. Eventually it ended up on a small ledge with its backside well wedged into a crevice of rock, and facing me.

Now it could only go one way – and that was towards me. If I remained where I was and the sheep decided to head in my direction then there was only one result. I would be knocked over the edge of the rocks into the water six feet below.

I decided to retreat, and rejoined Glen who was at least holding the third, and last, sheep that we had any hope of heading towards Kerracher. But I had given it some thinking time and as soon as I appeared it sprang into life and ran towards me – and towards its mate wedged in the refuge of the rock face below. Glen and the sheep both caught my legs as they rushed past and I ended up flat on my back in the heather. With Glen on its tail the sheep panicked as it reached the rocks and instead of jumping from rock to rock and ledge to ledge like its colleague, it launched itself bravely off the topmost rock and sailed like Icarus into the air. Glen stopped in his tracks. It seemed ages before we heard the splash as it entered the water below.

I struggled up and made for the cliff edge. I could see the poor animal swimming, but instead of striking out for the safety of a nearby rock ledge it was heading out to sea. There was only one solution. I had to get back to Kerracher, launch the boat and rescue the animal.

Rapidly I explained the situation to Ruth as I pulled the boat in from its mooring, yanked the rope and fired the engine into life. I headed the bow of the boat towards Reintraid, leaving Ruth and Glen, who refused to enter any boat, standing above the mooring.

It was only a matter of minutes before I reached the sheep. This time there was no escape as it needed all its energy to keep afloat. I pulled up beside it and made an attempt to haul it into the boat, but its heavy coat was waterlogged and it took all my strength finally to roll it over the gunwale and into the boat. The exhausted animal lay prostrate on the floor of the boat, no fight left.

When I reached the shore at Kerracher and pulled the boat up I expected the sheep to jump out but it remained where it was, quite limp, its eyes shut. Even when Ruth helped me get it onto the beach, it didn't respond.

There was only one thing for it. I turned it on its back and started a pumping motion with both hands on its chest. For the first few pushes nothing happened, then there was a splutter from its mouth followed by another, more of a cough. Eventually the sheep opened its eyes, lifted its head and surveyed the scene around it.

'I think it's going to live,' Ruth said with relief. 'Perhaps best to leave it to recover.'

We took Glen with us and walked up to the top of the beach, to watch the sheep from there. It lay still for a few more minutes, then, suddenly, as if prodded by an invisible stick, it jumped up and trotted off towards the croft where some of the gathered sheep were peacefully grazing.

'We must be mad,' I declared and headed back to the boat to secure it at its mooring for the night.

Next day I collected Lal and a cousin of his, Marion, a friendly helpful woman experienced in crofting matters. She lived near Dingwall but often came up to Kylesku to help Lal. She cooked for him, fed the helpers on sheep duties and even opened up his house for bed and breakfast during the summer months.

It took most of the morning, after some fun and games, to get the sheep gathered in the pen. Then Lal pulled out the first animal, sat it on its bottom and proceeded to shear it with hand clippers. He started at its neck and quickly worked his way down its body, deftly parting the wool from the sheep with a series of neat scissor movements. In no time at all the sheep and its clothing were parted. As he worked he occasionally explained to me what he was doing, and what I needed to watch out for.

He then sheared a second sheep while Marion whipped away the first fleece and demonstrated to Ruth how to fold it and then roll it up. Now I was the only one not actively involved.

'Ok, I'll do the next one.'

'Remember to keep the blades close to the body but be careful in the soft regions around the belly and under the legs,' he instructed. 'Mind to keep the animal still and calm.'

I pulled a frightened sheep from the pen and promptly sat it on its bottom with its back resting against my legs. It struggled briefly, but when it had settled down Ruth handed me the clippers she had bought me as a birthday present and I took the first tentative slice at the wool just at the base of the neck. The animal jerked its head around and caught the point of the clipper blades behind its ear. A small nick of flesh opened and blood oozed out.

'Keep her calm,' warned Lal.

'I thought she was!'

'Here dab this into it,' Marion said, thrusting her hand towards me with a dollop of greasy ointment.

Eventually the sheep settled again and I began to clip away. Very slowly, I made my way down the animal's body, taking what seemed an age to get the fleece off. As I made each cut I reassured the sheep that I intended it no harm. At last it was off and I was the proud owner of a fleece. I released the sheep and it joined its shorn companions grazing on the croft grass.

It was then that the results of my endeavours were clear. The four that Lal had clipped looked like normal sheep, smooth bodied and cleanly sheared. My poor sheep stood out forlornly from the rest looking as if it had been to some trendy hairdresser who had given it a punk-style clipping.

I managed, with a little improvement, to shear another two, while Lal polished off the rest. By the end of the afternoon Ruth and Marion had a good bag full of sixteen fleeces ready to transport to the Wool Growers Company, to bring us a small income.

As I returned up the loch after getting Marion and Lal home at the end of what had turned out to be a hot sunny day, my body ached and I longed for the soak in the tin bath that was waiting for me.

The sheep were much harder work than we originally thought. How would we cope with the extra sheep that would be necessary to make shepherding viable? We'd worry about that later – for now we needed to increase the flock. The simple solution was to build it up by natural means, introducing them to a male of the species. I was told it was a simple case of getting in touch with DAFS (Department of Agriculture and Fisheries Scotland) and hiring a tup for the month of November when the sheep would be in season and responsive to his attentions.

Unfortunately that first year we were too late in applying and DAFS had no more tups available. When I told Lal he was quick to offer a young beast. He didn't say exactly why, but implied it wasn't ready to be let out on the hill along with his other tups. Without thinking too much about this, I gratefully accepted his offer.

Again there followed a protracted sheep gathering which lasted a good number of days longer than I would care to admit, especially to any other crofter. Nevertheless, Glen and I managed eventually to get sixteen of our sheep into the fenced area of the croft. Once they were in and grazing the scene looked quite peaceful, belying the mayhem and air-wrenching expletives involved in the gathering.

All we had to do now was collect the tup from Lal. We hobbled the terrified creature and loaded it into the bottom of the boat where it made a few vain attempts to struggle free. Eventually it resigned itself and the two of us chugged off up the loch towards Kerracher.

When we arrived Ruth was waiting with the barrow, as agreed, at the water's edge. We rolled the young tup over the side of the boat and into the barrow and wheeled it up the length of the beach to the waiting sheep in the field. To make it easier to push a heavy barrow-load up the incline of the soft stony beach we tied a long rope to the front of the barrow and Ruth walked ahead with the rope over her shoulder, pulling to ease the burden of my pushing. The young tup was then unceremoniously tipped out into the field beside a group of curious ewes. Immediately it was untied it ran off to join the others.

Over the next few days Ruth and I kept looking to check if the tup was performing as required, but there was hardly an occasion when we caught it in action of any kind. There was *no* occasion when we spotted it doing what it was there to do. We began to wonder if he was a fellow who liked his privacy. After a week I had a chat with Lal who reckoned that it was still a young beast, which might need some time to get used to a new flock and surroundings. We decided to give the tup the benefit of the doubt and left him to get acquainted with his new companions.

Over time the tup did seem to merge in with the other sheep but he never seemed at all lively or indeed enthusiastic. All in all, he was a pretty sheepish type of sheep.

About six weeks later Ruth told me she couldn't spot the tup when she was over at the far side of the croft letting the hens out. When I made a quick reconnaissance of the field, I found the tup on its back with its legs in the air. It was dead.

'Perhaps it did all the sheep at once,' I suggested when I

got back to the house.

'I wouldn't think so on the evidence so far,' Ruth answered. 'Are there any marks on it – as if it's been attacked by a fox or something?'

But the tup was unmarked, and even looked quite peaceful. But what were we going to tell Lal? We decided we'd just have to tell the truth – the tup died in the night.

'But he'll need compensation,' Ruth said. 'It's going to be an expensive way of increasing our flock, if there *is* any increase.'

That afternoon I told Lal what had happened. I also explained to him again how the tup had been reluctant to service the sheep and indeed seemed lethargic in its whole approach to life.

'I'll pay you for the loss of course,' I added

'Och, there's no need, laddie,' Lal said. 'I thought there was something not quite right about that sheep. Some just don't have it in them to do what it takes.'

By the following spring the sheep were getting used to us and were now using the grazing on the croft more often, which made it easier for us to monitor them for lambing. We were still hopeful.

Then one morning Clare came back from letting the hens out and announced, 'One of the sheep is having a lamb.'

'What do you mean?' Ruth asked.

'It's got a head sticking out of its bottom,' she said. 'I watched it for a while but nothing's happening. I think it's stuck.'

'I'd better get over and see that it's ok.' Ruth dashed out of the house with Clare in her wake, leaving Ruthie and me to continue our breakfast, with no desire whatsoever to join them.

It wasn't long before Ruth and Clare returned with the good news that we had a new arrival at Kerracher – our first lamb. Our optimism had not been entirely misplaced: our ewes produced six lambs that spring. So our short-lived tup had managed to do some of his duty after all. Perhaps it had all been too much for him.

Because of Glen's limitations in shepherding we were persuaded to take on a young collie pup. The girls were delighted at the prospect of a puppy but I had to explain that the puppy would be a working dog and had to be trained as such. It would live in the shed with Glen. We found out very early that Glen was not accustomed to living indoors, having lifted his leg as soon as he was allowed in the house. From then on, he lived in the shed, where he was quite at home.

We decided to call the new pup Jamie. When he arrived, carried over by his owner, we found him to be affectionate and mischievous. For the first week we made a bed for him in the house but he soon disgraced himself by chewing up a pair of Ruth's slippers.

Jamie and Glen bonded well and we soon introduced Jamie to his own bed in the shed alongside Glen. Donald, the librarian, recommended a good book on the training of dogs and for some time I referred to that as I tried to bring Jamie on in the skills of basic dog conduct – as well as future shepherding.

I was usurped at every stage. Jamie was not a diligent pupil. He couldn't sit still or absorb instructions, and he was too easily distracted, especially when Ruth was nearby. Eventually I had to bar Ruth from our training as she was inclined to mutter, 'Poor Jamie,' and 'He's being too hard on you,' as I struggled to hold the dog's attention. It was a long slow process to get him to obey the simplest of instructions, but eventually he began to improve.

Then one morning he couldn't be found. He was gone for the whole day and it wasn't until the following morning, when Hughie got out of the car to collect the girls, that I had some idea of where he had gone.

'Have you lost your young dog?' he asked.

'Yes. Have you seen it?'

'No, but I got a call from Walter at Kylesku that a young collie spent the day yesterday going back and forth on the ferry,' said Hughie. 'He's waiting for you to collect it if it's yours.'

I arrived at Kylesku as the ferry was about to come into the pier from its crossing from Kylestrome. There on the bow of the old boat was Jamie with his tail wagging, clearly happy to see me. He leaped off onto the pier before the boat touched the side and ran up to greet me. I got a great welcome with not a trace of guilt. Remembering the book's instruction not to scold him unless I was able to catch him in the act of wrong-doing, all I could do was return his welcome and bid him into the rear of the Land Rover.

Walter, the head ferryman, said, 'We'll miss him. He made himself quite at home and kept us and the passengers entertained.'

'Thanks for taking care of him. I hope you won't see him again, otherwise I'll have to tie him up,' I said. 'There's not enough for him to do, I'm afraid.'

When we reached Kerracher, Ruth made a great fuss of him.

'That's not a good idea,' I told her.

'Poor Jamie,' she said, giving him a big hug. 'I hope he

hasn't been bad to you.'

I decided I would have to tie Jamie up, so that he realised he had to stay at Kerracher. I tied a long rope to his collar, tethering him to the gate at the corner of the house. This lasted for a few days until I was bombarded with pleas at breakfast one morning.

'Did you hear Jamie crying last night?' Ruthie asked.

'Yes,' said Clare, 'he kept me awake with his howling.'

'I don't think he likes being tied,' said Ruth.

In the end I gave in, and freed him. But only a few days later he was gone again. This time he arrived home with a couple who were staying at Reintraid and who had a clutch of dogs themselves.

'I'm going to have to tether you for a bit longer,' I said to the tail-wagging Jamie, who was again very happy to see me.

However, after he disappeared for a third time and reached Kylesku again, we knew he would have to go. When I took him out along with Glen to check the sheep he was attentive and biddable, bearing in mind that I was a novice not only with dogs but also with shepherding. He had the working genes in him and was wasted spending most of his days sitting at the corner of the house. So I let the word out that I had a young dog with potential that needed to work. It wasn't long before a shepherd from near Lochinver got in touch and collected Jamie. We were all sad to see him go but agreed it was for the best. I kept in touch with the shepherd for a while after that and he said that in time Jamie would make a good sheepdog.

I worked the sheep for about three years but slowly we realised that it could never be more than a hobby and certainly was not the solution to earning a living at Kerracher. We finally abandoned shepherding after a lambing when I came across a gimmer (a young sheep), which had died giving birth. That was distressing not only because the sheep was too young to be lambing, but also because there was no one there to help when it was in difficulty. It had wandered onto a small island that was only accessible during a spring tide, so I hadn't spotted it. It also confirmed that there was a rogue tup wandering the area. I realised that I didn't have the control or the time to ensure this wouldn't happen again.

I made arrangements that summer to sell my remaining sheep at the Lairg sales and came away with a small overall profit of £380 on the whole venture. This Kerracher Man, like his predecessors, was not going to be a shepherd.

RUTHIE AND CLARE KEEP HENS

The high ground arcing around the back of the house was the girls' playground. They were forbidden to go anywhere near the sea, especially to the rocks because of the obvious danger. So they discovered places that were secret and tucked away from the routes tramped by everyone else.

Once when I was checking a wooded area for some sheep that had wandered in to dodge me, I came across toy cups, saucers and plates neatly arranged in a circle. An assortment of leaves and seeds had been placed on the plates. On opposite sides of the circle there were low-lying branches long felled from their parent trees, providing seats for the diners.

Was the meal left from their playtime or had it been left for the invisible inhabitants of the woods when they emerged? Suspecting the latter, I cleared three of the plates, leaving just a few seeds on one as if a fussy diner had pushed them aside.

I never mentioned what I had found and I never heard anything about it from the girls. It was part of their private world, which wasn't shared with their Dad.

I was needed for another pastime. One Saturday

morning Ruthie asked, 'Daddy can you build us a house?'

'I thought that's what I *was* trying to do,' I protested.

'No, not this one, a peat one like an igloo,' she said.

'Ok ... and where do you want it built?'

'Well, we've found a nice place near the mooring,' she said, adding as an incentive, 'it's facing down the loch so we can see if anyone is coming up to Kerracher.'

I promised to have a look, and Clare promptly got up from the table.

'Oh good, let's go and we'll show you where it is.'

'Finish your breakfast first.' Ruth helped her back onto her chair.

'Then after breakfast will you build us a house?' Clare pleaded.

The girls led me over to the chosen spot high above the shoreline near to our running mooring. There was a small indentation in a bank of peat that had been used by either sheep or deer as a shelter from a westerly wind.

'We want the door and windows to be on this side.' Ruthie pointed towards the long bite of loch stretching out away to the east.

'Ok, let's get started.'

The girls and I spent a whole weekend digging into the bank then cutting blocks of peat for walls and larger turfs for the roof. We finally completed the 'house' on Sunday evening just before dinner. It wasn't exactly an igloo, but it made a satisfactory refuge for the girls.

It was only a shout away from the house, so Ruth could keep an eye on them, and easily summon them home for meals or bedtime.

Ruthie and Clare explored the surrounds of Kerracher with great freedom, and they learned about the natural world when they were very young. Their proximity to nature meant they discovered at first hand what other children could learn only from books. But they did acquire and use books, which helped explain further what they were coming across out of doors every day.

One of their early finds was what they described as 'a mysterious mound'. When I gave in to their pestering and went with them to have a look at this, I found it *was* a large mound with a series of openings like entrances.

'There's definitely something living in there,' said Clare, peering into one of the small openings.

'Watch it doesn't jump out and bite you,' I warned her, in case there was some creature in there.

'Look here's *another* hole,' exclaimed Ruthie from the other side.

A large tree coming down in a gale many years before had created the mound. The trunk and branches had long disintegrated and the surrounding fauna had invaded and merged with the root system.

'Daddy, come and look here – there's animal droppings,' Ruthie called.

Clare and I went round to where she was and we all bent over a pile of black dried-out droppings on a patch of bare earth close to one of the entrances.

'What animal could it be?' Ruthie asked.

'Let's take them home and I'll look in my book.' Clare promptly scooped them up in her hand.

'Ugh – you silly girl,' said Ruthie in disgust. 'You'll get a disease from them.'

'All right – let's get home and check out what it could be.' I kept an eye on Clare who had the droppings in cupped hands held out well in front of her.

Ruth was not too pleased with me when we returned home. Clare was sent to scrub her hands as soon as she'd deposited the animal evidence on a sheet of paper.

After a good look through some of the wildlife books, we came to the exciting conclusion that they might have found a badger sett. For weeks after that they checked for sight of badgers, but without success.

Animals were integral to our lives. We had of course arrived with Penny the cat, who had quickly established the surrounding territory as his own. Our first ever cat, a female, was Penny, but she met an untimely end in the jaws of an Alsatian. Her replacement was a neutered male, also named Penny in memory of the first. He didn't seem to mind. He certainly enjoyed life at Kerracher, keeping control of the mouse population. He also caught a number of stoats, which he deposited at the front door as evidence of having earned his supper.

Our first hens came as a gift from a local crofter who was introducing some young pullets to her stock and was looking for a home for her old brood. We packed the six bantams into a couple of boxes and transported them to Kerracher where we introduced them to the hen house I had built from an assortment of fish boxes.

Housed at the furthest reach of the bay away from the house, the hens soon settled into a routine, but their numbers dwindled as the winter set in and predators became hungrier. We assumed a fox took some, though none of us ever spotted one.

The girls tended to the remaining two scrawny birds as if they were pets, until one freezing winter's day they found them both as stiff as waxworks on the floor of the hen house. When the hens had been buried with ceremony we decided that come the spring we would invest in some of our own. Now only the cockerel was left.

A few mornings later Clare came running into the house very upset. 'The cockerel's gone,' she cried sobbing, 'and there's a huge badger in the hen house.'

'Don't be silly,' Ruth said.

Through her tears Clare insisted, 'But there *is* a badger.'

Realising how upset she was, Ruth put her arms round her. 'But how could a badger get into the hen house?'

'The door was open,' Clare sobbed.

'I forgot to shut the door last night,' I had to admit.

'Well, you'd better deal with the badger,' Ruth told me.

Clare was right. There was a very large badger taking up most of the floor of the hen house. It was fast asleep. But there was no sign of Harry, our cockerel.

'What are you going to do with it?' Clare whispered.

I was stumped. 'I don't know.'

'It's killed poor Harry. Are you going to kill it?'

'I'm not so sure it did get Harry,' I poked my head a little farther into the hen house. 'There's no sign of a struggle.'

Clare too peered in. There wasn't a feather to be seen. 'Maybe he escaped before the badger got in.'

'Well, we have a badger now instead of a cockerel, whatever happened. Harry might come back.'

It was time for Clare and Ruthie to get off to school. Clare was reluctant to leave without a search for the cockerel, but she perked up at the thought of having some exciting news to tell everyone. We left the badger sleeping soundly in the hen house, the door wide open. When I returned from walking the girls over the hill I went back to check: it was still fast asleep. But when the girls returned later in the afternoon they found the hen house empty. In the middle of the floor lay a pair of cockerel's feet and a bloodstained cockscomb.

It was April and approaching the second anniversary of our arrival at Kerracher when the twelve Rhode Island Reds we had ordered from a firm in Skye were left at the Post Office in Drumbeg.

I delivered the girls to school and called in at the Post Office to be greeted by Non.

'Good morning. Have you come to collect your additions to the family?'

Non MacLeod had lived all of her days in Drumbeg and ran the local Post Office from a wooden hut at the edge of her front garden. Her husband Pal had a creel boat that he worked with his son Donnie. Non was a kind woman with a cheerful and sometimes mischievous outlook on the world, which she often applied when she imparted some local news.

'I hope they haven't been a nuisance,' I said, since she'd had the hens for the last day or so.

'They've kept me company and we've had some interesting conversations. I told them all about you and where they're going,' she said without a trace of a smile.

'Thanks, I'm sure that will have settled them!' I bent down to pick up the first box of clucking birds. They were packed six each in cardboard boxes lined with straw. They were clucking away and seemed in good health, but they were now beginning to smell. Another day in the confines of the Post Office would have made it uncomfortable for any visitor – far less poor Non.

'Could you call into the hotel? Angus needs a haircut and wants to go with you,' Non said as we were leaving.

I collected Angus, whose parents owned the Drumbeg Hotel, and with the hens in the back of the Land Rover we set off for Kerracher. I was glad to have him with me as the hens were becoming agitated and I wasn't sure how long the bottoms of the boxes would last. Eventually we reached the safety of the bay at Kerracher and offloaded the hens into the freshly prepared hen house.

Ruth was pleased to see a visitor, especially one who needed a haircut. As she set to giving Angus a trim we suddenly realised he was our 'first foot'. We hadn't had anyone visit since before Christmas, nearly four months earlier.

'That calls for a dram,' I announced.

'You can't give Angus a whisky, he's too young,' Ruth said.

Angus looked disappointed. 'I am allowed a beer sometimes,' he suggested.

'That's no problem – our New Year drink is still intact,' I said, knowing that it was all in the cupboard where it had been stored at the back end of the previous year.

So Angus and I toasted in the New Year with a couple of cans of beer and Ruth with a Babycham, in April, a week before Easter.

The girls were delighted with the new arrivals and by the end of the week had given them all names. That weekend they spent most of their time herding the young hens around. They fed them and observed each one carefully so that they could get to know them. It was the start of a lasting relationship.

By summer the hens had started to lay an egg or two in the hen house but mainly, we discovered, out on the croft in the long grass. It became the girls' job at the weekends to search for eggs. In the meantime, Ruth changed the routine from feeding them first thing to leaving them in the hen house until she reckoned that most of them had laid their eggs. Slowly but surely this worked and most of their eggs were produced in the hen house.

These were completely different to ordinary eggs. They were very large with rich yolks whose deep orange colour came from the hens scratching in the seaweed on the shore and feeding off the plentiful shrimp-like creatures they found there. This added taste and texture to our eggs and a great deal of natural goodness. Some visitors were put off by the appearance, until they tasted the difference.

One winter day Ruthie was helping Ruth with baking when she exclaimed, 'These eggs are off!'

'They shouldn't be,' Ruth said.

'Well I've opened three now and they are all off.' Ruthie was quite indignant. 'I've thrown them all out.'

'Let me have a look,' said Ruth and peered into the bowl with the discarded eggs.

'Look how pale they are,' Ruthie pointed out.

'They're not off. They're shop eggs and that's their normal colour,' explained Ruth. Our hens had gone off laying for a short spell in the winter and we had had to buy eggs like normal people.

Eventually, we bought another cockerel to help keep the hens in order. It was easy to find one as people who had hens often got rid of young roosters. Our first was a fairly timid sort of bird but he seemed to keep the hens from squabbling with each other. He didn't last long, disappearing one day never to be seen again. The second rooster, Henry, was a little older when we got him and he soon established his pecking order – not only with the hens but also with the girls. He didn't take kindly to the attentions Ruthie and Clare paid the hens.

Life with the hens had become part of our routine. One of the girls, usually Clare, went over in the morning with their feed: egg-laying concentrate and any vegetable leftovers. Shutting them up at night was my duty, but when I was settled down for the evening it was hard to get up and go out, especially if it was wet and windy, even to walk 400 metres. I guess it did give old Glen a little more exercise for the day but often he was too settled in his kennel to bother.

One pitch black night, very late, having pulled down the hatch on the hen house to the muted sound of a few goodnight clucks, I set off back to the house. Suddenly from nowhere came a loud *squawk* and a large dark object flew past just above my head. It was a heart-stopping moment, shattering the tranquillity of the bay and giving me the fright of my life. As it flapped away across the water I realised it was nothing more than a heron, which I had disturbed.

Another night as I walked out very late to shut the hens in I was captivated by the northern sky. There were all kinds of rainbow colours spreading out from the horizon. I had never seen anything like this before so I hurriedly shut in the hens and ran back to the house to summon Ruth.

'What is it?' she asked as we both stood gazing.

'I don't know. I saw the Northern Lights when I was a young lad in Dingwall but they're white lights that shake across the sky like a long stretch of curtains.'

'Well, if it's not the Northern Lights what is it?'

'It could be an atomic explosion in northern Russia.'

'That's not the least bit funny,' Ruth replied. 'What if it was?'

The show was going on with bright green, cream and yellow lights mushrooming up and out of the north sky with the occasional splash of red and purple radiating across from west to east and mingling with the original colours. It was as if an invisible hand was mixing paints on a giant palette.

'We've got to let the girls see this,' I said. 'We may not get the chance again.'

'Wrap them up well,' Ruth said.

I ran upstairs to wake the bewildered children, who must have thought they were dreaming. Wrapped in dressing gowns and thick blankets they stood on chairs at the front door, facing the northern sky. There were gasps and cries of amazement, as we all tried to take in the magical Aurora Borealis.

———

Poor Ruthie had a few misfortunes with the hens, in particular with Henry, who had taken a dislike to her. One morning she came running in crying, blood streaming down the back of her leg from two fierce-looking holes. Henry had punctured the back of her leg with his spurs.

This time his aggression had gone too far, so he was destined for the pot. I duly dispatched and plucked him and

Ruth stuffed him into the chicken brick – just, as he was a good size – and cooked him. He was a little tougher than other birds we had eaten and there was a lot of him left over. However, Ruth used that to make a superb chicken curry.

The dispatching of hens was my responsibility. The first time we took a chicken for the pot (after protracted consultations as to which it should be) was not an easy task.

I caught the chosen hen and carried it over to the shed next to the house where I had propped *The Complete Book of Self-Sufficiency* on the workbench, open at the page on how to kill a hen. I held the feet in my right hand and, with the hen vertical and upside down, I slipped its head between two fingers of my left hand and pulled down swiftly with a slight twist, as the book suggested.

The hen pawked gently and looked up at me, blinking its eyes as if to say, 'What are you trying to do?'

I tried again, and again. By this time the hen was almost comatose and giving a gentle 'pawk' with each attempt.

'Have you done it yet?' Ruth enquired from the other side of the door.

'No. The thing has a rubber neck,' I said, exasperated.

'Come out here and let me see what you're doing.'

I emerged with the hen under my arm, handed Ruth the book and proceeded to demonstrate, in the hope that she would tell me where I was going wrong.

After watching for a moment she said, 'I think you're being too gentle with it.'

'Ok,' I said. I looked down at the now totally confused hen. 'Sorry, I'm going to have to be a little harder this time.' I pulled down sharply with my left hand. The hen started to flap around and jerk quite violently.

Eric's grandfather, the original 'The Kerracher Man', at Kerracher in the 1950s.

On the way to Kerracher, towing the caravan

The house as it was in 1976 when Eric and Ruth arrived

Eric's parents help with peat cutting

The girls dressed for the walk over the hill to school, circa 1978

The house at Kerracher, renovation complete

Ruth feeding chickens, 1978

Ruth with the first turnips from the market garden, 1978

Clare on Charlie, 1982

Penny by the fireside

Ruth's parents arriving by boat, 1986

The house viewed from the running mooring

Smolts delivered by road from Scourie, 1986

Ruthie and Clare as teenagers outside the house 1986

The fishpens on wavy seas, viewed from the house

Graham and Eric harvesting fish, 1988

John Blunt and Eric with the biggest salmon - 17lbs

Leaving Kerracher for the last time, 1991

'You've done it. That's its nerves kicking in,' Ruth told me and headed for the house.

When I plucked the still warm creature I was depending for this skill on a combination of the book's instructions and a memory of my first job, as a butcher's delivery boy at the age of twelve in Dingwall. At Christmas and New Year chicken and turkey were in great demand, and I was taught how to pluck the birds killed on the premises and prepare them for the front shop.

That first Kerracher hen turned into a very tasty meal but it was eaten in silence. We got used to this, though, and over the years eating what we killed became normal practice.

NOT ALL THE PETS ARE LAME DUCKS

A procession of children's pets came through our lives. Penny had come north with us, and now we had Glen. Glen adopted the girls, following them wherever they went unless I was around. Ruthie and Clare would vie to see who could get him to jump the highest when they threw sticks up for him.

The first of their own pets was a rabbit, for Ruthie's seventh birthday.

'The next time we go to Inverness we can go to the pet shop and choose one,' she decided.

I agreed without giving it much thought.

'The pet shop has cages too,' she added.

'Mm.' I still wasn't paying attention.

'And it has lots of things for it as well,' put in Clare.

'Well, we'll have to see about it.' I suddenly realised the implications of this shopping trip. 'I can build a cage for it myself.'

'Do you *know* how to build a rabbit cage?' Ruth enquired.

'Ruthie, get me the Reader's Digest manual and we'll have a look.'

Ruthie struggled back with the heavy manual I had received as a parting gift when I left my job. We opened it at the Projects section.

'Hurray!' Ruthie had found instructions for constructing a hutch.

'Right, I'll build the hutch first and then we'll see about getting a rabbit.'

I had most of what was needed amongst the wood for the house renovation, so all I had to buy were hinges, a sneck and wire mesh, all of which we could get from the chandlery in Lochinver. The hutch was built just in time for Ruthie's birthday.

As this was a school day, I arranged with Hughie that I would collect them. They were surprised to see me but I often tied in what I was doing with being available to walk the girls home over the hill. This time there was to be a small diversion – to visit a man we knew who bred rabbits. The girls were familiar with the place, as we'd often bought a rabbit for the pot there.

'Where are we going?' they asked.

'Wait and you'll see.'

When we arrived at the breeder's house they were noticeably disappointed.

'Are we having a rabbit for dinner?' sighed Clare.

'No.'

'Why are we here then?' asked Ruthie.

'Wait and see.'

They cheered up when they were asked if they'd like to see the young rabbits. As they peered through the wire mesh of the cage at the fluffy white rabbits I asked Ruthie which one she would like.

This took some time, but eventually she chose one, which she named Snowy, and we set off home. Ruthie was pleased not just with her birthday present but also because they had saved a poor baby rabbit from getting the chop.

Another early pet came from a visit to Moira and Stan's. Moira offered to show the girls her 'new arrivals', and disappeared to her hen house, down among the trees at the back of their property. When she strode back a few moments later she was followed by a mallard, with a line of ducklings waddling behind.

'Oh, they're so tiny and fluffy!' exclaimed Ruthie.

'Aw, look at that one – he's struggling to keep up.' The last duckling in line lagged behind the others.

'Mum keeps telling it off,' said Moira, giving the girls tit bits to feed the ducks.

As they did this, Clare observed, 'She's not a very good mother. It's as if she's trying to chase the slow duckling away.'

'She certainly gives it a hard time compared to the others,' said Moira.

'The poor wee thing needs looking after.' By now Clare had persuaded the marked duckling to feed straight from her hand.

'Perhaps you could do that?' Moira suggested.

'I'd love to.' Clare looked up at her mother, pleading. '*Could* I take it home and look after it?'

'It's unlikely to survive with the treatment it's getting at the moment,' Moira said, 'and I have enough animals to look after.'

All Ruth could do now was agree to this, so I resigned myself to building a house for a duck next. With the duckling safely tucked into a small cardboard box, Clare and Ruthie attended to it carefully all the way home.

'What are we going to call it?' Clare asked as we bumped along in the Land Rover.

'Why, Kerry of course,' Ruth said. 'It's going to Kerracher after all.'

At first Kerry was housed in an old sheepskin slipper in a cardboard box in the kitchen, and she remained there for several weeks with Ruth as her surrogate mother. I was amazed at Ruth's tolerance. She always kept her domestic surroundings spic and span no matter what renovating disruption there was around her, but when it came to animals, I believe she would have had them all live in the kitchen if possible. Eventually Kerry was deemed grown up enough to be housed in the new pen I had constructed, like many others at Kerracher, from wooden fish boxes washed up on the beach. For safety the pen was located close to the back of the house near Snowy the rabbit.

She was well cared for by the girls, but as she grew it became clear why the mother had rejected her. Poor Kerry had a hip and leg malfunction. She managed to waddle a bit but she couldn't go far. But she was very much part of the family. When we let her out of her pen in the morning she would quack incessantly, impatient for her breakfast.

Kerry had her adventures like the rest of us. One morning she made a tremendous commotion. We couldn't think what was wrong until Ruth spotted a group of mallards swimming along the shoreline. They visited the bay from time to time but we hadn't seen them for a while. There were about eight of them, six females in their drab brown coats with a touch of white under the chin, just like Kerry, accompanied by a couple of males who were much more striking with their metallic green heads and prominent black and white markings. The tide was well out and they were all busy foraging amongst the exposed seaweed.

'I wonder what Kerry would do if we introduced her to

the wild ducks?' I said.

'Don't be silly,' Ruth said. 'They'll attack her.'

'Not if I keep an eye out. She's desperate to get to the water.'

When we had taken Kerry to the sea previously, she'd enjoyed the chance to hunt amongst the stones and seaweed at the water's edge when the tide was low. However, she didn't last long in the water before retreating to the stony beach, quacking loudly to let us know she was ready to be lifted back to the safety of her pen.

'All right then,' Ruth relented. 'As long as you stay with her.'

I lifted the now frenzied Kerry and carried her struggling to the water. The wild ducks swiftly abandoned the shore, swimming out of reach of danger. Before I could place Kerry in the water she flew out of my hands in great excitement. When she settled on the water, I retreated to the side of the bay.

At first the other ducks stayed away but then slowly and surely they returned. They didn't seem too interested in Kerry and certainly weren't aggressive towards her. They were in fact keeping a discreet distance. Suddenly Kerry became agitated, quacking loudly and alarming the wild ducks so much that they sped away again until she quietened down. After a few minutes they drifted back into the edge of the shore but again when they reached a certain point, Kerry started her uproar. It wasn't long before the visitors decided this spot was too noisy for them and they swam off into the distance. Kerry then decided to come out of the water. Clearly, she didn't tolerate other ducks invading her territory.

She was a nuisance at times, managing to get under our feet whatever we were doing. If she saw me digging she would start her incessant quacking until she was moved near me, then she would pick off any worms which appeared in the soil I was turning over. One day she was burrowing away at the edge of the soil I was clearing at the back of the house, when I drove the sharp edge of my spade into the hard earth only to miss her neck by inches. I hadn't seen her topple into the hole beside me. She was banned from getting too close after that.

Kerry survived her first winter with us very well. Ruth felt guilty at times when it was freezing cold but Kerry's sleeping quarters were well insulated with dried bracken or hay. At the end of March that year Ruth and the girls went to stay with my parents for their Easter holidays and I was left to feed the animals and myself – in that order.

I awoke on the first of April to a thin blanket of snow. I let the hens out and fed them and when I returned to the house I could hear Kerry making her usual din. She seemed even more vociferous than normal, but I assumed she wasn't too pleased about the snow. I let her out and gave her food and then fed the rabbit, but she continued to quack so I thought it best to check her pen. And there was the reason for her excitement. In the middle of her bed I found a beautiful light green egg. Was this some kind of April fool? For a mad moment I thought someone had come along and put this egg in Kerry's bed. Somehow I had assumed that because she was disabled she wouldn't be able to lay an egg. But for the rest of her long life with us at Kerracher she continued to lay her pale green eggs. By the time the girls and Ruth returned there was a small bowl of Kerry's eggs awaiting them. Ruth maintained that Kerry helped her to bake cakes as well as any of the hens.

CHARLIE COMES TO KERRACHER AND CLARE GOES TO LONDON

The girls' fascination with animals, especially Clare's, brought us into contact with creatures great and very small indeed.

'Mummy, close your eyes. I've got something to show you,' said Clare one day, as soon as they got home from school.

Warily, Ruth closed her eyes.

'You can open them now! Look what I got from Lynne!' Clare thrust a tiny velvety object at her mother.

'Er – what is it?'

'It's a mole.'

'It's not alive is it?'

'No.' She sounded disappointed. 'Lynne's cat caught it but couldn't eat it, and so she brought it into school to show us.'

Ruthie wasn't impressed. 'Clare gave Lynne a plastic horse and a wagon for it.'

'What are you going to do with it?' asked Ruth, taking a closer look.

'I'm going to stuff it,' was the confident reply.

'Um … how will you manage that?'

'One of my books tells you how to do it.' She made to put the mole on the kitchen table but Ruth stopped her.

'It can't stay in here. It'll be full of tiny fleas. Keep it outside.'

Clare laid the animal carefully on the kitchen windowsill then ran upstairs for her book.

At dinner later she gave us a detailed account of how to preserve mammals by stuffing them, listing all the necessary items. Perhaps fortunately we had very few of them to hand.

'I'll have to bury him,' she concluded with some disappointment.

'I'll help you,' said Ruthie. 'We'll put him next to the bumble bees.'

Intrigued, I asked, 'Where are the bumble bees?'

'In our little graveyard up the back,' Ruthie said. 'When we find a dead bumble bee or butterfly or anything we bury it and put a little pebble as its headstone and write what it was on the stone.'

The mole had the honour of becoming the first mammal in their graveyard, after Clare made us take several photographs for her records. The graveyard eventually became the resting place for all departed pets.

These were the usual childhood pets, including mice and hamsters. From an early age, Clare also had an obsession with horses. As a baby she loved to be held close to the head of a horse poking its nose over a fence. At the age of three when asked what she wanted to be when she grew up she answered, 'a horse'.

Before every birthday and Christmas she dropped many hints about how good a horse would be on the croft. I suspect she was always slightly disappointed in the presents she did get, apart from the Christmas when she was given a plastic horse and trailer. She made a good deal of miniature tack to fit the new animal in her life. One of the gifts that gave Clare more pleasure and continued enjoyment than any other was a bag of leather off-cuts from her grandfather. My father was a devotee of the local auction rooms and he often came home with odd things he considered useful, but which my mother dismissed as mere rubbish. However, on this occasion the 'rubbish' was a great treasure for Clare.

Another treasure was the old leather horse feed bag that we found in our clearance of the barns. I didn't recall my grandparents having a horse but they must have had at one time. Clare was delighted with it, but eventually we had to beg her to stop hanging it round her neck in imitation of a horse feeding.

Describing this fascination of Clare's one day to someone I knew in Lochinver, I was asked, 'Are you looking for a horse?'

We weren't, of course – we couldn't afford it. But she knew someone who wanted a new home for a horse, and price wasn't a factor.

She put me in touch with the owner. He had bought the horse for his daughters but they hadn't kept up their early enthusiasm. As a result the animal was left to its own devices, running wild on an isolated hillside. When we took the girls with us to see it we didn't tell them why we were going there. As we passed the hill where the horse roamed, I said, 'Was that a horse I saw?' and stopped the Land Rover in a lay-by. 'I thought I saw something big and black in the bracken.'

We all got out, and from the fence that edged the croft we scoured the hillside. But there was nothing to see but bracken, rushes and patches of sparse Highland grass.

'You must have been seeing things,' said Clare, adding dismissively, 'No one would keep a horse here.'

The girls wandered back to the Land Rover. Ruth murmured, 'What are you going to do now? You'll have to tell them.'

I gave as loud a whistle as I could to see if it would summon the animal. There was nothing in response other than my echo. I tried again. Then we all heard it – a whinny, away in the distance further up the hillside. The girls ran back to the fence and suddenly a sturdy pony appeared, hairy and black. It galloped down to where we were standing, neighing all the way, its mane and long tail flowing. It pulled up before the fence with nostrils flaring and dark brown eyes wild in excitement and fear.

'Wow, he's beautiful!' exclaimed Clare. The animal was clearly nervous, but it didn't take Clare long to soothe him. She held his head against hers, stroking his long nose and rubbing behind his hairy ears.

'You need company, don't you?' she whispered.

'What do you think of him?' I asked.

'He needs care and attention,' she said firmly.

Ruth couldn't stand the suspense any longer. 'How would you like to look after him?'

For once both girls were speechless.

'Do you mean take him home?' Clare eventually found her voice.

'Well, not today, obviously, but yes, we could keep him at Kerracher.' Then I added, to include Ruthie, 'We would all have to look after him.'

We gave him a good look over, and eventually persuaded the girls to bid him goodbye until he was brought to live at Kerracher.

As we got into the Land Rover I said, 'By the way, he's

called Charlie.'

We left Charlie with his head leaning over the fence watching the Land Rover disappearing into the distance, the girls waving madly from the back calling, 'Bye Charlie. See you at Kerracher.'

I agreed a price of £150 for the horse, his saddle, a riding hat and tack, and delivery to Kerracher. Clare confirmed that a new saddle for Charlie would cost as much as that. It was clear that the owner wanted the horse off his hands. He told us Charlie was a Highland/Exmoor cross, and I wondered if there was something else he wasn't telling us, but decided to take the risk.

Charlie arrived at Kerracher on Ruthie's eleventh birthday when we were in the middle of holding a party with eight of her friends. I had collected them by boat from Reintraid and we had a treasure hunt before they tucked into the table-full of food. Through the noise Ruth heard a knock at the front door and went to see who it was. When she opened it the black hairy face of Charlie greeted her, the owner on his back. Charlie had arrived, with the owner's wife and three children in tow, a week before he was expected.

The birthday party disintegrated as the children started to spill out, eager to see Charlie. Clare was ecstatic but Ruth and I felt for Ruthie whose big day this was supposed to be. She didn't say anything but after being the life and soul of the party she became very quiet.

There was nothing else to do but to get Charlie, who was enjoying all the attention, safely secured in the field, and then invite the extra guests to what remained of the party.

Although we maintained that Charlie was a pet for all the family, it was Clare who took charge of him. She tacked him up early next morning after a rushed Sunday breakfast. Charlie was biddable and seemed to enjoy the new-found attention. Clare took him around the field for a short ride and he responded in a way that suggested he was used to being ridden. When Ruthie had a go he still behaved impeccably. I kept a close eye on them but by the end of the day, it was clear Charlie enjoyed the company of people and basked in the grooming the girls gave him.

It wasn't long before we discovered his real nature. On the weekend following his arrival Clare felt confident enough to take him for a short ride around the croft, but she returned in tears soon after.

Charlie had brushed close to a tree and pinned her leg against the trunk as if trying to get her off. Clare had tried to get him to move on but he ignored her, pulling her into the branches of the birch trees at the back of the house. Then he rolled over. Clare had been very frightened and afraid she would be crushed.

'Did he fall on top of you?' I asked.

'No, but he hurt my leg before I managed to get free.'

'I think it's just bruised,' Ruth said, inspecting the leg. 'But this means you can't take him out of the field, and someone will have to be with you when you ride him again.'

'Did you give him the whip?' I asked.

'No, I didn't have time.'

'Are you all right to get back on him just now?'

'I don't know.' Clare hesitated. 'I'll try.'

We returned to Charlie who was standing calmly by the gate where he had been left tied. I led him into the field and helped Clare get back into the saddle. The horse seemed fine so she trotted him across to the end of the field. I followed and went through the gate, hiding behind the wall that sheltered the hens. Then I saw him rub up against the large anchoring post at the gate.

'Give him the whip!' I shouted.

Clare tapped his flank with her crop but he continued to rub her against the post.

'Harder than that!'

The horse then made to get down on its hocks as if preparing to roll over so I ran out from behind the wall and through the gate, grabbed the crop from Clare and gave him several sharp smacks on the flank.

Charlie stood stock-still, eyes flinching, as I grabbed his collar and held his head close to mine. 'Oh no, you don't,' I shouted into his face, wielding the crop in the air above his head. He didn't move. 'Clare, you'll need to smack him harder if he tries that again.'

I suggested she ride him back and fore in the field, to let him know he hadn't won, so she rode him for a little longer before taking his saddle and tack off, and leaving him to graze.

He did try this trick again and it was some time before she was confident enough to take him out of the field for a ride. She persevered though, and eventually managed to control him.

Charlie had a wilful and mischievous streak and he went on trying his tricks from time to time. When I trimmed his hooves he would lean heavily against me so that I ended up supporting him. That I didn't mind, but I did object when he put his hoof down hard on my toes. I responded by stamping my welly-booted foot down on his hoof. He always stopped whatever he was trying on when he encountered retaliation.

Ruth wasn't so firm, and as a result he tried lots of dirty little tricks with her. Sometimes when she was attending him he would snatch at one of her buttons – successfully. As a result Ruth's jackets always had to be re-buttoned. Another trick was to wait until she came into the field, ignore her for a minute or two then suddenly gallop up at full speed, before coming to a halt right in front of her.

But for all his faults Charlie became part of the family and quite an attraction for anyone visiting with children. When there was a crowd and he was the centre of attention he was the best behaved of animals and comfortable with anyone on his back.

He proved to be an asset as a means of transport too, enjoying the trek over to our Snoopy box at the top of the glen and back again with a package strapped to his back. It was a slow journey as he had a fear of crossing even the smallest streams. Perhaps he had slipped into a heather-covered stream when he was younger and was trapped or injured as a result.

It was thanks to Charlie that Clare had the trip of a lifetime for an eleven-year-old rider. Ruthie's usual comic was *Bunty*, but for Clare it had to have something to do with horses. As a result she joined a club that was run by Crown Paints who sponsored a couple of show jumpers and described their activities in a magazine they published. It was the highlight of Clare's month when she received this through the post. When there was a competition for the most interesting letter from a reader about their horse Clare wrote about Charlie and their life at Kerracher. She ran along to the Post Office in Drumbeg on a school day and handed it personally to Non.

A couple of magazines later she discovered that not only had her letter been published but she had also won a trip to London to attend the Olympia International Horse Show and meet the two show jumpers sponsored by Crown Paints. Accompanied by an adult, she would fly from

Inverness, stay in a four-star hotel for three days and attend the Show.

Ruth didn't much want to cope with negotiating London on her own, so we decided I would go with Clare.

It was mid-December and snowing when we left Inverness. As the plane approached London the weather was clear and dry, and Clare was invited into the cockpit by the captain to view the city. We were well looked after by Crown Paints and Clare met several famous show jumpers. We also managed to take in the first viewing of *ET* and do some Christmas shopping in Oxford Street. Clare seemed to take all these new experiences in her stride. The only hitch was on the way back.

While we were waiting at Gatwick for our boarding call Clare wandered away out of my sight to explore the airport terminal. For ten long minutes I searched in vain and eventually had to enlist the help of two police officers and get a message broadcast over the tannoy system for her to report to the British Airways desk. After covering almost every square metre of the crowded terminal I discovered her looking up transfixed at a massive screen, which was replaying the highlights of the Olympia Show. She had been standing there the whole time, unconscious of all the drama. I was very grateful that she was safe, but even more grateful that I'd been the one to accompany her and not Ruth. But probably it wouldn't have happened with Ruth – she wouldn't have let the eleven-year-old Clare out of her sight.

For months afterwards Clare talked of nothing but this visit.

PASTIMES AND PLEASURES

The seashore was a constant source of treasures and excitement for Ruthie and Clare, and they often scoured the beach at low tide, examining the sea creatures they discovered there. One afternoon they came rushing into the house, Ruthie with her hands cupped.

'Look what we've found!'

She slowly opened her hands to expose a tiny pearl nestled in her palm. 'We'll be able to make jewellery,' she declared.

'How did you manage to find that?' I asked, knowing pearls weren't just sitting on the beach ready to be picked up by the odd passer-by.

'We opened a mussel,' admitted Clare.

'How?' Ruth asked.

'With our knife,' Clare said sheepishly.

'What knife?'

'This one,' and Clare slowly took her hands from behind her back to show us an old tea knife, which had been put out with the rubbish for dumping but had clearly been 'rescued'.

Ruth and I looked at each other. We had a pact that

whatever one of us decreed the other would not counter in front of the children. I was willing to let them use the knife, old and blunt as it was, to help them explore, but if Ruth was going to err on the cautious side then I would let her decide.

'Oh all right then,' she said to their delight. Then she added, 'But remember the rule.'

Their faces froze.

'But Mum, we don't *like* mussels.'

'You've never tried them,' I said, teasing.

As a solution, Ruth suggested that any they opened should be given to the hens. 'That way you're not killing something without a purpose.'

Relieved, the girls ran off to search for more pearls.

Our rule for anyone at Kerracher was simple – if you killed any creature then you had to eat it unless there was a very good reason. No one was allowed to kill something for decorative purposes. It was an early experience of this that had led to the rule in the first place.

When we were new to Kerracher many of our visitors would collect sea urchins, dry them out, clean the shell and take them away as ornaments. I felt uneasy about the practice, apart from the terrible smell that came from them drying out, and declared that if anyone wanted to take home a sea urchin then they would have to eat the innards. The practice of taking ornamental sea urchins from Kerracher ceased at once.

Now the hens had another wholesome seafood added to their diet and the girls soon collected an array of small blue-tinged pearls.

Also, as a result of this, Ruthie developed a penchant for the cockles that nestled under the small sandy patch in the corner of the bay. She found a recipe for cockles in vinegar and presented them at dinner one evening. Both she and I enjoyed them, but Ruth and Clare did not.

I was the only one who would eat winkles, despite being the least adept at picking them. When I was a child my father sometimes came home with a bucket full of winkles. He would boil them and then empty them into a large bowl for us to pick off the hard entrance to the shell, pull the creature out with a pin and pop it into our mouths. We ate them with brown bread and butter.

So we decided to try this. I demonstrated how easily it was done by pulling out a blackish-grey wormy creature from its shell. Ruth and the girls didn't even get to this stage. Fortunately, we had other foods to help us survive. Winkles were for sending away to people in foreign parts to eat.

A big part of the girls' life was the one and a half mile walk over the hill that had to be endured to get to school and indeed any event that happened outside Kerracher. Either Ruth or I would accompany them over to the school car where Hughie waited for them. Because there was a good vantage point just after the climb up and over the cliff, where almost the whole walk could be seen, Ruth would often wait there in the afternoons and watch the girls make their way home.

When the weather was bad they would have to be togged out in wellies, yellow raincoats and sou'westers. There were always moans and groans when they had to walk over in those conditions, so I would try to take their minds off the long trail ahead of them.

'Don't think of the whole journey, just concentrate on

each individual step,' I advised, a philosophy lost on them under the circumstances.

They became very interested in the plant and animal life we encountered along the path. Often when they walked home they came across a herd of deer and far from being afraid, they were always keen to get as close as possible to the anxious animals. They used every tactic they could, like offering them outstretched handfuls of grass, or singing to them softly.

'What took you so long to get over the hill today?' Ruth would ask at the dinner table, to let me know the girls had been straying from the beaten track.

'We saw some deer,' Ruthie said.

'We sang to them,' Clare added.

'That would make them run away,' I joked and got a frown from Ruth. I was supposed to remind the girls that deer were wild animals and not to be treated as if they were pets.

'No, they stopped and listened to us,' Clare said. 'We sang them the new Gaelic song we learned in school today.'

'They understood that better and didn't run away,' Ruthie explained.

These distractions meant that sometimes when Ruth was waiting for them at the top of the cliff above Kerracher she could see them in the distance weaving their way home only for them disappear from sight. When they reappeared further along the track their anxious mother would be told they had been 'exploring'.

Sometimes, however, one would hurry ahead of the other and declare to their mother when she breathlessly reached her that she was 'bursting for a wee'. Neither of them ever practised the age-long habit when caught out on an empty hillside of going behind a bush. Considering their surroundings and the time it took for us to achieve 'normal' living conditions, the girls retained a surprising degree of modesty. It came, of course, from their mother.

The girls were given chores and responsibilities which were perhaps beyond their years, but that was how it had to be. Very often these chores would take a lot longer than expected but Ruth and I learned to be patient, confident they were exploring or just lost in a world of their own. We wouldn't have been able to survive at Kerracher if we had become over anxious about their safety.

Our insurance was that there were two of them and, if there was any accident, one would come rushing into the house to tell us the other was injured. Mostly it was Ruthie who would enter with the news, as it was Clare who tripped and fell on stones, blunt instruments, sharp instruments, glass, into holes and bogs, off rocks or boulders – and walked into cars. It was Clare who helped us get through more tins of Germoline than any other family in western civilisation.

Perhaps the biggest disadvantage to the girls from living at Kerracher was that they weren't as streetwise as other children.

We were shopping in the nearest big village, Ullapool, one busy summer's day. The village was buzzing with tourists and both girls were at a high pitch of excitement as they were going to spend their long-saved pocket money.

Ruthie had crossed the road from the side of the street lined with shops to the pavement that ran alongside the seafront. There she beckoned to her sister, but I told Clare to wait until the road was clear. She ignored my warning, made a dash for it and was instantly hit by a passing car. She seemed to spin off the nearside front wing and landed in the road by my feet.

There were gasps and cries from passers-by and a shriek of fear from Ruth. The driver of the car appeared, badly shaken and full of apologies. Clare was also badly shaken, and in shock. Ruth gave her a quick inspection but thankfully didn't find any injuries. It was the driver of the car who seemed to come off worst and it was some time before we managed to assure him that it wasn't his fault.

The girls' lives centred on their school and friends in Drumbeg, with excursions at special times as far as Inverness. The Christmas Pantomime was a big event that meant staying overnight with Moira and Stan. Sometimes it wasn't the event that they enjoyed as much as all the attention Moira gave them.

These events had to be planned well in advance. There was no just getting dressed, then straight into a car to be whisked off to wherever they were going. There was the packing – good clothes for the event, and also clothes for staying overnight and perhaps the next day, depending on the weather and how we were going to get to the roadside, be it by sea or overland trek.

We did try to make their lives as normal as possible. Because it was often such an operation to go out of Kerracher, weekends were more often spent at home. This meant no church on Sunday and for the girls, no Sunday School. However, an aunt of Ruth's told us about a Sunday School by post. When they were enrolled they spent part of each Sunday on whatever the postal Sunday School had sent that week. The girls enjoyed the stories and activities and when they were old enough they attended the summer camps which were organised through the Sunday School.

During their teenage years we took them to these camps throughout the Highlands for a week away from home, where they could mix with other children, strangers who became friends and sometimes pen pals. Initially they did suffer from home sickness but over the years these holidays helped both girls adapt to the outside world and meet and mix with a great variety of people.

The girls' school days had the usual playground upsets and fallouts, which happen even in small schools. The teacher, Mrs Matheson, was local, so she knew all the families in the community, and was firm in her running of the school. I disagreed with her on one thing. Ruthie could not grasp numbers and she especially had difficulty with multiplication tables. I was trying to get her to learn the tables by rote as I had been taught but Mrs Matheson did not agree with that method and Ruthie agreed with her. My attempts were futile as Mrs Matheson was the champion of her domain and the girls revered her every word.

Our conversations on the matter always ended with me trying to impress upon Ruthie the need to know the tables by heart. But she would say, 'I'm going to be an artist when I grow up and travel all around the world and paint pictures, so I don't need to know my times table.'

'Ok, so how are you going to travel?'

'In my big camper van.'

'And when you need to fill it with petrol and you pay for it and get your change, how will you know it's the right amount?'

'Daddy, I can add and subtract *easy*,' she sighed.

'Right,' I would persevere, 'how about when you need some new brushes and go into an art shop and ask for five of the small ones, seven of the medium ones and three of the big ones. How are you going to know the shop assistant is charging you the right amount?'

Her mother pointed out that she was more likely to need foreign languages than multiplication tables.

But I persisted. 'If the small ones cost seven pence each, the medium ones eleven pence each and the big ones fifteen pence each, then what would you do?'

'I would use a calculator or watch the prices on the till,' Ruthie explained. 'Anyway, I'll be so rich by selling paintings I won't need to worry about a few pounds for paintbrushes.'

As a result, my daughter Ruthie, living abroad now and selling her paintings for substantial figures, if asked what seven times nine is, still works out seven times ten minus seven!

———

The primary school years were cocooned in a cosy world of play and exploration. Later, as the girls became teenagers, things had to change. But for the meantime they thrived in their life at Kerracher.

WE HAVE VISITORS GALORE AND ARE ENTERTAINED

Not long after we had arrived at Kerracher, Ruth's mother and father came to see the place, accompanied by an uncle and aunt. The girls and I met them at the top of the glen on what was fortunately a sunny day in summer. The walk over was leisurely and all was well until we reached the point at the top of the cliff where we started our descent. From there, the panoramic view of the loch below and Kerracher bay is stunning. For someone who suffers from vertigo it is also fearsome: you stand on what seems to be the edge of a precipice. Ruth's mother suffered from vertigo.

While the rest of the party marvelled at the view and the girls began leading the way over the rocks that marked the faint pathway, Ruth's mother edged back along the track.

'Isn't there another way to get down?' she asked.

We had to tell her there wasn't. Realising her grandmother was afraid Ruthie came back up the path to help her down. 'I'll hold your hand and show you the way, Grandma.' It took some persuasion before Grandma was gingerly led down the side of the cliff, Ruthie one step in front and Clare behind encouraging her as we went. We eventually made it to the bottom where Ruth was waiting to welcome her very shaky mother.

Perhaps it was this experience which made her burst into tears later when we took them through the dilapidated and neglected house. She said the state of the house was far worse than she expected, and she had broken down at the thought of the huge mistake we had made by coming here.

When it was time for them to leave I took the party back down the loch by boat to Reintraid and we walked up the short but steep track to where the car was parked. For Ruth's mother it was a choice between the devil and the deep blue sea as she was also terrified of water and the boat wasn't exactly a passenger liner. However, Ruth's Aunt Minnie and Uncle Les were boating people and they were able to reassure her as we made the short journey on a calm loch.

Ruth's mother and father visited us regularly after that but her mother never got over her fear of the walk down the cliff or the boat trip. When she visited Kerracher one or both had to be endured. Once she got there she at least had the consolation of seeing her daughter and grandchildren, as well as being revived by a welcome glass of whisky.

Ruth's mother and some other visitors found it difficult to cope with the quiet and the absolute darkness of Kerracher. Many of our visitors were used to living in streets with a constant background of noise and activity, as well as street lighting. All that could be heard at night at Kerracher were the wind and the sea. Even on a calm night there was the sound of water lapping on the shore, and for many people this was soporific – they slept like babies. However, a few insomniacs found it irritating enough to keep them awake. Ruth's mother was one of them.

My own mother also had a problem at night.

'I can't get your curtains to close,' she told Ruth at

breakfast after her first night.

'They're my curtains from the house in Kelsall, and they don't stretch all the way over,' Ruth explained.

'Why would you need them closed when there's no one to see in?' I asked.

'Well, a passing fishing boat might,' was the reply.

Ruth, sensing my mother's discomfort, offered to put a blanket over the window.

Our living conditions might have been strange to our visitors over the years, but they all came back for more. Initially the biggest problem was with the chemical toilet and the fact that we didn't have a bathroom. The middle room downstairs was allocated for this and we had a sign attached to indicate whether it was occupied as there was no lock on the door. Until we installed running water in the house many of our visitors enjoyed the chance to rough it and wash their faces in the morning from the water coming off the hill.

When that dried to a trickle during the height of a hot dry summer we had to walk to what we called the sea beach where there was a fresh water loch. It was a five-minute walk across our peat fields, and out to the seashore that faced north west towards the Minch. The path had been constructed with beach stones by my grandfather as he cut the peat from the bogs between there and the sea beach. At one point the sea and the fresh water loch were separated by only a small strip of grassy land twenty metres wide. The grass which straddled both the sea and the loch was a favourite place to sit and it was high enough to enjoy both stretches of water.

That fresh water loch was our bathing place on many hot summer days. If there had been passers-by they would have been intrigued at the sight of us busily working up a lather and having a good scrub in the warm water of the loch. There was some discreet skinny-dipping, though not everyone was willing to risk exposing so much.

One afternoon we were bathing there with our friends Hazel and Ian and their young children.

'Come on Ruth, get your clothes off and come in,' Hazel urged. The rest of us were already in the water. But Ruth protested that the water was still too cold, and stayed at the edge, only ankle deep.

'I didn't take my swim wear,' she said.

'That's no excuse,' said Hazel, who was in her bra and pants. 'Neither did I.'

After some coaxing Ruth stripped down to her underwear too, and waded in. She started splashing about like the rest of us, revelling in the freedom of bathing in the open air, the late sun warm on our backs.

After a while, Ruth said she was getting cold, and made her way to the shore. Having dried herself, she sat down to absorb the last heat of the day, propped up with her arms behind her, head inclined towards the sun and eyes closed. Suddenly two heads appeared from nowhere over a small hillock to her left. She didn't hear them at first, but when the two men acknowledged us with a 'Hello everyone. Enjoying your swim?', Ruth panicked. She jumped up, grabbed the towel and ran away to the other end of the beach, wrapping the towel around her as she escaped. She stopped abruptly when she realised that she knew the man who had greeted us.

It was Frank Myrtle, a local crofter who had sheep on the Assynt estate land, accompanied by a friend. They were clearing some of his sheep which had strayed towards Kerracher.

As Frank reached the frozen Ruth he murmured, 'No

need to be worried, Ruth. We're both old married men who've seen it all before,' and passed on his way.

But that was enough for Ruth – she never stripped off for a dip again.

—

Over the years many friends and family came to stay with us. One year we had people with us thirty-six weeks out of fifty-two. A lot of Ruth's time during these visits was spent in the kitchen preparing meals, which took longer than normal because of the lack of facilities. She managed so well with limited resources that she became the victim of her own success. But eating a good meal with convivial company in such a stunning setting was something we enjoyed as much as our guests.

We had many visitors who called in after a walk over the hill or a trip by boat, not just because we were there at the end of the journey, but because Ruth's baking would be a reward for the effort. One of these visitors was Phillipa Jellicoe, who would walk over from Reintraid with an assortment of family and friends in tow. She loved Ruth's fruitcake, which she declared 'marvellous', so much so that each time they came to Reintraid Ruth would bake a fruitcake especially for her.

After our first encounter with the Jellicoes over the creels, we became good friends and their visits to Kerracher were reciprocated at Reintraid. They often invited us to join them at meal times round their kitchen table. The table had been built to seat a dozen or more, and was often crowded.

Phillipa was no cook but she was never daunted and would attempt the elaborate menus of a TV chef. I recall a fish pie that seemed to have more bone than fish. Then there was the cake from Ruth's recipe that she proudly presented at the start of one of our meals. As he was head of the table it fell upon George – with great ceremony – to cut into the cake. He plunged the long knife in to cut a substantial wedge. A landslide of crumble cascaded out. He made another attempt but that too disintegrated into a pile of crumbs. Since he was making such a poor job of it he passed the knife and the responsibility on to Phillipa who completed the demolition. Soon it was no more than a mound of crumbs on the plate.

'I think you may have misjudged the recipe in some department, darling,' said George.

'I followed Ruth's instructions with *dedication*,' Phillipa said, gathering up a small handful of crumbs. She popped them into her mouth. 'It tastes marvellous,' she said, adding modestly, 'if I may say so myself.'

Ruth tasted some crumbs. 'Phillipa, the cake is lovely. It just needed to sit a little before being cut.'

On another occasion we sat round the table talking over the day's adventures while Phillipa set out the vegetables and trimmings for the chicken we were to eat. Then she took the chicken from the oven and placed it in front of George to be carved.

'Darling, I'm not sure this chicken is quite ready for consumption,' he said. 'Indeed I wonder if it's not still alive.'

We inspected the trussed chicken on the salver in front of George. It was as pale as when it had just been plucked. Indeed it seemed to be shivering slightly after emerging from the heat of the oven!

'But George, it's been cooking for more than the time in the book,' Phillipa pointed out.

'Perhaps, darling, it's an *old* bird so it really needed a

little *more* time.'

'Everything needs more time in that oven,' she sighed.

'Perhaps there's something wrong with it,' I suggested. 'Can I take a look?'

'Oh that would be *marvellous*, Eric.'

I opened the oven door, lit a match, offered it to the row of gas vents at the back and turned on the oven switch. Suddenly it burst into life – a single white streak of flame came from somewhere near the middle of the row. It was no wonder it was taking so long to cook the food – the vents were completely blocked. I turned off the gas and extracted the burner. After giving it a good clean, I replaced it, switched on the gas and relit the oven to produce a long regular row of blue flames.

'You are absolutely *marvellous*, Eric,' Phillipa declared. 'George, pour Eric a very large glass of wine. He deserves it.'

We didn't have chicken that evening but the stuffing and bread sauce went very well with potatoes, peas and red wine.

The Jellicoes always expected us to look in if we were passing Reintraid. One day, knowing they had guests, I tried to sneak past without being seen, but Phillipa spied me from the kitchen window. Then George appeared.

'Eric, how are you? Have you got time to meet some friends we've had to lunch? They'll be delighted to meet you – anyway I think Phillipa needs your advice on the cooker again.'

Diverted from my task of collecting the girls at the top of the road, I followed George into the house, remembering to duck as I passed through each doorway. George didn't have to, as he was less than six foot tall. We entered the large kitchen where two elderly gentlemen were seated at a table scattered with the remains of a meal.

'Eric, I'd like you to meet Assynt and Durness who have just polished off three bottles of my very best wine,' said George.

Both men greeted me warmly as I shook their hands with a 'How do you do.'

'George omitted to say that he consumed at least of two of these bottles,' interrupted Phillipa. 'Eric, would you like a glass?'

'Yes please.'

'Eric is a MacLeod of local stock,' George informed his two visitors.

'Do you know Eddrachillis – I think he has some local connections?' asked the older of the two men, who both radiated mellow goodwill.

'No, I'm afraid not.'

'What about Tongue? He's in the same club as Eddrachillis and ourselves,' the other offered.

'No, again I'm afraid not.'

George came to the rescue. 'Eric does know Alistair.'

'Ah, our beloved builder,' exclaimed one of the gentlemen.

'Has he done any work for you?' asked the other.

'No. I only know him through the work he's done for George.'

'We found, that apart from our political leanings in the House, the other thing we three had in common was that we all used the most interesting builder in the Highlands,' said George.

There followed a lengthy and animated discussion about the unusual techniques Alistair Stewart had used in his building services to these three Lords of the land. There also followed a few more glasses of wine.

When I reached the roadside at the top of the track from

Reintraid I found Hughie and the girls patiently waiting for me. I apologised, and explained that I had been held up by the Jellicoes.

'A dangerous occupation, passing that house,' said Hughie, and without more ado sped off home.

There was another delay when we passed the house again to reach the boat moored at the Reintraid jetty. Phillipa came out and spoke to the girls – she was always interested in their lives. So when we eventually got home to Kerracher, we were much later than Ruth expected.

'I got caught by the Jellicoes both ways,' was all I needed to say as explanation.

'Obviously,' was her answer, my wine-tainted breath giving me away.

The relationship with the Jellicoes and Reintraid led to our meeting a host of people who walked over to visit, probably more out of curiosity than for the exercise. However, after Ruth's home baking and hospitality they always returned and we made many friends.

They ranged from country folk with dogs in tow to city folks who weren't completely adjusted to Highland life. Two of these were Philip Hammond and Colin Moynihan who both entered politics. Philip came to Reintraid for a good number of years, but I never saw him wearing anything but casual slip-on shoes, slacks and a suit shirt open at the collar. While everyone else took the opportunity to dress down Philip was always immaculately but perhaps inappropriately dressed for country life. He gave Ruthie a lift to school one morning in the early days when she went to Kylesku. That evening she was full of the sports car he had and how fast he had driven it. From then on she yearned to own a Porsche. I didn't have the heart to tell her he drove a Toyota Celica.

Colin, now Lord Moynihan, visited Reintraid only a couple of times and although he had a sporty background didn't give the impression that the wilderness of the north-west Highlands was quite to his taste. Walking up the track from the house to the road he happened once to pass a sheep in the process of lambing. It was a messy affair. 'Is that really necessary?' he enquired.

We enjoyed meeting the people who came to Reintraid, and eventually became even more involved with them when we took over the running of the property for the Jellicoes as a self-catering unit.

We had many people call into the bay at Kerracher by boat, some mooring overnight after a day's sailing and others on holiday cruising the loch and just curious about people living in such a remote spot. We made scallop divers welcome to use the place to set up their air compressors between dives, and as a result often had the most superb scallops to eat. However, when one pair started their air compressor at seven o'clock one Sunday morning I had to explain that no quantity of scallops would make up for being wakened at that time on a Sunday.

Most of our visitors were more considerate and in return for a cup of tea and some of Ruth's home baking would arrive on the shore bearing the fruits of their day at sea, very often mackerel but occasionally sea trout or lobster.

For all its remoteness, Kerracher provided us with more friends than any other place we had lived.

STRANGERS ON THE SHORE

Not all our visitors were invited, or known to us.

I was walking back over the hill towards Kerracher early one evening when I spotted something revolving out at sea. The view on the walk for the first half was panoramic. Away in the distance the Calvas, a group of small islands out in Eddrachillis Bay, could be seen beyond the land mass north-west of Kerracher. It was there that the object was circling in the water. When I got home I grabbed the binoculars and headed for the hill above the peat field to get a better view. It was a small inflatable dinghy, but there was no one in it. I watched it circle until the outboard expended itself and the dinghy was left bobbing in the water.

Unfortunately, that was the time we had our boat up on stilts getting new ribs put in so I was unable to rescue the abandoned craft. We didn't have a telephone so there was nothing for it but to get to Ardvar, where our nearest neighbours, the Paynes, lived. It took about twenty minutes to walk there by way of the sea beach. Jim and Margaret had taken up full-time residence in Ardvar since they had taken it over from Lord Buxton.

Jim's boat was the kind of thing you see at the Boat

Show in Earl's Court. It had the appearance of a luxury cruiser, but more importantly, it had a powerful inboard engine. So it didn't take us long to get to the spot where I had last seen the dinghy. After scouring the shoreline we came across the small craft bobbing gently against a rockface. When we pulled it up to the side of Jim's boat there was something odd about it that struck us both.

We expected the dinghy to be full of the paraphernalia of a diver or an angler but there was nothing to suggest the occupant had been either. There was a coil of rope with an anchor attached to one end and a plastic canister marked 'petrol'. The only other items were a couple of black boxes, which looked like crude home-made radios with switches and knobs on the side panels. They sat on the wooden floor at one side of the boat, with wires stretching to a car battery under the seat at the stern. It was a *Marie Celeste* in miniature. As Jim's boat had radio he was able to call up the coastguard but we decided to search the immediate area before instigating any call out.

We tied the dinghy to Jim's boat and aimed for the shoreline, coming in towards Loch Cairnbawn on the premise that the sailor, if there had been one, would have been swept in that direction by the strong incoming tide. The boat followed the coastline, eventually coming to the small inlet of Loch Shark. We stopped in the middle and scanned the shoreline edged with the pine trees of Duartmore Forest, but there was nothing untoward to be seen in the water.

As we passed out of the mouth of the inlet I suddenly spotted (tucked behind some rocks) a small tent pitched on the grass above the high tide mark. I pointed it out to Jim, and he slowed the boat, reversing enough to take the bow round, then edged into the tiny bay. Next to the tent was a length of rope tied between two trees with some clothes suspended from it.

'Hello,' shouted Jim. 'Is there anyone there?'

Only the echo of his voice answered.

'Hello, Hello!' we both shouted, our voices loud in the surrounding silence.

'I'll pop ashore in the dinghy,' I suggested.

Suddenly a figure appeared from the tent, clad in a wetsuit. A middle-aged man, rather paunchy around the waist, waved, walked into the water, and then swam out to us. He hauled himself into the dinghy and without any further greeting or acknowledgement, began to check that everything was there and in order.

'Is this your dinghy?' Jim asked, since the man still didn't speak.

'Yes.'

'What happened?' Jim tried again.

'I fell out and had to swim back.'

'Are you all right then?' I asked.

'Yes.'

'Is there anything we can help you with – or get for you?' prompted Jim.

'No. If you'll undo the rope I'll let you get on your way.'

I undid his rope and he settled into the bow of the dinghy. Then with his hands splashing into the water on either side he guided it back to the shore.

Jim and I watched in astonished silence. He hauled the dinghy out of the water and up onto the shore, pulled the roped anchor out and spiked it into the ground further up the beach on the grass verge. He then took the battery and the two boxes out and disappeared into the tent with them.

'What an ungrateful fellow,' I said as Jim put the boat into gear and moved us out of Loch Shark.

'Ungrateful and very odd,' he agreed.

As Jim headed across to Kerracher to drop me off, he related the events to the coastguard over the radio. He suggested they report the incident to the local policeman at Lochinver who might be interested.

As I tucked the girls into bed I told them about my adventure, but later shared my misgivings with Ruth. She was anxious, since this character was lodged just a mile away across the loch.

Next day, with the help of binoculars, we saw one of the local creel boats from Kylesku transporting the local bobby to Loch Shark and returning some time later with the dinghy in tow.

Jakie, the fisherman whose boat was used, explained to a hushed Kylesku Hotel bar later, 'The bobby told the guy he would have to pack up and remove himself immediately as the Westminster Estates were not wanting him on their land.'

It seemed the policeman had questioned the man, but even Jakie couldn't tell us anything more. This left everyone free to come up with their own theories.

'I reckon he belonged to MI6 and was a training to be a spy,' said one.

'He could have been a Russian agent sending secret signals to a submarine out in the deep waters of the Minch,' said another.

'More likely to be a drug runner checking out a quiet spot to land the stuff,' was a more contemporary suggestion.

A few years later some men were indeed caught using one of the small islands bordering Eddrachillis Bay as a landing point for drugs from the continent.

Loch Shark was a good spot for the occasional lobster pot. A few months after the episode with the stranger in the dinghy I was sailing into it to set some pots, when I noticed a small yacht moored in the middle. There was no sign of life, then or later when I laid the pots. However, a day or so afterwards, I caught sight of the same boat sailing down Loch Cairnbawn towards Kylesku. With some excitement at seeing suspicious people in Loch Shark again, I made enquiries at Kylesku only to discover that the boat belonged to a couple, Jill and Trevor, who had come up from Wales to live in their yacht in and around the Loch Cairnbawn area. The next time I was in Loch Shark and they were there, I called on them.

They emerged damp and forlorn from a galley running with condensation. They were about to spend the winter in their boat but even at the end of autumn the nights were frosty. Despite this, they were upbeat about their plans, and fiercely independent. Trevor was a wood carver and Jill was dreaming up ways to survive on whatever they could glean from land and sea.

They called into Kerracher from time to time but after that first winter the novelty of living on the sea wore off and they succumbed to shore life like the rest of us. They moved into a house, and eventually settled into the community, starting a business and then a family.

Often people wandered by on the beach in front of the house. Some would walk past quickly, trying not to engage us, but whether this was due to their need for privacy or a wish to protect ours we never knew. But others would stop, very often as a result of Ruth running out and seizing the opportunity to have a chat.

The oldest was a woman of nearly ninety who was walking the coastline from Assynt to Durness accompanied by her son. She didn't tarry with us long as she didn't want to disturb our peat cutting. Besides, if she didn't maintain her pace, she said, her joints might seize up. From the look of him, her son was the one who was ready to stop. He was only in his sixties but certainly not as fit as she was.

Another afternoon Ruth was disturbed by a gaggle of young people chattering as they walked across the stony beach in front of the house. She eagerly rushed out to discover about a dozen Gordonstoun school pupils on a trek of part of the Highland coastline. There were two teachers with them, one of whom talked at length with Ruth well after the rest of the group had disappeared over the skyline. Before he scampered off to catch up with the others he had arranged a stop for refreshments on their way back in a few days' time.

This time they were treated to the usual Kerracher hospitality, and in return the children carried over to the house as many of the dried peats as they could. It was a kind gesture, which meant Ruth and I didn't have to collect peats for nearly a week. For some time after that Ruth received postcards from the teacher as he traced his journey back to his native Australia.

We had many cosy evenings at Kerracher with house guests, mostly family. But there was a night when one of those comfortable evenings ended in tragedy. The wind was getting up a bit on the loch, but we were safely tucked in the warmth of the living room engrossed in a board game with Ruth's mother, father and sister. The hiss of the tilley lamp and our animated conversation made us oblivious to the rising storm. Then, during a lull, I heard an unusual sound.

'Hush,' I said abruptly.

We all stopped and listened.

'There it is!' Against the wind whistling through the trees behind the house and the thump of the swell against the sea wall, there came the distinct 'putt putt' of an engine.

Jumping up, I grabbed the torch and made for the door, followed closely by Ruth. Outside, the sea was right up to the sea wall, lapping the few steps that led to the beach. And there it was – the reason for the sound we had heard – an open boat with the outboard engine running. It was sitting with the bow into the sea wall and it was empty.

'Is there anyone there?' I shouted, moving the light around.

My shouting took Ruth's father, Bill, out to join us. I did a sweep of the immediate area of the bay with the torch but all I could see was the movement of the heaving sea and wisps of spray lifted upwards by the wind.

I looked into the boat again.

'I think I've seen this boat before,' I said to Ruth who had now brought another torch. 'Do you remember the guy who called in when Hazel and Ian were here – he was looking for a ceilidh? It's the same boat that went down the loch to Kylesku earlier in the afternoon.'

The boat was wooden and clinker built and its wide belly suggested it had Orkney origin. It contained what you'd expect a local fisherman to have: a plastic fuel container; a coil of rope; a small anchor; and a fish box with a miscellany of tackle, including a pair of rowlocks for the oars that were strapped to one side of the boat. The engine was still idling as I secured the lanyard to one of the larger stones at the top of the sea wall. I was about to enter the boat to throw out the anchor at the back to keep the stern in deeper water when Ruth said, 'What's that over there?'

Bill followed the beam from her torch with the torch I had just handed him. The two beams fixed on something orange floating in the dark grey water.

I jumped into the boat, urging Bill to come with me. Ruth untied the rope I had just secured and I put the engine into reverse. With Bill bundling in behind me I took the boat out to the orange object, spotlighted by Ruth's torch. I carefully manoeuvred the boat alongside. At first it looked like an empty fisherman's jacket, but then we saw someone in the jacket, floating face down in the water.

'Help me get him into the boat,' I said.

'What is it?' Ruth called from the shore.

'Switch off your light,' I shouted back.

The dazzle of her torch disappeared and in the gloom, Bill and I stretched over the side of the boat and grabbed an arm each. Silently, we tried to haul him in but although it was a sturdy boat, it was tipping dangerously to one side with our weight, combined with that of a saturated body.

'We'll have to tow him in. If I hold him, can you guide us back?' I asked Bill.

He took the boat slowly to the shore with me desperately clinging onto the back of the man's jacket at the neck, holding his head out of the water as we went.

Bill took the bow of the boat back to the steps and I gently guided the body towards the front and into the safety of the shallow water.

'We'll need Mum to give us a hand to lift him,' I called to Ruth.

Ruth's mother arrived and the four of us lifted the heavy body up out of the water and onto the grass at the top of the sea wall.

'Is he alive?' asked Ruth. I tried to detect a pulse by gently pressing at his neck, and I also tried at his wrist, but the dark blue lips and the blue tinge of his face told their own story.

I turned to Bill. 'Can you have a try?'

'I'm afraid he's dead – for some time I think,' he said after a moment. Ruth too tried to detect some sign of life but had to agree. I went on pressing down on his chest with one hand over the other in an attempt to resuscitate him, but after some minutes of this there was still no reaction.

We carried the body up to the house and laid him gently by the door. Ruth fetched a blanket, which she placed over him.

'I'd better get over to Ardvar and phone the police,' I said, taking one of the torches. 'I'll leave you to secure the boat.'

I headed for Ardvar, where I phoned the local police station in Lochinver and explained what had happened. Some time later that evening Jakie arrived in his boat with the doctor and police constable from Lochinver. After Dr Nairn checked the body, they all came into the warmth of the house. It was the early hours of the morning when the boat returned to Kylesku with the man's body aboard and his boat in tow.

When you are on the water there is nothing more disconcerting at night than a light shining from the shore. In our early days when I arrived home by boat in the dark, Ruth would eagerly rush to the mooring to help me secure it. After I'd shouted at her several times to turn off the light, she realised that the well-meaning gesture was in fact a hindrance. It's just possible the lights shining from the house that night disorientated the boatman enough for him to make a fatal error of judgement. No one will ever know what happened to cause him to part from the safety of his boat.

Most of our visitors saw our lives at Kerracher as a permanent holiday. Only a few witnessed the extremes of an existence that could be harsh and perilous.

IN THE WILD, ON LAND AND SEA

We were conscious from the start that we were sharing our lives with the wild creatures which had always inhabited this landscape – and the sea.

During daylight hours it was very rare to see any creature on the hill other than the odd grouse and occasionally a herd of deer. The deer were shy and if they caught wind of anyone they were off with heads held high as they ran gracefully out of sight. The grouse too were shy but they had an irritating tactic of hiding in the heather until we were almost standing on them, then taking off with a blood-curdling shriek – enough to test the strongest heart. I never quite got used to them, especially in the dark.

Where our path over the hill to the roadside left the top of the cliff it sloped down towards a small fresh water loch. At the bottom of the slope the path crossed a shallow stream that meandered away from the loch and towards Loch Cairnbawn.

One mild morning as I walked down the slope towards this stream I noticed a v-shaped ripple on the surface of the loch. I was on my own, heading for the Snoopy box to collect post. At the stream I stopped to get a better view when I saw a small brown head, hair plastered flat, coursing its way towards the dam of stones that partitioned the loch from the stream. A large otter surfaced and climbed up onto the dam. I stood stock-still waiting for it to see me. But it was oblivious; after a vigorous shake it began to groom itself in the early morning sun. At one point it raised its nose, testing for danger, but the wind was in my favour and blowing off the loch towards the sea. I remained, so far, undetected.

We had occasionally seen otters off the rocks at Kerracher but they were always so far away we needed binoculars to watch them. This time the otter was very close. I felt honoured.

I waited for it to re-enter the still water of the loch. But instead it climbed down the short slope of stones and into the stream, heading steadily in my direction. The stream was only deep enough for it to doggy paddle, and I was standing right at the edge, so it couldn't help but see me as it passed. What if it attacked me? My ankles would not win any beauty competition but they have done me well over the years and I certainly didn't want them savaged by a terrified animal.

I stood transfixed, watching the otter slink along the stream towards me. It was only a couple of yards away when it spied me.

Our eyes met; we froze. Then, in one deft movement the creature smoothly and purposefully turned and headed back up the stream to the dam. With its belly low, it slithered over the stones, cut sharply into the water and disappeared.

I followed the small hint of ripple that broke the surface as it swam towards the middle of the loch. Suddenly it jumped up, its body half out of the water, and looked back at me. Upright, it observed me for a moment, before diving again and vanishing into the depths of the loch.

I think the otter got more of a fright than I did. When our eyes met it was as if it believed that if it turned around quietly I might not even notice it was there.

Apart from this, I came across otters away from the seashore only twice. The first time I was driving along the single-track road coming from the Kylesku side when an otter appeared in front of me at the bridge at Torgawn. I slowed and watched as it scrambled onto the tarmac. Taking no notice of the vehicle it set off in the middle of the road in the same direction as I was travelling. I followed it slowly for as much as a hundred metres with it loping along ahead of me at a fair pace. I expected it to make a jump over the low stone parapet into the stream running towards the bay at Torgawn, but just as suddenly as it had appeared it vanished instead into the birch woods to the left. I stopped the Land Rover in time to see the thick brown tail vanishing into low-lying bracken. I still can't think what would attract an otter to birch woods away from its natural element of water.

The other time was early in the morning when I had set off for a day's shopping in Inverness. I was just above Reintraid when I spotted something moving behind a tree. I stopped the Land Rover and waited, thinking it was a roe deer. After a minute or two I realised that whatever it was, I had missed it. It had probably danced away into the wooded area, too shy to want to be seen by a passing human. Just as I was about to engage gear, a small brown head appeared briefly from behind a birch tree. At first I couldn't believe my eyes: at that point the road is about a hundred metres above sea level so the last animal I expected to see was an otter.

It peeped out again, this time from the other side of the tree, eyes wide open in surprise and an almost whimsical grin on its whiskered face. The head disappeared again and I waited. A few moments passed, then it popped out again on the other side of the tree and stared at me wide eyed before disappearing behind the tree once more. This went on for a good five minutes until I realised that our game of peek-a-boo could go on forever! Reluctantly I had to abandon the fun and head for Inverness.

We often observed otters from the shoreline at Kerracher, amongst many other sea animals, including seals, porpoises and, once, a particularly unusual visitor. I would have missed it if it hadn't been for Ruth meeting me when I beached the boat after a short trip in pursuit of some fish for our tea. I had just pulled the bow of the boat onto the soft seaweed at the low tide mark when she exclaimed, 'What's that?'

'What?'

'That fin behind you!' she shouted.

A black fin was smoothly cutting through the flat calm of the loch only a couple of metres away. I froze where I stood, water halfway up my wellies. Then the adrenalin kicked in and I hastily scrambled up the shore, slipping and sliding on wet seaweed.

Turning, I saw the fin veer away, following the contour of the beach before it turned sharply and headed out into the loch, slowly sinking into the water. The whole experience was over in a matter of seconds. Later we were able to laugh at my reaction when we read that the animal we saw was more likely to be a porbeagle shark on the hunt for mackerel or salmon than a man-eating predator!

However, the sea wildlife could be dangerous as we found out one day when we were walking along what we called the 'sea beach'.

'Daddy, Daddy, come quickly!'

The girls had found something. They went on shouting as we reached them, and pointing to a mass of entangled net.

'Oh poor thing,' said Ruth, as she bent down to stroke the head of a terrified and exhausted seal completely imprisoned in a mesh of netting.

'No!' I yelled. Fortunately, Ruth reacted quickly before a swift and vicious pair of jaws could catch her hand. The reaction of the trapped seal was to defend itself with all it had – a mouthful of teeth as powerful as any Rottweiler.

'We'll have to rescue it,' said Clare.

'Yes but how?' asked Ruth. 'Especially when it's so frightened – and ready to bite our hands off.'

We realised we somehow had to keep its head still before we could cut away the net. Otherwise we would have to leave it to die, and the girls wouldn't hear of that.

We plodded off to scour the flotsam along the high tide mark. There were lots of pieces of wood but nothing seemed suitable. It was Ruth who came back with the remains of a wooden fish box.

'You can wedge its head with this,' she said, 'and I can cut away the net.'

I opened my Swiss Army knife, an essential tool to carry, and handed it to Ruth. Very gingerly I placed the V-shaped piece of wood over the neck of the seal and pressed it into the soft bed of stones so that it held the animal's head still. The seal squirmed violently and I had to put my full weight onto the wood to restrict it.

'Quick, start cutting!'

Ruth sliced deftly through the thick tangle of net. At no point did the seal resign itself to being rescued; instead it struggled as much as it could to escape the lock on its head. Its exertions began in fact to loosen the stones underneath so that the fish box was becoming less secure. I wasn't sure how much longer I could hold it.

'I'm nearly there,' Ruth said at last, as she sawed away at the net. 'Get ready to let go when I give the word.'

'All right girls – stand well away,' I warned Ruthie and Clare, who had shuffled closer to get a better view.

'Now!' shouted Ruth. She grabbed the remaining piece of net and jumped to the side. I leapt off the wooden wedge and we scrambled up the steep slope of the beach with the stones giving way underneath like sand.

The seal twisted violently, trying to catch something or someone with its jaws, but instead began rolling down the slope now it was free of the net. It eventually came to a stop where the stones gave way to wet grey sand. Without even a look back it shuffled the short distance to the water and disappeared into the foamy wash.

'Well, not even a thank you,' exclaimed Ruth. 'How ungrateful.'

Later, we came across another creature in a sorry state, but this time we could do nothing for it – it was too badly injured. This was a huge sea lion, sitting up as high as myself. It had clearly been in a fight: half its face was torn away. It was making the most woeful sound, from pain and the effort it needed to breathe. Ruth and I kept it company for some time but eventually we had to leave the poor beast. When I looked next day it was gone.

During one of our early Christmases at Kerracher, when Jean and Steve were with us, I decided to take our creels ashore. The forecast was for gales and we thought it would be good to have some time off from the usual chores. So Steve and I took the boat across to the far side of the loch where we took up about sixteen creels, which we stacked in the boat. We had just enough room sitting either side of the creels at the stern to see where we were going by leaning out. There was a slight motion on the loch's surface but the wind was getting up and coming from the north west with a raw edge to it.

We were heading across the loch towards Kerracher and home when I spotted something in the distance away to our right, near where the loch joined the open sea.

'What was that?' I said more to myself than to Steve. 'Did you see it – something broke the surface of the water?'

We both strained our eyes to the distance in the fading light of the winter afternoon. 'There it is!' I exclaimed.

A huge black mass was breaking the surface of the water then dipping in again.

'What *is* that?'

'I don't know – but it's huge, with a dorsal fin,' I said.

It broke the surface again and this time seemed even bigger. The dark mass rose gracefully out of the water and just as slowly dipped back in, its long body seeming to go on forever.

'It must be a whale,' I guessed.

All Steve could say was, 'Whatever it is, it's big.'

I seemed to recall that the only big whales you could see in these waters were killer whales. Perhaps it was a mistake to say so, but I couldn't help myself.

'I think it's a killer whale.'

As soon as I spoke, a chill descended on the boat. Our

predicament was clear. We were cramped in the stern of an open boat heading across an expanse of darkening choppy water right into the path of a killer whale. And all we had to propel us was an eight-horsepower Seagull outboard.

'Could it attack the boat?' asked Steve, trying to keep his voice steady.

'I'm not sure,' I admitted, 'but either way we're heading for it and if it doesn't go for us it might just rise underneath. Then we're in the water.'

'Should we wait and just hope it goes past us and into the loch?' Steve wondered.

I watched as the mammal appeared again, its head breaking the surface then dipping down, the huge fin appearing and disappearing before its tail end in turn rose up and sank again. The beast was certainly bigger than the boat, but I gauged that by the time we got to the middle it would be well into the loch and past us.

'Let's carry on for now,' I said. 'It's either that or we turn back to the shore behind us and wait. But if we wait it's going to get dark and we won't be able to see it at all.'

I felt I would rather be able to see the animal and base our chances on that, than have to cross in the dark, unable to see anything at all. So we continued in silence, with only the swish of the water splashing off the bow as we cut through the waves to accompany the chug-chug of the underpowered outboard. The crossing seemed to take forever. We didn't see the whale again but that just meant it could be anywhere – even underneath us.

It was two very relieved men who disembarked on the Kerracher shore. We quickly stacked the creels at the end of the barns and moored the boat before reaching the warmth and safety of the kitchen where we related the story over mugs of tea, well fortified with whisky.

On a beautiful calm day the week after Christmas we sighted the creature again, on a trip out of the loch for a spot of fishing. This time it was well off shore and we could see it in a better light. It emerged from the water glistening black with a flash of white. There was great excitement in the boat, but none of the fear Steve and I had experienced. We had read up on killer whales by now, and it seemed there were no reports of anyone ever being attacked by them.

We all fought over the sole pair of binoculars. And then to our joy we realised that there were in fact two whales. The fishing was forgotten as we watched the show put on for us by the two mammals splashing and diving.

I never saw one again but one evening, when I returned home from a day away from Kerracher, Ruth told me how she had spent her day fascinated by a single whale out in the bay, emerging and submerging as if solely for her benefit. From her kitchen window she had enjoyed the antics of what we now knew to be an orca.

Porpoises were more common, and Ruth saw those too from her kitchen window as they played in the loch. On one trip, when I was heading for Kerracher from Kylesku, a couple of porpoises accompanied me, keeping well away from the boat but nevertheless dipping and diving slightly ahead on the starboard bow.

The bird life around the bay consisted mainly of gulls, sandpipers, the odd curlew, oystercatchers and a variety of ducks and divers depending upon the time of year. We had an annual visit from a small group of Canada geese taking a day or two out of their migration to pick at the grass around the hen house at the far end of the bay.

During the winter months we were often entertained by gannets chasing shoals of fish in the loch. The commotion they made took us to the window to witness a frenzy of activity. Above the water a swirling group of gannets took turns to feed, plunging into the foam in ones and twos while others were resurfacing. With a swift flapping of wings they were out of the water and airborne again, preparing for their next dive. We marvelled at the sheer energy of these birds. Their diving display usually lasted only a matter of minutes before they would suddenly fly off to another part of the loch or vanish altogether, off out to sea.

We were used to bird calls of all kinds, but our human visitors sometimes complained of being wakened early in the morning by a squadron of shrieking oystercatchers landing on or taking off from the shoreline.

We did once adopt a pair of seagulls we named George and Mildred after the old TV sitcom. One was docile and seemingly under the rule of the dominant screech of the other. However, the girls managed to get close enough to feed them and they regularly visited us at mealtimes, becoming a permanent feature of the life around Kerracher. When we got the hens George and Mildred were included in feeding times and they saw to it that other gulls were kept away.

Unfortunately when our second batch of hens began to lay eggs, the gull we thought of as George began stealing into the hen house to help himself to a newly laid egg. One might have been excused, but when it developed into his taking *every* egg then I was called in by Ruth to put a stop to it. I never did explain to the girls how George mysteriously disappeared.

Back on land near the house we had regular visits from the red deer stags which roamed the surrounding hills. Clare had the best view from her bedroom where she watched them venture down the slope at the back of the house. They were alert and never allowed us to approach them, but they coveted the lush green grass of the croft meadow. The deer fence, which we had to erect very early on in our occupation of Kerracher, surrounded this, but it didn't stop the stags from becoming a nuisance. They found a spot where the land was a little higher outside the fence than in and the more adventurous and agile of them would try to jump the fence at that point. They didn't all succeed, and the fence took such a hammering I had to raise its height. Even then the odd one would jump at the fence in a renewed effort to flatten it. They were like the sheep: when they were set on getting to better grazing it didn't matter what stood in the way, they would bang their heads off it until it caved in. Unfortunately this is what happened to our fence.

Although the girls had found evidence of badgers living near us – and had brought the evidence home to show Ruth – none of us had ever seen them. Then one evening, quite late, when everyone had gone to bed and I was reading, I was startled by a ferocious racket. There was screeching and wailing followed by a guttural growling, then another bout of screeching. I jumped up, aware that Penny was out. I grabbed the torch and headed outside, but as I followed the direction of the hullabaloo, Penny brushed by my legs and in through the open front door. The noise was still going on and I ventured gingerly towards it round the back of the house, where it appeared to be coming from a clump of bracken.

As I shone the torch into the spot, a large hairy creature shot off into the darkness in the direction of the caravan. I kept the beam of torchlight on the same spot and pinpointed a second large badger seemingly blinded by my light and whining in pain. It remained motionless for a few moments before making up its mind to move. But instead of taking the same route as its adversary, it headed straight for me. I had heard of the ferocity of badgers – and here I was effectively cornering an angry and apparently wounded one. I managed to hold the torchlight on it as I edged a safe distance away. The poor animal dragged itself, limping, up the slope at the back of the house where it disappeared into the trees, obviously not interested in picking another fight.

My next encounter with badgers was quite different. I was on my way home after depositing the girls with friends in Drumbeg early one summer's evening. I was walking along the flat area below the cliff towards the spot where our water tank system stood above Kerracher. The area was sheltered under the stretch of the rock face, and scattered with birch trees. Some of these had succumbed to the elements as their root base was weak for their size and they lay on their sides, roots protruding into the air like ghostly limbs.

It was under one of these that I noticed a movement – a slight flash of black and white and then another abrupt movement. I stopped. Then out from under the root system appeared a small bundle of silver about the size of a bulging hot water bottle, instantly followed by another. The second one jumped on the first and the two rolled around in a tight ball. Just as they parted a third body leaped into the space. When I saw their black and white face stripes I realised these were young badgers playing amongst the labyrinth of roots. They climbed up and over the root branches and ambushed their playmates below by jumping on them, then they rolled over and over clutching each other before suddenly falling apart and running away in different directions, all the time squeaking and yelping.

There was no other sound but the noise of the three badgers having fun and there was no sign of an adult badger. The westering sun split through the trees, lighting up the stony fingers of the cliff face as they played.

I turned as quietly and quickly as I could, then hurried home for the camera and to bring Ruth up to see them. She had never seen a badger.

Together we hurried back up to the base of the cliff. But when we reached the spot where I had stood moments earlier, there was no sign of the youngsters. I was pointing out the fallen tree and its roots when suddenly we spotted a full grown badger as it broke the cover of some bracken close by. It crossed the path and loped off in the direction of where the girls and I had previously found evidence of a badger's sett. A little way on, it gave a few barks, and in response three young badgers broke from the cover of the bracken, one after the other, and each, nose to tail, jogged along to the pace of the adult. I was glad Ruth was able to catch sight of them. We smiled at each other, quite delighted, until we realised we had completely forgotten the camera in my hand.

Animals came upon us in the most unexpected fashion. One afternoon Ruth and I were relaxing in the sun on a patch of grass that served as a lawn and place to hang the washing at the side of the house. Suddenly there was a commotion in the long grass and shrubbery at the end of the lawn, just at the base of the hill behind the house. A fully-grown otter spilled out of the undergrowth, landed in a heap and rolled onto the smooth grass of the lawn. As it found its legs it caught sight of us and froze with horror. Then it came to its senses and, still bedecked in strands of long grass and bracken fronds, it loped off past us, turned the corner and was off through the gate and down the beach to the sanctuary of the sea.

We weren't sure who got the bigger surprise – the otter or us.

Another surprise was the fox that we found lying dead over the wall from the hen house. It was in perfect condition and on its side as if fast asleep. We could find no mark on it to explain its death, and it wasn't an old fox. We were puzzled: it was just as if it had lain down on its side and gone to sleep. The girls had a short ceremony for it when I buried it in the ever-expanding animal graveyard.

Many of our guests who had heard these animal stories were disappointed if they saw nothing on the walk over the hill. The problem, of course, was that we were chatting so much during the walk that any wild creature would have heard us and disappeared long before we could reach it. I saw more simply because I walked the hill more on my own than anyone else. I was so familiar with the route that I knew if someone had visited Kerracher on foot that day just by seeing the extra footprints they left in the areas of soft peat.

Our guests were desperate to see some wildlife. Often someone would rush into the house eagerly exclaiming that they had seen 'an eagle'. When we checked it out it was always no more than a buzzard.

We had a resident family of buzzards at Kerracher and only once did I witness an attack on our hens. A buzzard swooping down on something in the middle of the croft took my attention. A hen was stranded out in the open field with a line of young chicks behind her, desperately running for the cover of some nearby bulrushes. She flew up gallantly at the predator as it swooped again and again in an effort to get at one of the chicks. By now most of them had reached the safety of the long grass nearby but she wasn't able to get the last straggler under cover in time. The buzzard swooped again and rose into the air with a small yellow package. It made for the fence and settled on the large corner post with the chick gripped in its talons. I found it difficult to watch any longer as the bird proceeded to tear the chick apart and no doubt enjoy the tender meat. Living at Kerracher certainly indoctrinated us in the natural order of things and the food chain was always evident.

Once, when we were all walking over the hill towards the road, Ruth pointed out a large brown bird, which was gliding away from Quinag in the distance and heading across Loch Cairnbawn in the direction of Kylestrome. There was no beating of wings, just a gentle glide. It took only a matter of seconds for the glider to cross the expanse of water and lose itself against the heather of the hills on the other side. It was clearly not a buzzard but something much more magnificent. We were sure then we had spotted an eagle but this turned out to be the one and only time.

The road to the south over Quinag was high and in winter could be treacherous but also quite wonderful. I did encounter whiteout conditions several times. There was one evening when I had to stop the Land Rover and wait a full twenty minutes before there was enough of a break in the snow to pick out the next snow pole at the side of the road. I was, thankfully, without the girls or Ruth but I did have the back of the vehicle packed with provisions for Christmas. I did wonder if I might have to pull one of the Christmas crackers on my own.

However, there were other times when the crisp beauty of a moonlit night, white and sparkling, was enough to make me stop just to take in the scene. Doing that gave me the chance of watching two animals that otherwise I would never have seen.

One was a mountain hare. It was pure white and larger than any hare I had seen before. It loped gently from behind a clump of snow-covered rushes and stopped in the middle of the road. My headlights were full on it but nevertheless it sat erect with ears straight up and sniffed the air as if to check where the hum of the engine was coming from. But it didn't seem to be bothered, for it just loped off to the other side of the road. It wasn't long before it raced into the white hillside and was lost to sight.

The other creature I spotted over Quinag, again on a moonlit winter night, was a large bird foraging under some snow-laden heather at the roadside. It looked like a grouse that had donned a white coat for the winter but I knew that grouse weren't likely to be this high up on the mountain. I realised it could only be a ptarmigan. Like the hare, its white coat merged naturally into the backdrop of snow. It was shy and didn't wait around long to check out the parked Land Rover: as quickly as it had appeared it took up and flew off.

I had only glimpses of these creatures that shared the wild and often hostile land with us, so that each sighting, each encounter, felt like a privilege and something to treasure.

ELECTRICITY COMES, AND SO DOES THE DOCTOR

It seems to me there was a defining moment at Kerracher when our established routines and way of life began to change. We had lived there for seven years when Ruthie left primary school to go on to secondary education. She had to travel to Golspie High School on the east coast some sixty-five miles away. That in turn meant staying in a hostel with other girls from the west coast. So from the age of twelve she was driven every Sunday afternoon to where the road south from Kylesku over Quinag met the road from Lochinver. There she joined the school bus taking a group of forlorn-looking children to Golspie for the week. They returned again on the following Friday evening.

During the summer she was still upbeat about leaving the younger children at Drumbeg behind and going to secondary school, but when the time came the reality of being wrenched from the comforts of home was almost too much to handle.

For the first two or three weeks there were tearful moments when she waved goodbye to Ruth and Clare, and then again at the door of the bus when I watched her embark. The tears flowed again on the first few Friday evenings and she protested that she couldn't ever go back to Golspie. Gradually, a mixture of loving sympathy, more from her mother than father, coupled with the reality of having no alternative, and (perhaps most effective) making friends with another girl in the same situation, helped her adapt to her new life.

Our routine changed too. The weekend became a more concentrated family time, with trips to deliver and collect Ruthie in addition to the normal weekday routine of getting Clare to school and back.

The other monumental change for us at that time was that we were finally able to get a supply of electricity. The power line was to be extended from Drumbeg to take in the township of Nedd and then through the houses at Glenleraig and Ardvar, ending up at Kerracher. It was to be done through a European-funded initiative and subsidised so that the residents wouldn't have to bear the full cost.

By this time the house had been almost fully renovated, including wiring throughout, so this was excellent news. It was always our intention to install some type of wind-generated power to the house, or if that failed then to fall back on a diesel-fuelled generator. But we hadn't yet reached that stage. There were rumours that the cost was going to be only £400 for each house connected to the grid, which was even better news.

When we received our letter of offer the price quoted was £20,000. It was quite beyond us to find such a sum, which in any case would not have been economical. Apparently we were 'at the end of the line and therefore would incur extra costs to the scheme'.

We discovered that a number of the houses included in the path of the connection were holiday homes and therefore not lived in all the year round, nor occupied by local residents. Also included were a few commercial buildings, which were not even in use. So we wrote to our local MP, Robert MacLennan, pointing out that a local family with young children would be unable to bring their home up to the standard of modern living, while others who didn't even live in the area would benefit.

We soon received a letter from the Chairman of the Hydro Board admitting they had made some miscalculation in the cost. We were going to get electricity at the same price as everyone else.

Then, for the first time since we'd moved to Kerracher, we had to call on the services of the doctor from Lochinver. All our original detractors had warned us that it would be irresponsible to live in such an isolated spot with two young children.

'What will you do in an emergency?' they had all said.

We had lasted nearly seven years with only one emergency. When she was still quite small, Ruthie almost choked on an orange. Although my almighty thump on her back dislodged the piece stuck in her throat, we got a tremendous fright. As a result, I learned the Heimlich Manoeuvre, but thankfully we never had to put it into use. The incident could have happened anywhere and no emergency service would have arrived in time if Ruthie had gone on choking. To this day, she seldom tackles an orange.

So we didn't need the doctor for Ruthie, who soon recovered from her ordeal. Nor did we ever need him for Clare though she was the more accident prone of the children. As we were all so dependent on Ruth she, fortunately, never became ill. Apart from several surgical operations to remove cysts, she kept healthy.

The doctor had to visit Kerracher for me – the Kerracher

Man himself. All the time the helicopter was plying back and forth between Ardvar and Kerracher with electricity poles dangling beneath, I was lying in bed in a delirium, sweating, and unable to swallow anything but warm water.

I was ill for almost a week with Ruth constantly changing the bedclothes and tending to me. When the bout of flu, as we thought it, didn't get any better, she decided to call the doctor. While Clare was at school she walked across to Ardvar. There was no one there, so she went on to the manager's house. Alison, the manager's wife and a good friend, was not in either so Ruth had to go as far as the newly established fish farm work shed. There she found Jim Payne and his small team of workers – four local lads and Peter his manager.

'Hello, Ruth,' Peter welcomed her. 'Alison's just gone along to Drumbeg shop but she shouldn't be long.'

'Oh I haven't come to visit. I've had Eric in bed all week and – '

No one caught her next words – *and I need to call the doctor* – which were drowned in an outburst of laughter.

'Lucky Eric.'

'Doesn't he have the strength left to walk over?'

It was a few minutes before she managed to convince them it was serious, and the doctor was needed.

Dr Nairn, having driven twenty miles from Lochinver, walked over the hill to Kerracher later that afternoon. He diagnosed a virus and prescribed pills, which eventually arrived the following day via Clare when she came home from school.

We considered ourselves fortunate to have survived so many years at Kerracher without a doctor's visit, other than when the tragic drowning occurred, but I now had to suffer jibes from family and friends that I was the softy who'd called him out. But I didn't care – I was only too relieved to be able to get up and out to witness the last pole being delivered and dug in at the back of the house in advance of the power coming.

———

The power line had now been established between Drumbeg and Kerracher and overnight all the tilley lamps and generators in the area became redundant. Our local electrician, Kenny Stewart from Nedd, had installed the wiring with me as his 'apprentice' but even so Ruth and I were strangely reluctant actually to switch the power on in the house. All it meant was pushing down the big switch on the fuse box and then turning on a light. Whether it was because we didn't trust the job that Kenny had completed or the fact that it meant an end to the comforting hiss of the tilley, I am not quite sure.

Eventually, after some hesitation, I switched on the power at the fuse box, then pressed one of the kitchen light switches. Immediately, the room filled with brilliant light. We rushed to every other room in the house switching on lights. They all worked! We ran outside to witness the phenomenon. The house had become a beacon in the dark isolation of the bay. We were like children celebrating the lights being lit on a Christmas tree.

Now we could try out our new washing machine, which had been standing in the kitchen ever since we knew for certain we were getting electricity. Ruth was keen to put it into use after seven years of hand washing. She loaded it and set the programme. It began filling with water, which rose slowly up the window on the door. Then the drum started to splash gently from side to side creating a frothy sea through the glass. Fascinated, we gazed at it as if we were seeing television for the first time. Even Penny joined us sitting in front of the machine, his head going back and fore in time with the washing.

The other gadget Ruth was eager to put into action was the vacuum cleaner. For the first week after electricity came to the house the disc in the fuse box spun like a dervish. We all particularly enjoyed the fridge freezer that we eventually added to the kitchen, especially for the fresh milk. Gone were the days of long-life milk, though we had become quite used to it, unlike most of our visitors. The girls enjoyed being able to make ice lollies and trying out the ice creams Ruth started to produce. It made a pleasant change to put a bottle of white wine or beer into the fridge instead of walking up to the stream to immerse them in cold water hours before they were needed.

As well as the kitchen mixer and other gadgets, Ruth was delighted to be able to use a steam iron at last. She had been pressing our clothes with a gas iron. It was always a nuisance when I had to disconnect the cooker from the Calor gas canister and connect the tube extended from the iron. Now, thankfully, those days were over.

Two nights after the electricity was switched on we had a power cut, something we had to get used to over the years. As we were at the end of the line we suffered whenever there were any problems such as high winds, heavy snow on the lines or maintenance work.

For a long time after that whenever we switched on a light we stopped for a moment and marvelled at the wonder of it. To this day when we enter our home in the dark and switch on the light we feel grateful that we don't have to go through the palaver of getting a tilley lamp going.

It had taken seven long years to renovate the house. We never envisaged when we began how tortuous the road was going to be. Without power, everything had to be done by hand and my power tools were redundant until we got electricity, by which time most of the work had been done.

OUR LIVES BEGIN TO CHANGE

Getting in and out of Kerracher was always fraught with complications, and often affected by the weather. As the years rolled on we found ourselves using the hill more often than the boat. Often we would take the boat down to Kylesku and find when we returned later in the day that the weather had turned and was no longer suitable for going home by the loch. That meant a journey to the top of the glen then the walk, carrying whatever we had bought that day. The problem then was that the boat was stuck at Kylesku and the car at the top of the glen. That wasn't as bad as when the car was at Kylesku and we weren't able to take the boat out. That resulted in a walk over the hill of a mile and a half then a six-mile walk to retrieve the car at Kylesku, unless we were lucky enough to have a local person going in the right direction.

I did have sympathy for the girls when that was the case. It happened more when they went on to secondary school in Golspie. We seldom saw any cars on the road late on a Sunday afternoon. We were always laden with their baggage and often wet, so it was a rare treat to get a lift.

While the girls were at Drumbeg Primary School there

were winter days when Ruth or I would walk over in the snow to collect them, only to find the school car hadn't arrived. We had no telephone and there was no means of communication to tell us what was happening. It was a case of simply waiting for half an hour and then walking home. We had an agreement that if the weather was bad and Hughie couldn't make it to the top of the glen, the girls would be dropped off at Moira and Stan's at Glenleraig. If they were away then it would be back to Drumbeg to find a spare bed with one of their friends.

Once I arrived at the top of the glen in a blizzard to spot Hughie arriving at the road on the other side, but not venturing any further. I managed to get his attention and proceeded to walk down the glen and up the other side, a distance of about a mile, to collect Clare. Clare and I then walked down the far side of the glen and on up to our Snoopy box ready to walk the mile and a half over the hill. However, by this time it was very much darker and because of the increasingly heavy snow visibility was almost nil.

We began carefully picking our way across the hill. We found ourselves facing the oncoming snow, which made it difficult to see. Only a few minutes into our walk there was a large outcrop of rock. I decided to shelter there, thinking the snow might let up. After five minutes it was just as heavy so we set off again towards Kerracher. But this time we walked backwards. It was the only way we could make progress. I sheltered Clare as I walked before her with one arm outstretched and touching her shoulder. It was painfully slow but we trudged from vanishing landmark to vanishing landmark. It wasn't a total white out and the snow hadn't been falling for too long so we were able, just, to discern our route home. When we eventually reached the house, Ruth was very relieved to see us.

'You're just like a couple of snowmen.'

———

Clare coped well with Ruthie being away for the gap of two years between them. She busied herself with Charlie during the week and caught up with Ruthie's news when she came home for the weekend.

In Clare's last year at Drumbeg School, close to her leaving day, there was a change in Charlie. It started with a runny nose, which developed into breathing problems, so we called out the vet. We were given some antibiotics that Ruth had to inject him with over the period of a week but it didn't make much difference. We called the vet back and there was some talk of getting Charlie off to Glasgow to see a vet there. When Clare came home from school each afternoon she kept Charlie company until it was time for bed. He seemed to be responding and picked up a bit. But one morning we found him standing up against the fence in a distressed state. His eyes were glazed, he could hardly breathe and blood and mucus were streaming from his nostrils. 'I'll ask Hughie to call the vet and get him to visit today,' I promised Clare.

Clare stroked Charlie under his ear. 'I don't think he'll be fit to go to Glasgow now.'

'It doesn't look good,' I admitted, hoping she realised how serious it was.

'Poor Charlie. I want to stay with him today.' Clare bent her head close to his hairy neck. I could see she was on the verge of tears.

'I think it would be better if you weren't here – in case the worst has to happen,' I suggested.

Ruth too thought it best for Clare to go to school. So Clare got ready, but as she left she gave Charlie a long hug before reluctantly falling in step with me to trudge the walk over the hill. As we walked we talked about Charlie, recalling when he'd been mischievous but also his endearing and friendly ways. We talked about how much he and Clare had come on since he had arrived almost four years earlier. She was very upset though, as Hughie whisked her off in the school car.

At home Ruth was still tending to Charlie, who was by now producing white foam around his nostrils. He was breathing with difficulty and Ruth kept wiping his nose and mouth, whispering away to him. He stood quietly by the fence, accepting Ruth's care with resigned dignity.

'I hope the vet comes,' was all she could say.

I busied myself servicing the outboard in the shed. Every so often I went out to check how Charlie was, but he was not improving. Thankfully the vet arrived around lunchtime. He didn't take long to conclude there was nothing he could do for the horse.

I thought the vet would end Charlie's misery with an injection like a cat or dog. But when he explained the method I wasn't certain I would manage to hold Charlie for him. Ruth gave Charlie a last hug before heading into the house in tears.

I led the horse slowly to the corner of the field where so many other animals had been interred over the years. It was going to be my job to bury him so we decided this was the best place.

Poor Charlie was submissive and docile at the end. While I held him gently by the head the vet inserted a bullet into the implement he was going to use. He placed the bell-like part on the forehead of the horse and then hit the end of the pin that protruded from it with a hammer. Nothing happened. Charlie didn't flinch and let his head down a little when the vet took the tool away to check it. The horse was oblivious to what was happening, so when the vet adjusted something on the tool and placed it once again on Charlie's forehead there was no reaction from him.

I held Charlie's head steady with my arm around his thick hairy neck and the vet hit the tool end with the hammer once again. Charlie went limp and slowly slumped to the ground. There was no sudden jerk or shock. There was no loud noise to frighten him. He just quietly passed away. At least he was no longer in distress.

The young vet apologised for the first misfire, visibly upset. So, after laying Charlie's head gently on the ground I took the vet to the house for a cup of tea. He didn't stay long before setting off over the hill to his car.

Ruth came with me to see Charlie, stretched out on his side as if he was napping in the sun. She cut a long piece of his tail for Clare and then left me to get on with the job of digging a hole.

It took me three hours in hot sunshine to dig a hole big enough and Ruth helped me slide Charlie into it only moments before she had to go up the cliff to catch Clare coming home from school. By the time they both reached Kerracher I had almost refilled the hole. Clare was upset but she was also keen to help me put the last of the soil on top of her companion of more than three years. Then she went into the house where she started to pleat the hair from Charlie's tail, a keepsake she has with her to this day.

About four months later Clare rode into the field at Kerracher on the back of a new companion, an Arab Connemara cross. She had saved up her own money to add to the amount we were able to pay for this gentle mare from Ruthie's best friend, Eleanor. Clare rode Juniper home the sixteen miles from Achmelvich along the single track road to Ardvar and then over to Kerracher. Juniper had a very different nature from Charlie and was easier to handle, but, for Clare, her first horse was always special.

Ruth's world changed when eventually Clare joined Ruthie at Golspie. Suddenly there was no purpose in making an early start in the morning. The morning after they had both gone to Golspie for the first time, Ruth was in the kitchen when I came downstairs.

'What would you like for breakfast?' she asked.

'I'm just going to have my usual,' I said, surprised.

'But I can get it for you,' she said, grabbing a cereal packet.

She poured cereal into the bowl in front of me and was about to add milk when I interrupted. 'Thanks, but I can manage that by myself.'

She fussed about the kitchen like one of our hens that was agitated for some reason or other. Eventually I said, 'You can have a longer lie in now that you don't have to see to the girls any more.'

'Are you saying you don't want me to get up with you for breakfast?'

'No, I'm not saying that. But I can do my own breakfast, so you've got the chance of some extra beauty sleep.' This attempt at a joke failed utterly.

'So I need to improve my looks now as well as not being needed,' she retorted.

There was a long silence before I ventured to dig myself into an even deeper hole. 'You know morning isn't my best time for conversation. I just like a bit of peace to get going for the day.'

'Is that just for breakfast or does it include lunch and dinner as well?' She stomped out of the kitchen, leaving me with the distinct feeling that I had not handled the matter too well.

From that day Ruth let me see to my own breakfast but as a peace offering I have always made her a cup of tea before she gets up. The pain for Ruth was not that I could look after myself but that she had lost a large part of her life at Kerracher – caring for the girls.

As the house renovation was nearing completion I found more time for work outside Kerracher. I was acquiring a number of small jobs such as painting, constructing built-in cupboards, landscaping and general odd jobbing. I enjoyed the outdoor work but I also found that more and more accounts work was coming my way. I had established a number of clients: small businesses such as crofters, fishermen, hoteliers and shopkeepers. I began going out of Kerracher on an almost daily basis and sometimes, for one particular business, I would travel to Bonar Bridge and spend a couple of days updating their accounts. I eventually moved their accounting machine (a forerunner of the modern-day computer) to a spare room at Lal's and did their work from there. I kept the books for a couple of shops in Lochinver, which was convenient as we did most of our shopping there. The Lochinver Fish Selling Company also gave me work. Over a period of five years this expanded from a couple of days a month to my becoming their accountant three days a week. I resisted the opportunity to become a full-time employee, as I wanted to retain my independence and the time to do other things.

The many new experiences this work opened up went further than learning about how business operates in a rural economy; it meant I encountered some interesting people.

Simon Macleod who had the butcher's shop in Lochinver was probably the most energetic man I have ever met. He never outgrew his childhood hyperactivity and carried it into his daily work. While he was on the phone he would simultaneously be cleaning the worktops in the back shop. He was non-stop. He was also creative in his marketing and always coming up with a new ploy. He showed me a short letter in the *Sunday Post* praising his establishment – sent in by 'A. Brown of Paisley' who had clearly been on holiday in Lochinver.

'That's great,' I said. 'It's a pity more customers don't do that.'

'They don't do it at all,' he answered with a wry smile.

'What do you mean?'

'I write one of these a week and send them off to different papers or magazines,' he confessed. 'I'm helping my customers do what they *intend* to do but never get round to.'

Another character was another Macleod who owned a small local hotel and was also a shepherd renowned for his winning of sheep dog trials. He was a brusque and hardy man with a very short fuse. I was getting on with the accounts one day in the office of the hotel when he barged in, his teenage son in tow.

'Another one lost to these maniacs!' he shouted.

'What's happened?' I looked at his son for some clue as I could see John wasn't in any state to give me an explanation.

'Another dead lamb at the side of the road,' the son muttered.

'That's ten I've lost this past week to those damned tourists,' John raged, pacing the office floor. 'I'm going to get even though.' He stormed out and could be heard ranting and raving elsewhere in the hotel.

His son sat down in a corner and picked up a newspaper while I continued quietly with my work.

Suddenly John barged into the office again, this time brandishing a huge kitchen knife. He was now in full flow, waving the knife back and forth in the air, his eyes bulging with frustration and rage, and shouting, 'I'm going to kill someone!'

I tried to look sympathetic, while making myself as inconspicuous as possible. His son went on stolidly reading the newspaper.

'If I don't get one of *them*, then I'll kill *myself*,' John shouted, making stabbing motions towards his chest with the knife. Then he spun on his heel and tore out of the room, the knife scything the air.

'He'll surely not carry out his threats?' I gasped.

'It would be a relief for us all if he carried out the second one. But he never does,' his son replied, unperturbed.

I noticed that the piece of paper I was holding was shaking slightly. I tried to carry on working but an ominous silence had descended. Was he going to carry out *either* threat? My fears were allayed later in the day when I came across John enthusing to a couple of tourists about how wonderful a place this was to live.

I wasn't all that sorry to lose the work when some time later he decided that being an hotelier was not for him, and he sold up and moved from the area.

As a result of our friendship with the Jellicoe family we took on the caretaking of the house at Reintraid, which in turn led to my suggestion that we let it out for them while it was empty, which was for a good part of the year.

So Ruth and I established Reintraid as a self-catering

business and from Easter through to the end of September we prepared the house for new guests at each changeover.

We made lots of new friends and the work was enjoyable, but the house itself was fraught with problems. We always had to make regular checks on fuel for the generator, water in the tank on the hill, gas in the bottles for cooking, logs for the wood-burning stove and petrol for the Land Rover, which was available to ferry guests up and down the steep track to the house. There was also a dodgy septic tank which didn't quite operate to supposed capacity, so when a large number of people were staying in the house, the system tended to get blocked. The one respite we had from emergencies was that the guests couldn't contact us immediately but had to walk all the way over to Kerracher or wait until I happened to pass by. We were fortunate in that all the guests had come through personal contact and took a delight in making the place their own. They were mostly happy to muck in and try to sort out any problems themselves.

Now when I filled in my tax return I had to account for at least six different sources of income. Our lives at Kerracher were becoming rather frantic. But we were well settled into a routine with the girls away all week. Ruth and I were living almost like normal people in a house that now had electricity and running water, and with me going out to work on a regular basis. What more could we ask for?

Perhaps it had become a little too much like being back in the real world and we were missing the activity of developing our lives at Kerracher. That's when we started to question these new routines, and we began to look at ways of earning a living, one living, at Kerracher.

WE PLAN THE FUTURE, AND TRY TO
WATCH TELEVISION

When we sat down to plan the future, there was no shortage of ideas.

In our early years at Kerracher we had thought of farming lobsters, but that meant learning to dive, and we didn't want to tackle that. I now carried out extensive research into farming mussels, which was better. To make it viable we'd have to invest a good deal in machinery, but it was a possibility. We also flirted with the idea of farming oysters after Ruthie and Clare's science teacher, Mr Joyce, sent them home one weekend with a tub full of oyster spat and a net, with directions for me to set them in the bay.

For several months afterwards we measured the growth of our oysters. They grew, but the lantern net we were using was not ideal and the young oysters didn't grow quickly enough for commercial use. We enjoyed a few almost fully grown survivors about two years later, but this was clearly not the best bet for a business.

In the midst of this research and experimentation a number of fish farms began to appear in the coastal waters of the north-west Highlands. The Paynes had recently started one in their bay at Ardvar. Sometimes when we were talking to them, the discussion would get around to our plans, and gradually, the idea of fish farming at Kerracher began to take hold.

Jim was helpful with initial information and statistics and I carried out further research. We visited a number of other fish farmers supplying the fledgling industry and I also attended a fish farm conference in Inverness. The initial idea developed into a plan, then into a business plan. Not only was it a feasible idea because we could start it as a cottage industry, but it also, in the mid-1980s, looked extremely viable.

We also had another quite different idea, to build a few self-catering chalets at Kerracher for the increasing number of people who wanted to come and holiday each year. This business plan was much easier to construct, as the concept was simple. It also meant little physical work, whereas fish farming would mean constant labour. Both would need considerable financial investment, but we now had a house that was at last up to modern living standards, and, as we had bought it from my father and the croft from Ardvar Estates and had no mortgage or debts, we could borrow against this asset.

I worked for more than a year on different business plans, but we finally came to the conclusion that we had to decide between fish farming and the self-catering option. Then at the last moment I suggested a third possibility, that we should all emigrate to New Zealand and start a new life there, based on our ability to survive in an extreme rural environment.

I threw this in one Saturday morning when the four of us were sitting round the kitchen table after breakfast, discussing all our options. The girls were now in their middle teens and well able to contribute to the debate.

'Ok,' I said after we had gone over the pros and cons of each option, 'let's take a vote on what we do. Hands up who wants to go to New Zealand.'

I shot my arm up in the air followed rather more slowly by Ruthie, then even more tentatively by Clare.

I beamed at them. 'Looks like we're going to be off down under then.'

'Well, you lot can go if you want. I'm staying here.' Ruth was adamant. 'Kerracher is my home and I'm not leaving.'

'You'll be on your own then,' I said, fingers crossed that she would change her mind.

'You can send me a postcard when you get there,' Ruth said, undeterred. 'Anyway, I thought we were looking at ways of making a living at *Kerracher*. Throwing in other options is not allowed.'

I had to admit defeat and come back to the alternatives of self-catering or fish farming.

'If we choose self-catering it won't be a living,' I had to admit. 'I'll still have to go out of Kerracher to earn.'

'Then that leaves fish farming,' Ruth decided.

'Alright, hands up those who want to start a fish farm at Kerracher,' I said, resigned to the inevitable.

Four hands were raised. We were committed to a new adventure.

———

Once the decision was made, we set to work to establish a salmon farm in the bay. I'd done enough research to source suppliers for equipment and materials as well as the stock of smolts to start us off, but before I could start placing orders I had to organise finance for the business. We successfully applied to our bank for a mortgage then sent a copy of the business plan to the Highlands & Islands Development Board, applying for a grant and loan. When funding was agreed we were able to start ordering equipment, materials and smolts in a rush of activity, which reminded us of our first months of renovation at Kerracher.

As these preparations took us nearer to the actual start-up of the business, I had to reorganise my other work activities. Most of my accounts clients didn't need me on a regular basis, but I had to say goodbye to the Lochinver Fish Selling Company. I had enjoyed being with my fellow workers in Lochinver for the last six years, but it was time to leave. My colleagues presented me with a portable television, something we had never visualised at Kerracher. Nevertheless it was very welcome – to the girls and me.

They were very excited at the prospect of being able to watch programmes that all their friends talked about. They had lasted ten years without TV, but now in their teens they minded more about sharing the same experiences as everyone else. Ruth was less enthusiastic.

We tried it out right away, but the indoor aerial was not powerful enough to receive a signal. I consulted someone in Ullapool who had a small telecommunications business. He had a piece of equipment which could detect the best spot for a signal: a heavy-duty car battery with accompanying meter.

One Saturday afternoon, while Clare was riding round the field with Juniper, Ruthie and I walked about on the croft with this apparatus. It fitted into a backpack that I strapped to my back so that all I had to do was carry the portable TV until something appeared on the screen.

We tried all afternoon with no success until we had

walked to a spot above the peat fields where there was a clear view of the western horizon. The TV screen crackled into life. Not exactly a picture but an animated series of lines and squiggles. There was obviously a signal coming from the transmitter on Lewis.

'You'll get the best view at the top of the hill at the back of the house,' Ruthie suggested.

'Ok, let's try it.' I switched off the equipment, disconnected it from the battery and prepared to climb the steep slope that loomed up behind Kerracher. Struggling up a precipice with more than the weight of a car battery on my back and clutching a portable television in one hand was not quite how I'd envisaged watching my new TV. But we reached the top. Settling down on a slab of rock, we connected the equipment together and switched on the television.

'It works!' exclaimed a happy Ruthie, as an almost perfect picture appeared on the screen.

In the waft of a spring evening breeze with the sun setting low across the Minch, we sat absorbed by a Saturday night light entertainment show

It was a success of sorts, but we were not going to be able to get that signal down at the house without some sophisticated relay system, which would no doubt cost a small fortune. Ruthie and I walked home despondently with the news.

Shortly after that my father gave me an old TV aerial and we rigged it up outside the house in the forlorn hope that we would get something from it. For almost a whole morning calls of 'how about that?' answered by 'nearly, yes, no it's gone again', rose from the house as Ruth and I attempted in vain to attract a signal. I had the aerial stuck to the corner of the house, manipulating it in all directions while Ruth was inside glued to the flickering screen.

Suddenly she shouted, 'Yes, stop, hold it there.'

'Are you sure?' I shouted back.

'Well, if you don't believe me come in and check it yourself!' she retorted.

'It's just that the aerial is pointing to the rocks at the running mooring,' I said as I came back into the living room. The television was poised on a bookshelf emitting a perfectly clear picture.

'Well, whether it is or not, you have a picture,' she announced as she brushed past me on her way to the kitchen, fed up with all the toing and froing.

The picture was now fluctuating between clear and grainy, but just good enough to make out what was going on.

'I think the reception is getting bounced off the rocks for some reason,' I said when I joined Ruth in the kitchen for a conciliatory cup of tea.

The girls were delighted when they returned home that weekend to find they could watch television. This new milestone in our lives at Kerracher was soon to disrupt the usual weekend harmony. The small white box flickering away on its shelf in the living room transfixed Ruthie, Clare and me. Spellbound by the magic of the screen, we couldn't pull ourselves away.

It all came to a head on a Saturday evening long after Ruth had gone to bed. The living room door burst open on the three of us gazing at the flickering screen.

'When are you lot going to bed? Do you know the time? It's nearly midnight,' Ruth demanded.

'When this film finishes,' we assured her.

'What are you watching?'

'It's the *Best Little Whorehouse in Texas*,' sixteen-year-old

Ruthie told her blithely.

Ruth swiftly pressed the off button and immediately the screen went dark to a chorus of '*Aw Mum!*'

'You can't let them watch that.' She faced me sternly, hands on hips.

'It's not what it seems,' I protested.

'It's really funny,' added Clare.

'Dolly Parton is in it,' said Ruthie, as if that would make it all right.

'Well, I don't approve,' Ruth said, defeated, and headed back upstairs muttering, 'Don't moan to me when you're all tired in the morning.'

We switched the magic box on again to enjoy the rest of the film while no doubt Ruth lay in bed above kept awake by bursts of laughter until the film ended.

I suppose the good thing about the advent of television at Kerracher was that the picture was often so bad we were unable to watch it. It operated best when there was a high tide, so clear viewings were intermittent. We raised a lot of false hopes for visitors who thought they would now be able to keep up with their favourite soaps when they came to stay. Certainly everyone who ever watched television at Kerracher declared that they never again took their own television for granted.

When he visited us soon after this, my brother Billy was keen, like myself, to watch an evening football match. It was well into the game when he observed, 'Odd that none of the snow's actually lying on the pitch.'

'It's not snowing, Billy. That's the interference we get from the poor reception,' I explained, as we peered to pick out the players running back and forth in what looked like a horrendous blizzard.

'I did think it odd the commentator never mentioned

the terrible conditions,' he admitted. At that point we had to concede defeat and switch off as the players had become totally obliterated by 'snow'. We were by now fully occupied in setting up the fish farm, so there was, in any case, less time for television.

We were advised to get a rifle to scare off predators. As a crofter I was entitled to apply for a gun licence to deal with vermin. When I was granted my licence, I bought a .303 rifle with telescopic sights from the gun shop in Inverness.

We had been given many gifts of venison over the years, and I told Ruth I felt it was time we tried our own.

'You'll need to shoot a stag then,' she pointed out.

'I spotted a few up behind the house. They look in good condition.'

'Are you sure you know what you're doing?'

'Well, if I don't try, I'll never know, will I?' I said, getting the rifle out of its secure storage. I was about to head out of the door when Ruth asked,

'Haven't you forgotten something?'

'I have my rifle and ammunition. What more would I need?'

'Well, what will you do when you shoot one?'

Then I remembered that of course the beast would have to be bled immediately, as I had obviously explained to Ruth at one time.

'Oh yes, I'd better take a knife.'

Handing me the sharpest knife we had, Ruth gave me a little smile. 'Best of luck – and take care.'

I picked my way through the long heather, approaching

the deer from down wind so that my scent wouldn't reach them. I knew they would move towards me as they grazed, so I lay flat on my belly in the heather and waited. I had never shot a deer although I had seen others do it. My arms began to go numb with holding the rifle in readiness, so in the end I laid it down beside me.

They had to come up a slope before they reached the flat where I was positioned, but nothing happened for what seemed ages. Suddenly the tips of the first deer's antlers appeared on the horizon of my vision. I picked up the rifle and extended it, peering through the telescopic sight. There were now five or six deer leisurely grazing with heads down, unaware of any danger. An occasional head would jerk up and sniff the air, then lower again to continue feeding.

Most of the pack had now reached the flat and the leader was checking out the area. He wasn't as absorbed with feeding as the others and held his head high, sniffing and looking around. I carefully aimed the cross on the sights at his forehead and pressured the trigger of the rifle with my finger. The deer held his position as I pressed the last section of the trigger. The bang of the rifle rang in my ear, echoing around the hill above me and out across the loch. The deer dropped to the ground.

There was a split second of frozen shock before the other young stags sprang into action. They jerked one way and then another before, to my horror, they stampeded in my direction. My first thought was that they were attacking me, then I realised they were running in blind panic. My next – fleeting – thought was, do I take this opportunity to bag a second one? I decided to show myself and hopefully divert the terrified animals. As soon as they saw me they veered off and up the hill, well away from me.

I ran over to the animal lying on its side on the heather.

To my great relief it was stone dead. I certainly didn't want to confront a wounded stag. I pulled out the knife I had taken with me in preparation and slit its throat to let it bleed. Now I had to summon help to gralloch it.

'Did you get one?' Ruth was keen to know when I reached the house.

'Yes. Now I'll have to go to Kylesku for John.' I put the blood-stained knife in the sink, handed her the rifle and then set off towards the boat.

John Clark, a friend at Kylesku who often worked at an office in his home, had said that if I ever managed to kill a deer, he would be happy to help me deal with it. Unfortunately, he was not at home that day. I returned to Kerracher and faced Ruth in the kitchen.

'We'll have to do it ourselves. Are you ready for this?' I said.

'What will we need?'

'The sharpest knife in the drawer.'

Although we had tackled hens and fish, and I had even dissected a rabbit many years before, neither of us had ever disembowelled an animal as large as a stag.

The dead animal was lying where I had left it and I set to by cutting the leathery skin in a line down its belly from throat to tail. I recalled an old crofter explaining that the only crucial thing was not to pierce the bladder as that could result in spoiling the taste of the meat later. I therefore spent an inordinate amount of time cutting around this balloon-like organ.

Eventually, with Ruth holding the animal steady for me, we cleared the body of the internal organs, which were left on the hill as a meal for some other predator. Now it was time to get the animal home. I attempted to lift it across my shoulders but it was too heavy. There was only one way – we had to drag it across the heather-clad hill and down to the house.

All went well until without warning my footing disappeared under me and I slid deep into a narrow crevice. The animal followed by falling on top of me and for a few moments I struggled to escape its empty belly, which enveloped my head.

'Are you all right?' Ruth called, trying without much success to suppress her laughter.

'Yes – if you can get me out of here,' I spluttered, wiping trails of blood from my face. After a moment she managed to compose herself and free me from my victim so that I could scramble up out of the peat and heather.

We struggled with the carcass down to the flat of the beach without any further incident. I collected the barrow and bundled the stag into it, then wheeled it the rest of the way to the shed where it was to hang for a few days. It was well after midnight when I finished attending to the now headless and skinned carcass, which we suspended from a beam. I trudged into the kitchen exhausted, but I had provided us with a source of excellent meat for some time to come.

As I sat recovering in the kitchen I was reminded of my father's stories about watching his father through the slits of the bedroom floor above. As young boys, he and his brothers slept above the kitchen and the bare floorboards were broken with chinks of light from the room below. Whenever their father shot a beast they would peep through the spaces in the floor and watch him dissect the carcass below. When the job was done, my grandfather would have a good dram before going to bed.

'Here's to blood in the heather,' I pronounced to the ceiling above as I swigged down the last drop of whisky from my glass in the tradition of the Kerracher Man.

The girls were fascinated with the hanging carcass when they arrived home at the weekend and were keen to help with its dissection. By then both were well embedded in the crofting culture and had grown accustomed to the sight of a dead animal waiting to be dispatched to the cooking pot. However, they hadn't seen such a large animal before, and, as both were interested in anatomy, they took some time studying it before helping to divide it into the different cuts of venison which would eventually grace Ruth's, and a number of friends', cooking pots.

My having a gun led to Ruth's Uncle Peter bringing his rifle with him when he came to stay with us. Peter was a former tax inspector who had retired with his wife Anne to Strathpeffer. They had a croft in Applecross, so they too had the right to apply for a gun licence. Peter, who was now in his sixties, had survived a number of heart attacks and had had major heart surgery, the evidence of which he was inclined to show people by lifting up his shirt and exposing the scar that ran from his sternum down the centre of his belly – thankfully ending no further down. Peter was one of those characters always at odds with the world. The reasons why became clearer to me the more he visited.

Arriving home during one of his early visits to Kerracher, I found that all the young birch trees that had grown up around the water and filter tanks as a natural screen and shelter had been felled. I couldn't understand what had happened. When I got into the house I asked Ruth if she knew.

'What do you mean?' she asked, puzzled. 'Who on earth would cut them down?'

At that moment Peter came shuffling through from the living room into the kitchen to join us, his eyes trying not to meet mine.

'I thought they were in the way of the path. Anyway, they were the right size for the fire,' he said.

'I'd appreciate it if you checked with me before you cut down any more of our trees,' I snapped, striding past him out of the kitchen.

Peter sulked after this like a schoolboy, but at least he didn't attempt any more tree felling. His complete fall from grace happened another time when he came to stay with us on his own.

In the middle of one night Ruth and I were wakened by a knocking on our bedroom door and Peter's voice whispering. 'Ruth, Eric, are you awake?'

'What's the matter, Peter?' Ruth was instantly alert but I took more time to surface.

'I'm OK, but I've shot a deer and I can't find it.'

'What time is it?' I asked, trying to bring my brain into gear.

'About half past three.'

'You'd better get up and see what's wrong,' Ruth sighed.

I groaned. 'Hold on Peter, I'll be with you in a minute.'

In the dark I struggled into my clothes. I opened the bedroom door to find Peter fully dressed in outdoor gear. As we went downstairs he started to explain what had happened.

'I wasn't getting to sleep so I thought I'd go out for some fresh air. That's when I saw the herd on the croft, so I got my rifle and went after them. I shot one but it got away – I think it could still be on the croft. I tried to find it but then I had to come in and put some clothes on. I was still in my pyjamas and it's cold,' he added.

Silently I donned a jacket, grabbed a torch and headed out for the croft with Peter following. We scoured the field with our torches until eventually we came across a stag lying among bulrushes near the far corner of the croft.

We approached it cautiously in case it was able to get up and make a run at us, but the poor brute was not in any fit state to move. It was badly wounded, its breathing laboured.

'I'll get my rifle,' I said.

'You can use mine.' He held up his .22.

'It's not powerful enough,' I told him through gritted teeth.

When I went into the bedroom to unlock my gun I told Ruth briefly what was going on.

I went back out, and with a sense of sorrow, loaded my rifle. Standing a little distance away from the distressed beast, I raised the gun, aimed at its forehead and fired. The shot broke the silence of the night and the body of the once proud animal slumped into the bed of rushes. Silently I apologised to the beast that it hadn't been dispatched cleanly in the first place.

I gralloched the animal, all the time impatiently asking Peter to hold the torch one way and then another to help me get the job done. It took some time in the dark and to add to the discomfort, it began to drizzle. Finally, exacerbating the whole situation, the midges began to appear. With the disembowelling done we each took hold of an antler and began to drag the carcass across the wet grass in the direction of the house.

'It's a heavy beast,' Peter said, breaking the silence.

After a strenuous effort which got us very little distance, I realised I would have to cut it in two – it was the biggest stag we had ever had at Kerracher. When the two halves were finally hung, skinned and cleaned, we convened to the kitchen where Ruth was preparing breakfast for us. It was seven thirty.

There was no dram that morning and all I had to say to Peter was, 'If you visit again, don't bring your rifle.'

He did visit again but always with Anne and never with his rifle. Strangely, he never made any reference to the magnificent twelve pointer stag that he had felled on the croft.

He brought his fishing gear instead. After hours spent on hill lochs surrounding Kerracher he often came home with a meal of brown trout. His pride and joy was a five pounder, which was never bettered, not even by Clare who had taken up angling and who also contributed many a good meal to the dinner table at Kerracher.

Now we were embarking on a venture that would provide us with a fish every day if we wanted. This new development would require full-time commitment. There would be less time for activities such as fishing and lobstering.

I talked this over with my father one autumn evening as we sat together in the middle of Eddrachillis Bay with lines extended from each side of our boat. The sun was setting slowly into the horizon of the Minch and we were admiring the salmon pink and blue grey sky it was leaving in its wake, rather than fishing for the elusive ling we had intended to catch.

'If all's well this time next year it's the pink and grey of salmon that we'll be seeing more of, I guess,' I said. 'There won't be as much time for doing this.'

'Oh well, I'll just have to visit more often to do your fishing for you,' was my father's reply. He relit his pipe and in the gathering gloom the flame from his lighter revealed the satisfaction on his face.

'Time to head for home I think. We've got an early start in the morning,' I said. The next day Ruth and I were to visit a fish farm at Lochcarron, which built salmon pens, as we were planning to place an order with them.

WE BECOME FISH FARMERS

In April 1986, ten years after we had towed a caravan to Kerracher on a raft, we amassed a stack of fish cage sections, nets, chains, anchors, buoys, ropes and other equipment at Kylesku pier for our new fish farm.

By this time Roddy had sold his fishing boat but Walter and Andrew from the Kylesku Hotel were there to help us. They had a creel boat moored at Kylesku so they towed all our materials to Kerracher and left them high on the beach ready for us to construct two fish cages. Compared to other fish farms we were going to be a small operator but we thought it best to start in a way we could manage and afford.

We also bought a boat that would be more suited to fish farming than our open clinker. The girls were delighted when I arrived at Kylesku pier with the new twenty-foot Taskforce. It was equipped with two forty-horsepower Mariner outboards, which, according to the catalogue, would get the boat to a speed of thirty knots on the plane. It had a trihedral hull, which meant that without a heavy load, it could plane on top of the water, which cut our previously tedious journey of three-quarters of an hour to around fifteen minutes. The boat was constructed of fibreglass and had a small cabin up front to house the steering wheel and a cross seat. The main well of the boat was empty and at the stern a separate section held the petrol cans for the outboards attached to the stern plate.

We had a deadline to get the cages into position as the smolts had to go in the water not later than May, a date also governed by the supplier hatchery's timetable. Ruth's father came up to Kerracher to help us make up the cages, which had already been built by a larger fish farm. They were delivered to us in four walkways, which we had to put together, adding upright railings. That part wasn't difficult and we had them ready moored at the top of the beach in plenty of time. Next the anchors, ropes and buoys had to be organised in such a way that they could easily be set in position. After that, the challenging part of fixing the two cages in position in the sea was all we had to do before the smolts arrived.

When the day came for us to get the cages positioned out in the bay, the weather turned really foul. It was early May but we were hit with sleet and winds from the north. I had arranged for Walter and Andrew to help us with their heavier and more powerful fishing boat, but before they arrived I had to get the cages off the shore and into the middle of the bay in readiness. The wind coming from the north across the bay into Kerracher made this very difficult, but with assistance from Ruth on shore, I managed to manoeuvre the system out into the water and slowly began to nudge it ahead with the new boat. I was progressing quite smoothly when a rope fell from a walkway and began to trail out towards the boat.

Throttling down the boat into neutral, I jumped onto the floating system, picked the rope from the water and secured it. But when I turned to get back on the boat it had drifted away and was being driven slowly shorewards where the windswept Ruth still stood.

'Did you not tie the boat on?' she shouted. 'What do you want me to do?'

'You'll have to get in the boat and take it out to me,' I shouted back into the raw wind.

Eventually the boat reached the line of seaweed where Ruth was standing and she managed to turn it broadside enough to scramble in. The worrying thing was that the engines were upright in the water and could get damaged if grounded on the seabed, but Ruth was quick to grab the boat hook and push the stern of the boat out, away from any damage to the propellers. By this time both engines had stopped.

'Best to lift the engines up until you can push the boat into deeper water,' I instructed. 'Push the grey lever at the base of the engine down, hold the top of the engine and haul it up towards you.'

I watched Ruth struggle with pulling the heavy engine to a position where the propeller came free from the water. She then did the same with the other engine, all the time the cold wind sweeping her nearer to the shore again. The floating cage system was also getting closer to the shore but not as quickly as the boat, so I could see she was never going to be able to get the engines into upright and start even one in time to get it back out.

'Try and push the boat out with the boat hook again!' I urged.

She did this, but without managing to come any closer to where I was standing out on the cage system. I decided to throw her a rope so that I could pull her towards me, but the rope landed short of the boat each time. Eventually, I shouted, 'I'll see if it will float towards you. Just wait.' By this time she was almost ashore again.

Sure enough the rope slowly edged its way nearer and nearer the boat until at last Ruth was able to lean over the side and pick up the spliced end. She secured it to the bow of the boat and slowly I pulled her towards me. I had just enough time to get the engines down and started before the propellers were grounded again. Then I set off, slowly pushing the system out towards its final resting place.

'Why didn't you tie the boat?' said Ruth, who was now of course a passenger alongside me.

'Because you can't manoeuvre the system if it's tied,' I explained.

'I meant when you jumped off to rescue the rope.'

'Ah. I forgot,' was my only defence.

'You'll not do that again,' she predicted.

We eventually got the system out to the marker buoy where the first anchor was to be dropped. By this time Walter and Andrew had arrived as planned to help with the whole operation. Not long after, Eddie Hughson, a local scallop diver, also appeared with his diving mate and we all set to the task of installing the two fish cages in the bay.

It took us nearly five hours of working in a cold north wind, hampered with rain and sleet, before Eddie was satisfied that the sixth and last anchor was safely in place. It was the seventh of May and our introduction to fish farming had been wet and cold. And yet, as I rowed the small tender in and looked back towards the newly installed cages, and the new boat on its mooring, I felt a shiver of excitement at what we had achieved.

'Well, that's us started, at least,' I said to Ruth, who sat facing me in the stern.

She shivered too. 'I can't wait for a hot bath and a bowl of soup.'

The weather improved after a few days and we managed to complete the system by hanging the nets in place. We were ready now for the arrival of the young salmon in the form of smolts, but we had a bit of bad news from the smolt supplier, as they weren't able to deliver the full amount we had ordered. This meant a frantic search for a supplier for the missing balance, but when we found one they were unable to deliver the fish by boat. We would have to take the fish from tanks delivered to the pier at Kylesku.

The only way to deal with this was to tow a cage to Kylesku, fill it with 5,000 smolts and tow it back to Kerracher. We were worried that they might not survive the journey to Kerracher, but we were assured they would if handled properly.

The first intake of 3,000 smolts arrived by boat and we watched with great excitement as they slid down the chute into the cavernous net. We were very disappointed a few days later to lift the net and find almost 300 hadn't survived the experience. We were told that was not unusual.

The second intake was going to be a much more complicated exercise. The day prior to the smolts' arrival at Kylesku, I disengaged the empty cage from the system and towed it to Kylesku where it was left overnight moored by the pier.

The following day started with a calm loch and fair weather. The lorry arrived and, with the cage in place at the side of the pier, the driver and his mate, assisted by a small group of local helpers, began the task of getting the smolts into the net, which had to be only half its full depth because the water wasn't deep enough. They were all transferred safely, so the next critical stage was to tow the cage out into the Kylesku narrows and let the net down to give the smolts more room. Again we had Walter and Andrew's boat to help and they had to 'park' the cage full of fish out from the pier until the tide turned and the net could hang vertically. The strong tide forced the net to a severe angle, threatening to trap the young fish.

Once the tide turned and started to go out, Andrew slowly edged his boat out of Kylesku and through the narrows before we set off towards Kerracher. My job was to follow the towed cage in our boat and ensure that the net was kept as vertical as possible. Although Andrew's boat was inching forward at a snail's pace, the mass of tiny fish had to swim as they had never swum before to keep from getting caught by the back wall of the net. We could only travel as fast as they could swim. I watched in amazement at their ability to keep going, but they did this for more than three hours before they reached their new home at Kerracher. It was midnight when Ruth and I eventually finished off by placing a bird net over the safely reinstalled cage of smolts.

We now had two cages full of young salmon we would grow until they were ready to sell in fifteen months' time. It took us back to when we first arrived at Kerracher, full of hopes and plans: here we were again embarking on a venture that would take us into the unknown.

During the following months we fell into a routine of feeding and caring for fish. For Ruth, life at Kerracher was renewed, as we were both again involved in spending most of our days working at home. At weekends the girls too were drawn into the work with the fish. Friends and family were also eager to visit us and help, especially with feeding the fish.

My father and mother came to stay with us for a fortnight a few months after the arrival of the fish. Dad thoroughly approved of our new venture and was eager to participate, even though he had just come out of hospital and was supposed to be convalescing. His health had suddenly deteriorated at the start of the summer and by the time he came to visit us we knew he had cancer of the liver.

Although illness had weakened him, he still very much wanted to take his turn feeding the young salmon their afternoon ration. My mother wasn't happy about it, but by this time she had no say – he wouldn't be deflected.

I made sure there was a bucket already filled with feed so that he wouldn't attempt to lift one of the heavy bags. It was painful to watch him rowing out to the cages as he struggled with each dip of the oars, and yet the look on his face told us he was utterly content in what he was doing.

By the time he was safely back on land he was exhausted and had to rest for the remainder of the day.

Before he and my mother went home to Dingwall, he insisted on checking the fish once more, so I stopped the boat at the pens to let him have a last look. The expression on his face as we sped off down the loch towards Kylesku reminded me of how he had looked ten years earlier when on the same journey we had first spoken about coming to live at Kerracher.

———

For six months the smolts fed well and grew to the size of trout. We had our usual bouts of bad weather when the boat had to be left on its mooring either at Kerracher or, as was often the case, at Kylesku, which meant we had to walk the hill. The windy weather seemed to happen more at the weekends when we were collecting the girls from the school bus or delivering them to it. Apart from the dreariness of having to walk the hill in foul weather, life fell into a comfortable routine. Then one Sunday morning in late October something happened to change that sense of security.

When I stepped out of the small tender onto the walkway of the first cage to feed the fish, I sensed something was different. I tied the tender to a railing, but before I went to pull the bag of fish feed from it, I looked into the cage to see how the fish were. There was a spreading circle of blue-green oil on the surface. Then I saw something else. A knot tightened in my stomach. Far down in the fish net was a large white mass: there were many dead fish at the bottom of the net. I walked across to the second cage. It was the same there.

We'd had mortalities before, but not to this extent. When the fish were first introduced as smolts quite a few expired but then there was only a slight suggestion of white at the bottom. We expected that: we knew a small percentage wouldn't have the stamina to survive the rigours of being transferred from the controlled environment of a hatchery to their new home in the open sea.

Now the fish were not behaving as they did normally, which was to circle up towards the surface looking for food. Instead they were keeping to a tight mass well down in the net. I scattered a few handfuls of fish food in from the bucket but there wasn't the keen response I had come to expect. Only one or two fish came up for the pellets, which were now sinking into the darkness of the net.

I rowed back to the shore, and beaching the boat, trudged over stony sand to the house. Ruth could see from my expression that something was far wrong. 'What's the matter?'

'I think we have a lot of dead fish,' I said. I felt stunned.
'How?'

'I don't know. I'll have to pull up the nets to find out.' I began to formulate a vague plan of action. 'We'll need the big boat to take them ashore.'

Ruth came with me, and the girls, overhearing us, also offered to help. It was with heavy hearts that we all set out in the boat to the cages for our first harvest – but not the one we had imagined.

In that first morning we took 764 dead fish from the nets, all with their soft young bellies torn open by two jagged V-shaped incisions. We had been warned about seal attacks, and were now witnessing the results of this very thing.

'What a waste,' Ruth kept repeating.

We had to take action. 'I'll need to have a word with Jim Payne to find out what we can do.'

'Yes, that's certainly the result of a seal bite,' Jim confirmed when I showed him one of our dead fish. He asked if we had predator nets in place. 'You'll need to get them. I'm sure we have some old ones you could have in the meantime. They're not in great condition but if you were willing to fix them they would help.'

'Will they keep the seals at bay?' I asked.

'Not entirely.'

'How can I keep them away altogether?' I said in desperation.

'You'll need to use your rifle rather more than you do,' was his simple answer.

During the following week we lost another 1,200 fish to seals, which left us with about seventy-five per cent of our initial intake. We prepared the nets Jim gave us and got them installed. I also increased my use of the rifle.

We took to sitting out in the boat moored to the fish pens for long stretches to try and discourage any predator seals. On a couple of nights Ruth and I sat out until the early hours of the morning and were only beaten into submission by the cold and wet of a late October gale. I stayed out another night until five in the morning when I was driven indoors by a thunderstorm.

The predator nets, combined with this vigilance, paid off, as we never had a seal attack of that magnitude again. To my mind the main factor was the rifle, which helped deter the boldest of seals.

Life now took on a different tempo. More time was spent on the water, and our journeys to and from Kylesku increased with the new boat. Fish feeding was a twice-a-day chore. I made arrangements with another fish farm based near Scourie to buy the 25kg bags of fish food from them as I required, for I couldn't justify the bulk order that a large feed company required.

Apart from the daily routine of feeding the fish we had to apply ourselves to fish husbandry, which included de-lousing them on a regular basis. This involved lifting the net of fish up to a depth of two metres and then slipping a tarpaulin underneath, thus cutting off the oxygenated water. It was a crucial operation, which had to be carried out with precision and speed. Most fish farms introduced oxygen to the separated fish as they were being treated but we decided to forego the oxygen and reduce the time factor. This made the whole job even more critical. The other vital part was the use of a highly dangerous chemical, which was used extensively in the cleaning of poultry farm premises.

The first time we had to deal with this was within a couple of months of introducing the young fish to the cages. I couldn't understand why they had become so active, continually jumping out of the water. At first I put it down to the increase in water temperature but soon it was clear I would have to get the local vet to visit. He said at once, 'You have lice.'

I was horrified, especially when we had low stocking densities of fish in a clean site, where the water flow was excellent and our nets were clean.

'It's inevitable,' he assured us.

Our first lice treatment was a Heath Robinson affair. We carried it out on a cold afternoon that turned very windy, making it even more precarious. Jim Payne came from Ardvar with an assistant to give us some guidance and help. Our friends, Ian and Hazel, who had just arrived that morning from Cheshire with their children, also joined in. It seemed to take forever, but we completed the job without visibly doing any harm to the fish. When the tarpaulin was pulled up and the fish net dropped back into place the most gratifying part was watching clouds of dead lice float away in the current.

Over that first year in the water, after the bloodbath in October when we lost so many to the seal attack, our fish began to develop well. What was pleasing was their shape. Many farmed fish do not develop a wedged tail because they don't have to do much swimming in their environment of four walls and the bottom of a net.

Our position, with a fast flow of through water, meant the nets at times were swept in the wake of the current from their vertical position to an angle of something like forty-five degrees. The fish had to swim so they wouldn't get washed up against the back of the net, thus developing their fins, and especially their tails. So we were producing a strong healthy specimen of farmed salmon.

We had to add to the cages before we could take in the next generation of smolts but this time we built and installed them ourselves. By the following May we had five cages when the Norwegian smolt boat called with a new intake of 10,000 fish.

That summer was busy, as we had to tend two generations of fish. We had to separate the grilse from the salmon and get them sold as quickly as possible. We also had to continue with the regular tasks of feeding, de-lousing and net changing and cleaning.

During June and July we began to sell our salmon, initially to friends and small local hotels. Our first harvest was a grand total of twenty-five fish. Like our first lice treatment and first grading it was another Heath Robinson effort, but it helped us to iron out the imperfections in our system and plan larger harvests for the future. Our next harvest was for a hundred and by the start of August we were harvesting 200 at a time, almost half a tonne in weight, in a manner that suggested we had finally made it as fish farmers.

The preparation for harvesting was laborious. The evening before, I had to go through to Lochinver to collect nearly half a tonne of ice, which had to be shovelled into polystyrene boxes, loaded on to the boat at Kylesku, and then unloaded at Kerracher ready for the following day's harvest.

The harvesting itself was easily established. Each fish was taken out of the cage by a hand net, knocked on the back of the head with a priest (an old police truncheon donated by our friend Ian), and then dispatched into a tub of iced water. They were taken out of there to be individually weighed and then packed into the polystyrene boxes, graded according to weight and topped with more ice. The boxes were then loaded onto the boat, transported to Kylesku and then delivered usually to a collection point at Ullapool, thirty-two miles away. It was very labour intensive so when the harvests became more regular we needed another pair of hands.

Our first employee was the son of the woman who ran the office at the fish farm where I collected my fish food. Jenny Sandals mentioned that her son was looking for something to do while he took time out from his studies. At first Graham travelled to and from Kerracher, but after Ruthie went to Art College in Aberdeen we had space for him to stay with us during the week. He made a tremendous difference to the work. He was always thinking one step ahead; working with him was like working with a twin.

That first winter, harvesting became progressively more intense in the run up to Christmas. At one point we managed a harvest three days running. It was hard work at that time of year because the work was almost always done in rain or sleet, with a keen wind. And yet our first season of harvesting fish, although diminished in quantity by the seal attack, was a profitable one, with prices averaging £4.50 a kilo. By Christmas some of the fish we were producing reached weights of four and five kilos.

It seemed at the time, despite the hardships and knockbacks, that we had made the right decision. The team of Graham, Ruth and me, supplemented by Clare and Ruthie when available, was working well together, getting through the daily routines at Kerracher to keep the fish tended and fed.

STORMS AND MISHAPS

Fish farming did have its crises, but most of them were minor. One morning we saw that two of our cages had been dragged close to the outcrop of rock at the north end of the bay. When we got out to check them, we found the nets were not fully extended because their bottoms were scraping on the seaweed in the shallower water. Fortunately, the fish had not been unduly affected. We managed to tow them back into deeper water until Walter and Andrew came with the additional power of their boat to help get the moorings back into place.

Then one Tuesday morning in October, two years after we had put the cages in, there was a much ruder awakening. We were still in bed when there was a shout from the upstairs landing window. It was Steve, who was up on holiday with Jean and their family.

'Eric, I can't see your boat. I think you'd better get up.'

Ruth jumped out of bed. From our bedroom window she could see there was an easterly gale blowing. 'Oh no! Eric, everything's getting washed up on the beach.'

I heaved myself from the comfort of my bed and joined her at the window. It was a strange scene – of beauty and devastation. Huge waves rolled in with a mist of spray and spume streaming from their crests, eventually crashing onto a beach strewn with littered fragments of fish farm cages.

'Where's the boat?' Ruth was hoarse with horror at what she was seeing.

'It's sunk on the mooring. I can just see the bow above the water,' I said.

For a moment we were unable to say anything more. Then I ran downstairs and snatched the binoculars from the kitchen windowsill. Back at the landing window with Steve and Jean, who had arrived only the day before, I focused on the fish cages, which were almost hidden by waves and spray. I handed the glasses to Steve. 'It doesn't look good. We'd better have breakfast, then think about what we can do.'

In the kitchen, we sat down to talk.

'If we took the tender out we could untie the boat and get it ashore.'

'If we could get out to the pens, then we could limit any further damage.'

As we ate, I thought over these suggestions, and tried to summarise the situation. 'There's no way we can get on that loch as long as this wind's up. All we can do is to get to the phone at Kylesku and let the insurance broker know we're going to have a massive claim.'

We considered this in silence for a moment, and then, unable to sit still any longer, I got up. 'It might be worth collecting the bits and pieces being washed up. We can take them over to the corner of the bay where they won't get blown away any further.'

'The forecast said we were going to get an easterly for the next three days,' Ruth said miserably.

'Well, in that case, I may as well wallpaper the

bathroom,' I concluded and headed off to walk over the hill for the journey to Kylesku.

By this time we had set up a phone point in John Clark's garage at Kylesku, where we also had an answer machine. This at least gave us a way of communicating with the outside world without having to scrounge the use of someone's phone or resort to a public call box, which was not always guaranteed to work.

I telephoned the insurance broker we used for the business and explained the situation. I also phoned Ewan MacKay at Drumbeg to prime him for action when the weather improved. He had established a diving business and had the equipment to refloat the boat. We hadn't any harvests planned so the broker and the divers were the only people I needed to contact immediately.

When I got home I made a start on wallpapering the bathroom, but the others continually interrupted me with a running commentary on what had been blown up on the beach. After a while they left me to my wallpapering, and spent the next two days eagerly collecting anything that had washed up.

The wind blew for three whole days. On Friday it calmed enough for us to row out in the tender to inspect what remained of the fish pens. Of the five pens three were still intact, but the other two had collided with each other. One was low in the water at one corner but the net looked all right – the fish were still swimming about in it. The other cage was broken up with the net ripped open. It looked very empty. Other than that the main damage was to the walkways around the cages where much of the rubber matting was ripped off and many of the polystyrene blocks underneath had been forced out. Steve and I managed to make a few running repairs that pulled the system back into shape, but we had to abandon the work when the wind started up again.

The easterly blew for another week but the cages didn't suffer any further damage. Our boat lolled vertically in the water throughout with the bow appearing and disappearing in the waves. It was a week before the divers were able to get to us and eventually float the boat by inserting and inflating huge balloon-like bags underneath. The engines were smashed and lying on the seabed, having been ripped off the stern, which now had a big chunk torn out, like a terrible attack in 'Jaws'.

Two weeks after the storm had started we towed the boat up on the shore.

As soon as the locals heard of our predicament we had a number of offers to use their spare boats. We took up Diarmid MacAulay's offer as his was a working boat used for tending his mussel rafts. It was available and moored at Kylesku, so for a period of six weeks we managed to carry on our fish farming with some magnificent support from local friends.

It was then that John Blunt came to work with us on the fish farm. John was a crofter from the local township of Nedd. He had a range of skills and like Graham, who had by now left to work in Glasgow, he was a hard and competent worker. John went on at a steady pace, interrupted only by the need to roll a cigarette. He had a prodigious appetite and strength, both belied by his lean frame. It was John who helped us get the cages back into shape after the storm and who was able, when not busy with his own work, to assist us with the harvesting.

It was a full six weeks before we got our boat back, nicely repaired with two brand new gleaming Yamaha engines. Our insurance covered all the cost of the restored boat and the repairs to the cages and nets bar an excess of £250. However, we had lost nearly 2,000 young fish. For these we were recompensed £3,000. If these fish had matured for another year they would have sold for nearly £20,000.

We were now able to get back into the daily cycle of harvesting again – going through to Lochinver for ice, sometimes getting back up the loch to Kerracher with it, sometimes not. At times, when the weather was bad, we had to leave the boxed ice on the pier at Kylesku, mooring the boat and driving to the top of the glen to walk home, very often arriving in the early hours of the morning. Then it would be an early start to get back to Kylesku and meet with John before loading the boxes of ice and making our way up the loch to Kerracher where the harvesting process began all over again. We always seemed to be doing our bigger harvests when the weather was foul and the daylight short, which invariably meant getting the fish away when darkness was falling. At least after Christmas the number of harvests reduced and became more spread out.

We had a few mishaps working with the fish but with no serious consequences. All of us except Ruthie fell into the water. Ruth did it when she was with John and me while we were making some repairs. One of the corners of a pen was open: the wooden decking that covered the square corner-piece of the pen was off as we were working on securing some bolts. Suddenly Ruth walked straight into the open space feet first and ended up to her chest in water. Her outstretched arms prevented her from being totally submerged, and she bobbed in the water for a moment until John and I managed to pluck her out.

'It's not as cold as I thought it might have been,' she said calmly as we ushered her to the small boat to be rowed ashore to change into dry clothes.

I stepped backwards one day when we were hauling up a net, forgetting for the moment that the walkway was only half a metre wide. I simply plunged down into the water and popped back up. I grabbed at the walkway and was hauled out by John. I emptied my welly boots then carried on with getting the net up before I headed to the house for a change of clothing. I was pleasantly surprised at how my feet warmed within the boots. The rest of me, although wet, kept warm as long as I carried on working.

The girls were always keen to help, especially with the feeding. At weekends this gave Ruth and me a welcome break. They always did it together as it took both of them to carry the 25kg bags of fish feed into and out of the small boat we used as a tender to and from the cages. We discouraged them from being out on the pens on their own. We discovered, some time after it happened, that Clare had fallen in the water in the same fashion as Ruth, skinning and bruising her arms.

'I can't remember you coming in wet,' Ruth said when she found this out.

'We didn't tell you at the time in case you wouldn't let us out to feed the fish again,' Ruthie confessed.

'I put all the wet clothes into the washing machine and pretended I was washing some things I'd forgotten to give you,' Clare added.

'It's just as well I didn't know about it,' her mother said.

It was rare for us to lose harvested fish, but one day as John was handing a box to me on the boat the bottom fell out with the result that the ten fish very quickly dropped into the water, each spiralling down before either of us could grab a net to salvage them. It was a painful moment watching the silver flashes disappearing into the December darkness of the loch. No doubt the crabs and other sea life fed well.

We had already lost another three fish that day. After we'd killed and thrown them into the tub of ice, they 'jumped' out and landed in the water before any of us could catch them. It was clearly an unlucky day – John nearly joined the Kerracher dunk club as he slipped badly, but just managed to catch himself before he ended in the water. Just as well, for it was cold and wet, with a north-westerly wind running through us, as we struggled to get 300 fish away for the Christmas market.

The only other time that fish went to the bottom was after a harvest. Helped by my sister Ann's husband Ruairidh, we landed twenty or so boxes of iced fish at the pier at Kylesku. I gently sidled the boat up against the side of the pier ready to moor it and Ruairidh stepped eagerly onto the gunwale and then jumped onto the pier. Because the boxes were stacked high in the boat this action of suddenly removing about fifteen stone in weight from one side of the boat had a dramatic effect: the side by the pier tipped out of the water as Ruairidh jumped, causing the opposite side to dip sharply downwards.

John and I instinctively grabbed at the tilting stack of fish-laden boxes. We managed to steady the pile but one box escaped, gracefully flying off the top. As it turned in mid air the weight of its contents knocked the lid off and several fish escaped. Although the polystyrene box floated upright on the water with four fish still wedged inside, John and I could only watch in dismay the remaining silver shapes drift down to the seabed below.

As it happened, we had in the boat the hand net we used to harvest the salmon. It took a little while but after safely unloading the intact boxes onto the pier I managed to locate each of the 'lost' fish and retrieve them with the net before packing them back into the awaiting half-empty box with their companions. Given the value of each salmon to our business, it was worth the effort!

We seemed constantly to be on the loch these days, and we had a few adventures with the boat.

One beautiful sunny afternoon Ruth and I were speeding towards Kylesku, the boat planing across the top of the becalmed loch, when all at once the bow dipped as one of the engines cut out.

For all the time she had spent at Kerracher, Ruth had never come to be at ease on the water, and she was instantly anxious. I thought it might be water in the fuel: when I had topped up the tanks with petrol at the Kylesku Hotel pumps it hadn't been flowing as well as usual. I also recalled Walter saying something about waiting for a delivery. I tried the dead engine again but there was no response. We would just have to slow down and get there on the other engine. Then a moment later it died too, leaving us sitting pretty in the middle of a loch of clear blue water sparkling in the sunlight.

'What are we going to do?' Ruth was beginning to panic now. 'You haven't got a radio or flares. What if the wind gets up? We haven't even got oars.'

I tried to reassure her. 'There's no wind forecast for

today. If the worst comes to the worst the boats coming back into Kylesku from their day's fishing will see us.'

'You'll have to stop getting petrol from the Hotel. Their tanks are far too old.' In her fright, Ruth overlooked for the moment all the help we had had from Andrew and Walter.

I leaned forward into the small bow space and picked out the two plastic buckets we used when feeding the fish. 'We'll paddle in,' I decided.

But Ruth didn't think much of this idea. 'Don't be so stupid.'

I handed her one. 'I'll sit this side of the boat and you sit the other and if we dip the bucket like this in the water it will move us forward.'

I demonstrated with a sweep of the bucket in the water, the open end facing towards the back of the boat. 'It's just like a paddle steamer action,' I explained, demonstrating again how easy it would be.

She shook her head. 'It'll never work.'

'We can only try and see,' I said, and to persuade her added, 'it's our only hope.'

She dipped the bucket over the side and made a desultory effort before declaring in exasperation, 'I'm not strong enough.'

'We can do it if we take our time. You don't have to put the bucket deep in the water,' I urged. 'Let's try together.'

We both swept our buckets like a paddle on either side of the boat.

'We've moved,' I said with glee. 'Do it again.'

The boat made another forward movement.

'Ok, we need to get this synchronised. We go on one, and one, two, three,' I said, in the hope that Ruth would get the rhythm and paddle in time with me.

'We'll never manage it,' she moaned.

'This is an adventure,' I exclaimed. 'Who else has adventures like this?'

She mumbled something unintelligible.

We inched our way towards the shore near Kylestrome, taking a full half hour to reach the rocky outcrop. I left Ruth holding the boat off the rocks and headed along the nearby road on the half-mile walk to Kylesku where I was fortunate enough to meet John Clark turning out of the village in his car. After collecting a full can of petrol from his garage he drove me back to where Ruth was waiting and we were able to continue on our boat journey to the mooring at Kylesku.

Our new boat served us well but apart from the time it sank during the gales, there were other occasions when it seemed it was about to meet its end.

I had just met Ruth's parents at Kylesku pier to take them to Kerracher for a visit. Not only did we have their baggage, but I had just been shopping for extra provisions, so the boat was well laden. Because there was some rain in the wind I packed most of the items up front in the cabin to keep them dry until we reached home.

As we edged away from the pier Ruth's mother said she would rather sit in the cabin with her back to the bow, facing the stern. This was so that she wouldn't see the oncoming waves. Because she was so nervous, Ruth's father sat beside her to reassure her as we sailed home.

As a result the front section of the boat sank further so that we were cutting through the waves with the bow deeper in the water than the stern, which still rode high on the surface. The mouth of the loch was boiling with wind-driven waves. I decided to take a line that was close to the far shore where we'd be most sheltered as we exited the Kyle. I throttled down as we approached the first large wave and the boat took it well. But Ruth's mother screamed in panic at the lurch of the boat, grabbing at her husband, and so dipped the boat to the left just as the next wave hit us.

Because we weren't exactly head into it, the bow of the boat was thrown high into the air and a vortex of green water cascaded over the cabin, much of it ending up in the well of the boat. Ruth's parents were both flung to the floor of the cabin along with luggage and boxes.

Then the next wave hit us, spraying over our heads. I had to get the bow back into the oncoming and increasing waves so I couldn't stop to pay any attention to my petrified mother-in-law. I quickly manoeuvred the boat in a one-eighty degree turn between the next two waves and shouted to my dishevelled and petrified passengers to join me on the seat so that we could even the boat out. They did this so promptly, I suspect they realised the horrific experience would soon be over now we were heading back to the safety of the pier.

I edged along the shoreline, all the time being washed along by waves, which were diminishing by now. Once in the quieter water I pulled the throttle back and swiftly made for the pier.

'I'll take you both to Reintraid where you can wait for me. I'll pick you up there with the boat,' I explained as we tied up at the pier.

This brought a little colour back to my mother-in-law's cheeks.

I now had to drive the two of them to the top of the track at Reintraid, load them (with luggage and provisions) into the old Reintraid Land Rover and drive down to the jetty. I then drove back up the track, into my car, back to Kylesku, parked the car and got back into the boat. By this time the great walls of waves were dying down, but I was also better able to control the boat as I manoeuvred through the narrows.

I picked up a pair of very relieved relatives at the jetty at Reintraid and we continued on a much calmer journey along the sheltered west side of the loch.

'Just give me a double whisky,' was Ruth's mother's response to her daughter's offer of a cup of tea when they arrived in the warmth of the Kerracher kitchen.

———

Loch Cairnbawn is not a yachting loch because of the eddies of wind that can suddenly rush down on it from Quinag. From a distance there was something magical about these sudden mini tornados flying across the water, very often when it was quite calm. They usually occurred across the wide bite of loch before it channelled into the narrows at Kylesku.

One afternoon after John and I delivered a harvest of fish to the pier at Kylesku and had seen it off on Lachie MacRae's lorry, I left him walking off to the car park in Kylesku for his car while I set off home to Kerracher on my own.

I cleared the narrows and headed towards the shelter of the opposite side, as there was a hint of a westerly wind appearing. I was about halfway across the wide part of the loch when suddenly from nowhere I saw a spray of water ahead of me, dancing up from the surface of the loch. It looked spectacular but innocuous as it swirled its way across to the left of me. It disappeared almost as quickly in a watery mist sucked up into the atmosphere. Then another appeared in the direction I was heading. It too danced up into a fountain of spray, twisting and twirling as it headed towards me. This one didn't disappear as the first had done.

Instead the fountain began to spread and in seconds the spray became a wall of water at least twice my height. I was heading straight into it.

I throttled down as it approached and held the boat steady. Suddenly with very little noise the grey hard force of this wall hit me. The surface of the loch boiled and it seemed as if I was momentarily in the middle of a washing machine. The spray was all about me, cutting out both land and sky. I was enveloped in grey. The boat was being pulled around as if caught in a whirlpool, but I had to try to keep it going ahead. At the same time a powerful force was sucking the stern down so much that water was beginning to pour over it into the boat.

I tried to throttle up a bit to escape but to no avail. The noise increased as if a host of phantoms was sweeping across the loch. It was the eeriest and most frightening experience I have ever had in my life. I struggled for what seemed liked an eternity but was probably no more than a matter of seconds. Then as suddenly as it arrived it passed on, to disappear in an ascending, spiralling spray.

I quickly emptied the water from the boat, which was now sitting dangerously low in the sea. But it was some time before I was able to continue, for I was considerably shaken. It was the closest I had ever been to going down with the boat. What was most frightening was the way it happened so quickly and with little warning of danger.

Katie-Anne Allan, who lived at Kylestrome, told me later that she had witnessed the event from her window and was about to phone the coastguard when she spotted me reaching the other side of the loch. She said she had never seen anything like it before, though she had witnessed the effects of wind and weather from her window over many years.

SUMMER AND WINTER BRING
CHALLENGES FOR SIMON AND CLARE

In our third year of fish farming we added a sixth cage and built three platforms to hold the system together. This made it a safer and more efficient environment to work in. Then we added a large work shed, built by Ruth's father and me in the 'old' garden. We also investigated building a jetty to ease our landing problems as the logistics of loading and unloading were always complicated and dependent on the state of the tide. Plans were drawn up but shelved for later since we couldn't manage everything at once – financially or practically.

Not all our fish farming was done in the wet and windy days of the winter months. We also had some very good days when the sun shone and we had fun alongside the hard work.

For most of the summers that we had the fish farm our nephew Simon came to stay and work with us. At first he followed me around like a puppy, enjoying the boat rides and any fun there was to be had. As time went on he became a great help, and never wanted to leave when it was time for him to go back to school. Like most of our visitors,

Simon enjoyed the better weather.

Some summers were miserably wet. One very drizzly evening when Simon and Clare returned from collecting our mail in the Snoopy box at the top of the glen, Simon was very excited about seeing a herd of deer.

'Where were they?'

'Just between the path when you come up from the small loch and the sea loch,' Clare said, swiping midges away.

Simon was convinced we could get one, but when I saw the grey haze of midges swarming around the kitchen window I wasn't keen.

'They're not so bad on the hill,' Simon insisted.

I looked at Clare but all I got was a wince suggesting that either she didn't quite agree with him or she was still suffering from the midges that had hitched a ride with her into the house.

Simon longed to witness the kill of a stag and since his arrival that summer he had pestered me at every opportunity. Every day he had scoured the hillside, even while he was working on the cages – so much so that I had to remind him on a few occasions to keep his eyes on the job. 'Otherwise I'll be pulling you out of the water.'

'No harm in having a look,' said Graham, who was also staying with us. There was a glint of mischief in his eyes. 'But if it's your first deer kill you will have to bleed it, it's traditional,' he reminded Simon.

'No way,' said Simon.

'Graham's right of course.' I thought I might have found a good excuse for not having to go out on such a miserable evening.

'What would I have to do?' Simon asked after a long silence.

'Just take the knife across its throat,' Graham said.

Another long silence.

'Ok then, I'll do it.'

Despite a few protestations from me about the poor weather and some from Ruth scolding Graham for suggesting such a thing, there was no way out now. As we left, she reassured Simon that really he wouldn't have to do anything but keep quiet and out of the way of the rifle.

The four of us, Simon, Clare, Graham and I, kitted in foul weather gear, trudged up the path towards the cliff and the hill beyond. Simon chattered so much I had to tell him if he carried on talking he wouldn't see any deer. Controlling his excitement, he fell silently into step with the rest of us.

Sure enough the deer were where they had said, in a group just down to the left of the path leading to the small loch. We approached them quietly until I felt we were at a distance where I would have a decent chance of a hit. I beckoned to the others to settle down in the wet heather and then I went a little further ahead to find a suitable spot from which to shoot. I slid the rifle out of its covering, fitted a bullet into the chamber and I settled down in the heather. A moment later, I aimed and fired.

The silence and calm of the hillside were shattered by the ugly report of rifle fire. Whether the poor beast heard it before collapsing on the ground it was grazing, I don't know. Thankfully my aim was good and a magnificent animal was dead instantly.

The rest of the herd scattered and ran away in the opposite direction.

'Wow,' was all I heard behind me as the others scrabbled to their feet.

We approached the dead animal cautiously just in case

it had been grazed and knocked out rather than killed but my instincts were right – it was dead.

The four of us stood over the beast, admiring its glossy beauty. Then Graham broke the silence. 'Here, you have to do it now,' he said, thrusting the large knife towards Simon.

Simon went white. He looked down at the deer in horror, unable even to speak. Taking pity on him, I took the knife from Graham and patting Simon on the back said, 'Don't worry. You don't have to do anything.'

We gralloched the animal before dragging it down to the loch shore. Taking it back up the hill and then down the cliff on the other side was not an option. Clare and Simon were willing to watch over the carcass while Graham and I headed back to Kerracher for the boat.

When we returned with the boat I felt more sorry for Clare and Simon than I've ever felt for anyone. They had been exposed to a ferocious midge attack and were almost in tears by this time. We hastily loaded them and the deer carcass onto the boat and headed for home.

It was a relieved Simon who got into the safety of the kitchen and the company of his Aunt Ruth. He didn't seem all that keen to join Clare, Graham and me when we went into the shed to skin and hang the beast. Indeed, he never again tried to persuade me to kill a deer.

He was happy to continue helping us with the fish and, like many of our friends who came to stay when we were fish farming, he was a great help with the hard manual work.

—•—

The girls grew up accustomed to the rigours of our life at Kerracher, and understood the need to kill for food. They also learned to face setbacks and hardship with equanimity. Perhaps there were times when I overestimated this resilience, or didn't quite realise the impact on them of some of our adventures.

One Friday evening, I met Clare from the Golspie school bus. By now, Ruthie was a student in Aberdeen. We headed for Reintraid where I had moored our tender, a two-metre boat with a small outboard engine, which I had taken along to collect her. By the time we got down to the pier the wind had risen from the west and it was almost dark.

'Is it not too windy for the boat?' she asked.

She sounded despondent, knowing the alternative was a trek back up to the road and then the walk over the hill.

'No, it'll be alright if we keep tucked into the shoreline,' I assured her.

I knew the rocky shoreline between Reintraid and Kerracher intimately by now, and I was confident we'd be fine if we kept into the side, sheltered from the wind. I had a torch to shine on the rocks to keep us right. I placed Clare facing me with her back to the wind in the bow of the craft, and we set off into the wintry night.

Immediately a sudden wave almost swamped us.

'Dad!' exclaimed Clare. Even against the noise of the wind, I could hear the quake in her voice.

I reduced the throttle and we slowed enough to ride the next wave. I shouted back to her, 'It's OK. I was just going a bit too fast. Trust me – we'll be OK.'

I hastily emptied out the excess water, looking out this time for the next wave. I throttled down as it hit us and the spray from the impact flew over Clare and into my face. Again I had to bale out. As the wave passed under the boat the water rose up the stern and over the engine so that it gurgled and spluttered as it emerged. We rode wave after wave like this, speeding down the other side of each one and through the trough. There was quite a swell building up by now and Clare had fallen silent.

I began to master the technique of going from wave to wave without taking in too much water. Now I could shine the torch on the rock face of the shoreline, my other hand firmly gripped on the throttle of the outboard. We were making progress.

Then it started to snow. Apart from fog, the greatest enemy of visibility on water is falling snow, especially in the dark.

The torch became redundant, the beam bouncing back as it hit the snowflakes. But the waves kept coming. Now I could only see the crest of each wave as it was about to hit the boat behind the silent shadow of Clare hunched up at the front. Progress was painfully slow and I became cocooned in a world that repeated itself like Groundhog Day. Each wave hit the bow of the boat and passed underneath us, leaving the outboard spluttering as we passed through the brief respite of the trough before the next wave hit. It seemed interminable.

At last we made the safety of the bay where the bite of the wind was diminished and the waves were gentle and rolling. After we moored we made for the security of the warm kitchen. Ruth couldn't understand why we were so wet.

'It was quite wavy.' I tried to make little of it, not wanting to alarm her.

'You didn't come back by boat?' she exclaimed.

'Yes,' Clare said. 'It was terrible.'

'I thought you must have decided to walk, you were so long.'

'We were so long because Dad took the boat,' Clare pointed out.

I discovered later that Clare thought of this as her worst ever boat journey. She had been convinced we were never going to get home. At the time, not knowing this, I said breezily, 'Well, it was an adventure and we're safe and sound. So what's the problem?'

If the experience had been a daunting one for Clare, for me it had been exhilarating and had even given me greater confidence in handling a boat.

Understandably, Clare was not available for feeding the fish the following morning. I rowed the small tender out to the pens on a flat pancake of a loch with a flurry of snow wisping around the bay. It was a total contrast to the rage of the night before. That's what working on the water was like. We were made even more aware of that in our fish farming life.

THE LAST KERRACHER MAN

Ruth had gone out to feed our new intake of pullets. When she burst in through the kitchen door a few minutes later, she could hardly speak for fright.

'I can't hear a sound but I'm scared to open the hen house,' she gasped.

I accompanied her back to the hen house where a month earlier we had installed new occupants: ten young Black Rocks. Ruth had always wanted these beautiful birds with their glistening feathers, not only for their looks but also for their renowned suitability as a free-range all-weather egg layer. The pullets had been reared in Skye and as usual were delivered through the post. They had settled in well without a cockerel and kept themselves active over at the far end of the croft, away from where we had the vegetables and Ruth's flowers.

When we reached the hen house, its door still unopened, there was a deathly silence. Something was far wrong. By this time in the morning the hens were usually keen to get out and clucking loudly in response to our presence. Slowly, I pushed the door open – to be met with devastation. Black feathers and blood were splattered everywhere. The hens lay scattered across the floor. Every one had had its neck ripped open.

'It's impossible,' I stammered.

'How did anything get in to attack them like this?' Ruth wept.

I looked around the hen house and checked for an opening of some sort. It didn't take long to discover how the culprit had entered. In a bottom corner I found a hole no bigger than a child's hand could get through. There was a little heap of what looked like wood shavings underneath it. Whatever had got in had gnawed its way through the wooden floor. I couldn't think what kind of creature it must be.

'Well, it's academic now. They're all dead,' was all Ruth could say as we went back to the house, my arm around her shoulders, trying to console her.

Later, we were sure it was a polecat that had massacred our hens, but we never saw any sign of the creature. I made tea and as we sat down with it at the kitchen table she said, 'I don't know if I can live here any longer.'

It was the first time I had heard Ruth say anything like that. Over the years it was Ruth who kept me going whenever I declared that I'd had enough. She was the one who had vetoed the idea of emigrating. She was the one who insisted that she would live out her days at Kerracher. And she was the one who wanted to be buried near her hens in the far corner of the croft.

Now I could barely take this in. I went out to dispose of the Black Rocks, to give us both time to think about it.

I threw all the feathered corpses into the barrow and took them over to our animal cemetery behind the vegetable area. I buried them deep so that a fox wouldn't disturb them. As I covered them up I reflected on this now crowded burial plot.

Our dog Glen and cat Penny were in there alongside Charlie, Clare's first pony, Snowy the rabbit and Kerry our duck. There were also Ruth's budgies and numerous other small creatures the girls had buried when their short lives were over.

Glen had grown old and one morning he died quietly in my arms, looking dolefully up at me as he slowly lost his hold on life. It was a peaceful end; he simply didn't have the strength to carry on any longer. Penny followed him shortly afterwards. At the age of seventeen he began to have fits, then went blind. That didn't deter him getting out and he would use the house wall and other landmarks to help him make his expeditions. This went on until it became clear he was in pain, so I took him through to the vet in Rogart. I carried him over the hill on my return as the weather was too foul for the boat, and buried him alongside the other animals.

Snowy, Ruthie's white rabbit, got to the point where she wouldn't eat and could hardly move. I would have preferred to take her to the vet like Penny but at the time it wasn't possible, so rather than prolong her suffering I had to take on the responsibility. I stood for a full half hour in front of her hutch, unable to make up my mind to it. The knock on the head that I eventually steeled myself to administer was not a hard one, indeed it didn't require much of a knock, she was so far gone. But it was the hardest kill I ever had to make.

Kerry was a good age for a duck and grew old with us among the other animals until one very frosty morning when I went to let her out of her house. There was no welcome, and when I pulled the top off the section where she was deep in her warm bedding of horse's hay I found her stiff as a board. Like many of our pets she had expired through the night of old age.

Our first budgerigar arrived as a present from Ruth's father after she complained she had no one to talk to once I was out working and the girls were away all week. Ruth was delighted with this bright yellow bird, and called her Sunshine. But Sunshine didn't quite live up to her name. She never ventured out of the cage and for all the effort Ruth made to get her to talk there was absolutely no return of affection or any sign of gratitude for being fed and cared for.

We didn't have her long. One afternoon Ruth heard a slight commotion from Sunshine's cage. When she turned round she saw the poor bird on its back at the bottom of the cage. She had literally fallen off her perch. She was dispatched in the animal cemetery with some ceremony that weekend when the girls came home from school.

Ruth actually missed this disobliging bird so the girls and I decided to get another from the Inverness pet shop for Christmas. I reserved a bright blue bird and arranged to collect it on Christmas Eve when we planned our last minute shopping. We were going to hide the cage in the caravan, covering it with a thick blanket.

As usual, the elements conspired against us and the loch was far too wild for a trip by boat. The girls and I reached the top of the glen to find there was a storm force wind blowing horizontal rain. Obviously there was no question of transporting the bird and its cage. In the end we made for Ardvar, where we left the bird with the Paynes, arranging to call back for it on Christmas morning. We also decided to leave some of the goods we had packed into the car.

The walk from Ardvar to Kerracher was more sheltered and less of a climb, and we weren't so exposed to the fierce wind. But the rain was relentless. We reached a point that crossed some lazy beds, a remnant of the way crofters grew their potatoes in olden days. The high ridges were under water, which made it difficult to follow the usual path. Ruthie and Clare scanned the area with their torches. Our options were to keep going across or to climb higher up the rocky crags of the hillside in an attempt to go round. In the end we decided to keep going.

So with Ruthie in front hidden by her backpack and shining her torch ahead, me in the middle with a heavy backpack and a couple of bulging bags in each hand, and Clare following also laden and shining her torch ahead of our feet, we began our trek across the flooded lazy beds. I tried to keep Ruthie on what I thought was the pathway but when we were halfway across she suddenly disappeared up to her waist in water.

'Grab onto my bag,' I shouted. She came stumbling and groaning out of the hole. 'Are you all right?'

'Yes, I think so,' she gasped.

'Shine the torches around,' I instructed them. The light bounced off murky water; it was going to be impossible to find the path. I could see, though, that the depth of the water would be, at worst, up to the girls' waists. We would just have to go for it.

So we did. I picked my way forward, wading into deeper water but at least I was holding my feet on the soft submerged heather, the water level just below my knees. The girls followed with a few complaints about the cold, but they too kept their feet, which was the important thing. At last we made it onto the strip of hard-packed grass which came up from the sea beach. We had a short stop there to check everyone was all right, before heading towards the peat bogs.

The rain was still lashing our faces, but the wind that

came off the sea also hit us with spray. It was like testing some new carwash system without the brushes. I was relieved to find when we reached the disused peat bogs that they weren't awash like the lazy beds. At least we would be able to pick our way across them on the familiar pathway. Even in the dark and with rain sweeping across our vision it always amazed me how we managed to cross a boggy hillside as long as we knew the safe route.

We eventually reached the last stretch – the reassuring safety of the narrow path my grandfather had built many years ago. As we trudged through the field towards the light of the house we spooked Juniper who neighed, then settled again, relieved to hear Clare's voice in greeting. Ruthie and I plodded on to the house but of course Clare had to spend a while with her soul mate.

As we approached the house the front door opened and a shaft of light cut across the lawn. Ruth appeared, starting when she saw the torch beams. Then she realised it was us – safely home.

'Well that was good timing,' she greeted us. 'I was getting a bit worried because you were so late. Where's Clare? You're soaking wet. Why did you come from the field? Did you have to walk from Ardvar?' She fussed like any mother hen gathering in her chicks. The 'chicks' in question were only too grateful for the welcoming warmth of the kitchen. It was a Christmas Eve journey the girls and I will never forget, but we appreciated the peace and comfort of the following day all the more.

The girls made Christmas dinner that day, which allowed Ruth and me to walk over to Ardvar to pick up some of the things left in the car but also to collect Ruth's Christmas present.

Ruth named her new pet Bluey and he was introduced

to Kerracher on Christmas Day. Bluey was much more gregarious than Sunshine and Ruth enjoyed his company. However, he didn't take much to anyone but me. When he was allowed out he would immediately fly to me and chirp away into my ear. I felt for Ruth as she enjoyed his company and his bright chirping when she worked in the kitchen. He tolerated her cleaning his cage and letting him in and out of it but never returned the affection she showed him.

On the next Christmas Day, a year after his arrival, we noticed he was unusually excited. Then, just as we took the turkey out of the oven, Bluey gave a shrill squawk, fell off his perch onto the floor of the cage, landed on his back with legs raised stiff in the air, and expired.

The following April Ruth lost her Black Rocks.

We had, of course, survived far worse at Kerracher in our fifteen years there. Although the deaths of many of the animals who had kept us company was distressing, we lived so close to the rawness of nature that we accepted this was the way of things. The significant change in Ruth's feelings was only partly caused by these setbacks.

———

There was another kind of ending that affected our lives and living at Kerracher. During the year after we set up the fish farm my father's health deteriorated. Living at Kerracher and operating the fish farm allowed us to make regular visits to my parents in Dingwall, which meant we saw a lot of my father during his illness. He suffered stoically in that typical old-fashioned Highland male way, but he was in constant pain. He was always keen to enquire how the fish were faring and looked forward to tasting one on his plate.

In the end, he had to go into hospital again, and we knew it would be for the last time. On the last evening of his life I was fortunate to be able to sit by him, holding his hand and telling him everything at Kerracher was going well – the fish were on their way to becoming good wholesome salmon. Although he couldn't talk much he was able to murmur 'Good' and squeeze my hand faintly in encouragement.

He passed away the following morning with my mother and sisters with him.

In some ways Ruth found it harder to come to terms with my father's death than I did. She had been very fond of him, but because she was at Kerracher when he died, she wasn't able to say her farewell as I had.

My father had greatly enjoyed Kerracher during the last years of his life and often lingered in the home where he had lived until the Second World War took him away and funnelled him into a different life. Now only two of his sisters, my Aunts Jessie and Jean, remained as the last Kerracher offspring of that generation. They continued to visit us when they were able. Since then many of the original Kerracher Man's grandchildren, great grandchildren and great great grandchildren have made their personal pilgrimages to Kerracher.

Fish farming slowly became more uneconomical and we had to find other means of generating income. This meant that I had to go out of Kerracher again to earn money. Ruth was once more left at home for days on her own, which of course wasn't what we'd intended when we started the farm.

There was also Clare's imminent move to Aberdeen as a student. Ruth became increasingly unsettled.

This was probably what made her decide to learn to drive at last, since this would give her the freedom to get in and out of Kerracher independently. Ruth took to driving lessons in Lochinver with enthusiasm and a determination to pass her test at the first sitting. I tried to supplement her lessons from the professional driving instructor, but this was a complete failure. After only two sessions we agreed that I would not make any further attempt to teach Ruth to drive. I left it to the professional.

On the day of her test, which was in Lochinver, a village devoid of traffic lights and roundabouts, I was to collect her afterwards. However, I was delayed and drove into Lochinver about half an hour late. She was waiting on a seat in the car park, very disappointed that I wasn't the first to hear the outcome, since she was convinced I didn't think she'd pass. Of course, the first thing I said was, 'Well, did you pass?'

'If you ask Anne in the butcher's she'll be able to tell you.'

'What do you mean?' I asked, puzzled.

'You're late and I couldn't wait any longer – I had to tell someone so I told Anne first. I passed.'

That moment opened up new avenues for Ruth and was an end to her dependence on me when she wanted to get out of Kerracher.

—·—

With the Black Rocks finally dispatched I walked back to the house where Ruth was still sitting at the kitchen table, staring out of the front window across the bay.

'I think it's time to leave,' she whispered.

'We can get more hens,' I reassured her.

'No it's not just the hens, it's everything. It's all going the wrong way now.' She looked down, gazing into the bottom of her favourite china teacup.

'Ok, if it helps, we can sell the fish farm. Then see how you feel,' I offered.

'Will you?' Still she spoke in little more than a whisper.

'Yes, definitely. I'll put word round that we want to sell up.'

Suddenly I felt a huge sense of relief. Because of a massive decrease in fish prices over the previous two years, the farm's finances were by now heading for disaster and Ruth's words were the catalyst which made me take action.

During the following weeks I contacted as many people as I could who might be interested and this produced a number of visits to the site. There were a few potential buyers, but the prices they offered were simply too low, reflecting the state of the industry at that time. It was becoming a struggle for the smaller farmer to survive and many others were getting out. It was not a seller's market.

We carried on through to the following year. But we did not take in any smolts and instead began to wind down the farm. We would leave it fallow for a year or so until we could see an upturn in the industry's fortunes.

This did not happen.

We couldn't see any economical future in remaining so we consulted with the girls. With their understanding and agreement we put the house and business up for sale. The time had come for us to leave Kerracher.

Both Ruthie and Clare had by now left home. Ruthie was at Art College in Aberdeen and Clare at the University in the same city. Although they were disappointed they were sympathetic – they understood our predicament and supported the decision.

We investigated a number of options to avoid selling Kerracher but by now Ruth had developed such a strong feeling against remaining there it was clear the best route now was to make a clean break.

We had a good number of enquiries, and a young couple put in an acceptable offer. The man worked at Ardvar and he saw Kerracher as the ideal place to set up his own mussel farm.

From then on we were winding everything down in preparation for the day when we would leave Kerracher for the last time. We had agreed with the Jellicoes to use Reintraid as a staging post to store our furniture and belongings prior to taking them to a new home. We packed box after box and over a period of two weeks we shipped them along the loch to Reintraid.

We had our last visitors a couple of weeks before we left and they helped us to move much of the furniture. Les and Peta, good friends from New Zealand, had visited us before, but now they had their young children with them. The children must have found the near empty rooms rather strange – or perhaps they thought this was how Highlanders lived.

After they left, Clare came home for the last time and spent a busy but reflective week with us. She had to return to her studies in Aberdeen the day before we were to leave Kerracher empty for the new owners. As I took her along the loch in the boat away from Kerracher and the home she had known for the past fifteen years, she was noticeably quiet. Ruthie had spent her last days at Kerracher between ending her summer job at the Kylesku Hotel and going back to college in Aberdeen, a few weeks earlier. If she shed any tears as she left Kerracher, I didn't see them, for these days she had the shoulder of her fiancé, Alex, to lean on.

The house was now left to Ruth and me. On the last morning we made a couple of boat trips to Reintraid with the remains of our life at Kerracher. When we had heaved the last item onto the boat for the last trip, we walked back up the beach and into the empty house to say farewell.

The emptiness echoed with memories of bringing up our children and sharing this place with many of our friends and family.

We had survived fifteen years longer than the most optimistic of our friends had given us when we left the south. As we looked around the empty rooms we recalled how Aubrey Buxton had reproached us for taking two young children to such a place. We smiled as we remembered the concerns he had about their health. The doctor had to visit only twice, and one of those times was for me!

After a prolonged tour of the rooms, supposedly to make a final check for anything left behind, we stood in the brightness of the kitchen, looking out onto the loch where the boat sat in the water, piled high with the last of our belongings. Although it was a dull October day the room seemed to be lit up, bright and glowing. Perhaps it too was recalling the many sunny times when it was filled with the aroma of Ruth's cooking, the hustle and bustle of young children growing up, the warm welcome it gave to wet and weary arrivals off a boat or off the hill, the chatter of people around a table enjoying a meal – the peace and solitude of a room with a view that slowed our lives to the pace of the landscape in which our home nestled.

We shook ourselves out of our silent reminiscing and

went from the kitchen to the hall, then finally out of the front door. Above it the inscription '1896' was etched in the lintel. We locked the door that had opened and shut to so many Kerracher men in ninety-five years, but was now shutting on this Kerracher Man for the last time.

We walked hand in hand down the stony beach that seemed to reverberate with sounds of the past, but would now fall silent to our comings and goings. We boarded the boat and pushed it out into the loch. I started up the engines and we pulled away from the place that had been more than our home and would be in our hearts forever.

With the boat's bow set towards Reintraid, I turned round and with Ruth leaning against me we looked back to the receding house and bay. I put my arms around her as I heard her sob, and murmured, 'We certainly lived there.'

WHITE RIVER
A journey up and down the River Findhorn
Jamie Whittle

Illustrated by Jo Darling and with a foreword by Alastair McIntosh

The new wanderers have at their feet an access to the world's wild places and manifold cultures such as no previous generation has known. A unity is in development that calls for a new approach and appreciation. Onto this ground steps Jamie Whittle, traveller, environmental lawyer and poet.

In this his first, great, book he returns to his origins beside the River Findhorn in Scotland to make the journey from its mouth to its source on foot, and to return again by canoe. It is familiar ground, but made new after his many travels about the world. From the interaction of traveller and river there arises a new lyricism that speaks of energy, dangers, wild places, of bounty taken from hard landscapes, of beauty and risk.

'A journey book in the tradition of Basho's *Narrow Road to a Far Province*, mixing poetry, prose and meditation. Jamie Whittle is never blind to modernity's grip on the river, but never deaf to the river's old magic either.'

Robert Macfarlane
Author of *Mountains of the Mind*
and *The Wild Places*

BETWEEN WEATHERS
Travels in 21ˢᵗ Century Shetland
Ron McMillan

The Shetland Islands sit where the North Atlantic Ocean and the North Sea meet, closer to the Arctic Circle than to London. Over the centuries they have been a vital staging post for Vikings, Hanseatic traders and merchant sailors from faraway lands. Yet somehow, the same islands remain 'off the map' of British consciousness. Ron McMillan spent weeks on the unbeaten Shetland tourist path, braving the weathers to explore scenic landmarks, archaeological treasure troves and remote islands so under populated that for centuries they have lived with the threat of abandonment.

A travel writer for more than twenty years, McMillan cast an inquisitive and witty eye over present-day Shetland to interweave the Islands' history, archaeology and 400-million-year-old geology with observations of a remarkably hospitable society that remains intricately connected to the outside world. His warm and generous narrative is the first original Shetland travelogue since 1869. Set amidst fascinating locations and soaked in history, filled with stories skilfully told, this is a book for lovers of lyrical travel writing delivered with informed authority and irresistible humour.

CAIRNGORM JOHN
A Life in Mountain Rescue
John Allen

For over thirty years John Allen was an active member of the Cairngorm Mountain Rescue Team and for most of them acted as Team Leader. In 'Cairngorm John' (his call sign when in contact with search and rescue helicopters) he recalls the challenges of mountain rescue and the many changes he has both witnessed and been a party to. His book is filled with exciting accounts of real-life rescues, discussions of mountain rescue topics such as hypothermia, first aid, and the use of helicopters and search and rescue dogs. Peopled with interesting characters his accounts are at all times humane and the book is laced with humour.

Filled with anecdotes and compassion this book takes the reader deeply into the world of mountain rescue, more deeply into the hills themselves than many more direct appreciations. Cairngorm John: A life in mountain rescue is by turns exciting, funny, informative and wise, an indispensable addition to the literature of the mountains. – Sir Chris Bonington in his Introduction.

'I had to put on several layers just to read this book. It makes Touching the Void seem like a pretty routine day on the hill.'

– Iain Macwhirter in the Sunday Herald

AT THE EDGE
Walking the Atlantic Coast of Ireland and Scotland
Joseph Murphy

AT THE EDGE tells the story of a 1500 kilometre walk from the southwest corner of Ireland to the northwest corner of Scotland. By following the Atlantic coast all the way, Joseph links the most vibrant Gaelic communities. Reflections on identity, culture and sustainability, and use of Gaelic in the text, make this a unique and memorable book. It will appeal particularly to those with Irish or Scottish heritage and no doubt some will want to do the journey themselves - although perhaps not on foot.

'This book is a glorious illustration of how the coastline will surrender its riches to the enquiring visitor. It encourages us to think hard about the meaning of sustainable development. Some will agree with its arguments and others will disagree. Perhaps it is only the starting point for debate. It is surely the case, however, that culture and language must be part of any meaningful definition of sustainability.'

– The Rt Hon Alex Salmond MSPMP
First Minister of Scotland

THE WEEKEND FIX
Craig Weldon

In this light-hearted coming-of-age tale Craig Weldon, directionless except for his love of the hills, wanders Scotland, Wales and England having fun outdoors.

This delightful book is a lively account of hill-walking in all weathers and up and down every possible terrain, braving Welsh farmers, Knoydart rain, the terrors of the Cuillin, and the real ales of Yorkshire. From Sutherland in the Far North to the rolling downs of Gloucestershire, Craig and his friends search out their Weekend Fix.

For hill walkers this is an easy guide to the hills, informative and amusing. If you've never been on a hill in your life this book will make you think again about the landscape around you, and the challenges to courage, determination and the human spirit to be found only a few miles from home, wherever you live in Britain.

'This is a young man's story and one that could be replicated almost endlessly. Any reader will see their younger selves in it, recognise the agony and the ecstasy, the turbulence of finding a place in society, of accepting the unknown challenges of the hills. We are given it straight, from the indulgent early days of a university club to the bitter realities of work (or lack of it), its demands even entailing a spell working in Birmingham (to Craig's credit the douce hills within easy reach of the city came to be taken at their own value). Life wasn't all Munros.'

— Hamish M. Brown in his Introduction

THE ANORAK'S
BOOK OF
KNOWLEDGE 1

Published by Aultbea Publishing, Inverness

Copyright details

The Anorak's Book of Knowledge 1

First published in Great Britain by
Aultbea Publishing Company in 2005,
28 Church Street, Inverness IV1 1HB

Second Edition

ISBN 1905517009

Printed by Highland Printers Limited
Henderson Road, Inverness IV1 1SP

CONTENTS

AIRCRAFT

Q: Which was Britain's major fighter aircraft of World War 1?
A: Sopwith Camel

Q: What was the most advanced bomber in the Second World War?
A: B 29 Superfortress

Q: Which is considered to be the most sophisticated and safest plane in the sky?
A: The President of USA's Airforce One

Q: The aeroplane Hercules HK1 built by Howard Hughes was known as what?
A: The Spruce Goose

Q: What was unusual about the Heinkel HE178?
A: It was the world's first jet plane

Q: What was notable about the Focke Wulfe 61?
A: It was the first successful helicopter

Q: Who designed the Lancaster bomber?
A: Roy Chadwick

Q: In which war did jet fighter planes first meet in combat?
A: The Korean War

Q: What was the RAF's first monoplane fighter?
A: The Hawker Hurricane

Q: Which device in a jet engine provides extra thrust for take off?
A: The after burner

Q: Which was the first airship to make a successful transatlantic crossing?
A: The R34

Q: Which was the first jet fighter plane to enter service?
A: The Meteor

Q: What was the world's first supersonic airliner called?
A: T144 (Soviet Russia)

Q: What was the builder's code for the Catalina flying boat?
A: P D Y

Q: What was the name of Britain's first jet propelled aircraft?
A: The Gloster –Whittle E28/39

Q: What was the fastest biplane ever built?
A: The Gloster 1VB seaplane in 1927

Q: Which aircraft was the first to test the ejection seat?
A: The Meteor

Q: Which type of aircraft did President Harry Truman use as a presidential aircraft?
A: DC6

Q: Which was the first aircraft to have air to air radar?
A: The Blenheim bomber

Q: What was the world's first jet powered bomber?
A: The Canberra

Q: Where is Mission Control for the American President's Air Force One?
A: Andrews Air Base

Q: What is the ground crews' name for the American President's Air Force One?
A: The Angel

Q: What was the call sign for the last Concorde to fly commercially?
A: Alfa-Foxtrot

Q: What was the world's first all metal aeroplane?
A: The Junkers J1

Q: Which type of aircraft sank the first German submarine by bombing in WW2?

A: The Blenheim bomber

Q: What are the three fundamental principles of flight?
A: Lift, power and control

Q: What was Britain's first jet aircraft called?
A: The M52

Q: What was the world's first swept back wing aircraft called?
A: The British DH108 Swallow

Q: How long did the first flight to break the sound barrier last?
A: 14 minutes

Q: What type of aircraft was the first to break the sound barrier?
A: Rocket powered Bell X1

Q: What was the world's first operational jet powered aircraft?
A: The Messerschmitt ME 262 (A high speed bomber)

Q: What was the number of Igor Sikorsky's first successful helicopter?
A: VS300

Q: Who created the world's first successful helicopter?
A: Heinrich Focke

Q: What was the number of Heinrich Focke's first successful helicopter?
A: FA 61

Q: Which was in 1968 the first supersonic airliner to fly?
A: The Russian Tupolev TU-104

Q: Which was the first vehicle to go into space like a rocket and come back like an aeroplane?
A: The NASA space shuttle Columbia in 1981

Q: What was the world's first rocket powered aircraft?
A: The ME 163

Q: Which British company designed the world's first rocket and jet-engined aircraft?

A: Saunders Roe

Q: What was the largest flying boat ever built?
A: The Princess flying boat

Q: Which British company built the world's largest flying boat?
A: Saunders Roe

Q: How many engines did the Princess flying boat have?
A: 10

Q: What was the name of the world's first jet seaplane fighter?
A: The SRA-1 The Squirt

Q: Which British company designed and built the world's first jet seaplane fighter aircraft?
A: Saunders Roe

Q: What was the name of the world's first rocket and jet engined fighter?
A: The SR-53

Q: What type of jet engine powered the SR-53 aircraft?
A: The Viper

Q: What type of rocket powered the SR-53 aircraft?
A: The DeHavilland Spectre

Q: What was the name of the world's first rocket powered fighter aircraft?
A: The SR177

Q: Which rocket powered aircraft superseded the SR53?
A: The SR177

Q: Which was the first American aircraft to be fitted with both rocket and jet engines?
A: The Lockheed Starfighter

Q: What was the number of the world's first Concorde?
A: 001

Q: Which was the first British jet powered aircraft?

A: The M52

Q: The M52 powered by a Whittle jet engine was the first aircraft to be fitted
   with which new invention?
A: An afterburner

Q: Which is the world's most successful fighter aircraft?
A: The American F-16

Q: Which is the fastest jet powered aircraft ever to have flown?
A: The American SR17 Blackbird (The Stealth Bomber)

Q: Which is the world's fastest aircraft?
A: The X-15 (rocket powered)

Q: Who piloted the world's fastest aircraft on its record breaking flight?
A: Peter Knight

Q: Which aircraft holds the world's altitude record?
A: The X-15

Q: How many flights did the X-15 make?
A: 199

AMERICA

Q: In the U.S.A. there are four time zones, can you name them?
A: Central, Eastern, Mountain and Pacific

Q: On which racecourse is the Kentucky Derby run?
A: Churchill Downs

Q: What is the name of the crack in the earth's crust in the region of California?
A: The San Andreas Fault

Q: Which U.S. State lies directly north of New Mexico?
A: Colorado

Q: What in the U.S.A. is the name given to a raised embankment to prevent a river from overflowing?
A: Levee

Q: In the U.S.A. the nation's gold is stored at Fort Knox. Where is the nation's silver stored
A: West Point

Q: The U.S. lawyer Francis Scott Key wrote a poem about a flag; this poem was later set to music. What is it called?
A: The Star Spangled Banner

Q: What is the American equivalent of a knighthood?
A: The Congressional Medal of Honor

Q: Which North American river was a major transportation route during the Klondike goldrush?
A: The Yukon

Q: When the U.S. President is in his Boeing 747 his radio call sign is Air Force One. What is his call sign when he is in a helicopter?
A: Marine One

Q: What is America's highest civil award?
A: The Congressional Medal of Honour

Q: Which is the smallest U.S. State?
A: Rhode Island

Q: What is the national bird of the U.S.A.?
A: The bald eagle

Q: Which room in the White House is the President's room?
A: The Oval Room

Q: On which river does Washington D.C. stand?
A: The Potomac

Q: Which two American tribes were both in the Battle of the Little Big Horn?
A: The Cheyenne and the Sioux

Q: Black Diamond could be seen on U.S. nickels until 1938. What was Black Diamond?
A: A bison

Q: Which American building can be found at 1600 Pennsylvania Avenue?
A: The White House

Q: In which street is the New York stock exchange?
A: Wall Street

Q: What was the aim of the Manhattan Project of 1942?
A: To develop the atom bomb

Q: In which city was Abraham Lincoln assassinated?
A: Washington D.C.

Q: In which American state is Death Valley?
A: California

Q: Where are the heads of four former U.S. Presidents carved in stone?
A: Mount Rushmore

Q: In which U.S. State are the Sierra Nevada Mountains?

A: California

Q: What was banned in the U.S.A. by the 18th amendment?
A: Alcohol

Q: Where did the Confederates surrender in 1865?
A: Appomattox

Q: What is the traditional yell of U.S. paratroopers when jumping out of aircraft?
A: Geronimo.

Q: In 1783 the signing of the Treaty of Paris ended what?
A: The American War of Independence

Q: Which river formed the Grand Canyon?
A: The Colorado

Q: Which is most southerly state in the U.S.?
A: Hawaii

Q: Which was the first American consumer product to be sold in the Soviet Union?
A: Pepsi Cola

Q: What is the minimum age for an American President?
A: 35

Q: In western frontier towns what was the cemetery called?
A: Boot Hill

Q: Which U.S. state has shores on four of the Great Lakes?
A: Michigan

Q: Four U.S. states border Mexico. Texas, California and New Mexico are three, which is the fourth?
A: Arizona

Q: Which trail was the pioneer route to the north-western United States?
A: The Oregon.

Q: The U.S. National Anthem is set to which tune?
A: The British song To Anacreon in Heaven

Q: Which is the only U.S. state with a one-syllable name?
A: Maine

Q: How many North American colonies originally became the United States of America?
A: Thirteen

Q: What were Hoovervilles in the U.S.A. in the 1930's?
A: Shanty towns for unemployed workers

Q: What is the largest state in America?
A: Alaska

Q: What was the original name of the Hoover Dam when construction started in 1930?
A: The Boulder Dam

Q: Who was the only U.S. President never to have lived in the White House?
A: George Washington (It wasn't built)

Q: In 1920 the Volstead Act came into effect in the U.S.A. What is it better known as?
A: Prohibition

Q: In America what is the Helms Burton Act in place for?
A: To punish any contract or trade with Cuba

Q: What is the connection between Camp David in America and Shangri-La?
A: Shangri-La is the former name of the presidential retreat

Q: What is America's oldest city?
A: Boston

Q: What was North America's first industry?
A: Glass making

Q: In which state is the Pentagon?
A: Virginia (Arlington)

Q: In 1927 the first bridge to carry cars over San Francisco bay was opened. What was its name?
A: Dumbarton Bridge

Q: In 1928 Herbert Hoover was elected President of America what was his electoral promise?
A: A chicken in every pot and a car in every garage

Q: Which was the first year since the end of the American Civil War that America was free of lynching attacks?
A: 1952

Q: Which is the only vowel that does not start an American state?
A: E

Q: In which state did the American Civil War start?
A: South Carolina

AMERICAN STATES ENTRY into the UNION

State	Date	Position	State	Date	Position
Delaware	1787	1	Michigan	1837	26
Pennsylvania	1787	2	Florida	1845	27
New Jersey	1787	3	Texas	1845	28
Georgia	1788	4	Iowa	1846	29
Connecticut	1788	5	Wisconsin	1848	30
Massachusetts	1788	6	California	1850	31
Maryland	1788	7	Minnesota	1858	32
South Carolina	1788	8	Oregon	1859	33
New Hampshire	1788	9	Kansas	1861	34
Virginia	1788	10	West Virginia	1863	35
New York	1788	11	Nevada	1864	36
North Carolina	1789	12	Nebraska	1867	37
Rhode Island	1790	13	Colorado	1867	38
Vermont	1791	14	North Dakota	1889	39
Kentucky	1792	15	South Dakota	1889	40
Tennessee	1796	16	Montana	1889	41
Ohio	1803	17	Washington	1889	42
Louisiana	1812	18	Idaho	1890	43
Indiana	1816	19	Wyoming	1890	44

State	Date	Position	State	Date	Position
Mississippi	1817	20	Utah	1896	45
Illinois	1818	21	Oklahoma	1907	46
Alabama	1819	22	New Mexico	1912	47
Maine	1820	23	Arizona	1912	48
Missouri	1821	24	Alaska	1959	49
Arkansas	1836	25	Hawaii	1959	50

AMERICAN PRESIDENTS

President	From	To		President	From	To	
George Washington	1789	1797	1	Benjamin Harrison	1889	1893	23
John Adams	1797	1801	2	Grover Cleveland	1893	1897	24
Thomas Jefferson	1801	1809	3	William McKinley	1897	1901	25
James Madison	1809	1817	4	Theodore Roosevelt	1901	1909	26
James Monroe	1817	1825	5	William Taft	1909	1913	27
John Adams	1825	1829	6	Woodrow Wilson	1913	1921	28
Andrew Jackson	1829	1837	7	Warren Harding	1921	1923	29
Martin van Buren	1837	1841	8	Calvin Coolidge	1923	1929	30
William Harrison	1841	1841	9	Herbert Hoover	1929	1933	31
John Tyler	1841	1845	10	Franklin Roosevelt	1933	1945	32
James Polk	1845	1849	11	Harry Truman	1945	1953	33
Zachary Taylor	1849	1850	12	Dwight Eisenhower	1953	1961	34
Millard Filmore	1850	1853	13	John Kennedy	1961	1963	35
Franklin Pierce	1853	1857	14	Lyndon Johnson	1963	1969	36
James Buchanan	1857	1861	15	Richard Nixon	1969	1974	37
Abraham Lincoln	1861	1865	16	Gerald Ford	1974	1977	38
Andrew Johnston	1865	1869	17	Jimmy Carter	1977	1981	39
Ulysses Grant	1869	1877	18	Ronald Regan	1981	1989	40
Rutherford Hayes	1877	1881	19	George Bush	1989	1993	41
James Garfield	1881	1881	20	William Clinton	1993	2001	42
Chester Arthur	1881	1885	21	George W. Bush	2001		43
Grover Cleveland	1885	1889	22				

ANIMALS

Q: To which family of animals does the hyena belong?
A: The dog family

Q: What animal gives us nutria fur?
A: The coypu

Q: Which domestic pet is descended from the cavy?
A: The guinea pig

Q: What sort of creature is a lynx?
A: A wild cat

Q: Which creature has the largest eyes in the world?
A: The squid

Q: What is the colour of a polar bear's skin?
A: Black

Q: What is the name of the only armoured mammal?
A: The armadillo

Q: What is the world,s largest marsupial?
A: The red kangaroo

Q: Which canine mammal is also called a prairie wolf?
A: The coyote

Q: Which animal lives in a citadel?
A: A mole

Q: At certain times which creatures form the biggest gathering of large animals on earth?
A: Wildebeest

Q: Which is the only mammal with no teeth?
A: The anteater

Q: What name is given to a young hedgehog? .
A: A hoglet

Q: What is another name for the grey or white wolf?
A: The timber wolf

Q: Which land animal has biggest eyes?
A: The horse

Q: Where can the largest population of wild camels on earth be found?
A: Australia

Q: Animals that eat grass are called grazers. What name is given to animals that eat leaves from trees?
A: Browsers

Q: Humans, bears and wolverines have what in common?
A: They all walk on the soles of their feet

Q: Which animal has the thickest fur?
A: The sea otter

Q: What is the largest migration of animals in the world?
A: The herring

Q: Which is the slowest mammal on earth?
A: The sloth

Q: What is the domesticated polecat called?
A: A ferret

Q: Which is the oldest domestic animal?
A: The dog

Q: Which animal has been responsible for more human deaths than any other in Africa?
A: The hippopotamus

Q: Which is the only breed of dog that can contract gout?
A: The dalmatian

Q: What is a male guinea pig called?
A: A boar

Q: What is largest animal found in the Amazon rainforest?
A: The tapir

Q: What is the fastest non-human animal in the world?
A: The peregrine falcon

Q: Which is the only animal with a four chambered heart?
A: The crocodile

Q: In Costa Rica which animals are the main predators of crocodile's eggs?
A: The raccoon

Q: What is the largest member of the weasel family?
A: The wolverine

Q: Which name is given to animals such as the gazelle, eland and gnu?
A: Antelopes

Q: What are believed to be the first animals to have developed muscles and nerves?
A: Jellyfish

Q: What is believed to be the world's first animal?
A: The sponge

Q: Where is the only place in the world you can find crocodiles and alligators together?
A: Florida

Q: The Australian honey possum is the only mammal on the earth completely dependent on what for its food?
A: Nectar

Q: Which mammal lives furthest south?
A: The Weddell seal

Q: What is a fox's den called?
A: An earth

Q: Cocker spaniels were originally bred to hunt which birds?
A: Woodcock

Q: What was the first animal to be exterminated by man in modern times?
A: The dodo

Q: What is another name for a leopard, particularly one with a lot of black pigmentation?
A: A panther

Q: Which group of animals are the most successful and adaptable on the planet?
A: Mammals

Q: What colour of teeth do beavers have?
A: Orange

Q: Which male animal is called a tod?
A: A fox

Q: Which animal's skin gives us Morocco leather?
A: Goat

Q: What do the greyhound, deerhound and the wolfhound have in common?
A: They hunt by sight not smell

Q: What is the most widely distributed of all mammals and is found on every continent including Antarctica?
A: The house mouse

Q: What is the world's tallest breed of dog?
A: The Irish wolfhound

Q: Which animal has the heaviest brain in the animal world?
A: The sperm whale

Q: What was the first cloned animal?
A: The sea urchin

Q: What animal lives in a sett?

A: A badger

Q: What is the largest group of mammals in the world?
A: Rodents

Q: To which family of animals does the polecat belong?
A: The weasel

Q: What are the most destructive animals on earth?
A: Humans

Q: What name is given to a male hare?
A: A jack

Q: Elephants are the only mammals that cannot do what?
A: Jump

Q: Kangaroos and emus cannot do what?
A: Walk backwards

Q: The domestic cat is the only species of cat able to do what?
A: Hold its tail vertically while walking

Q: The cheetah is the only cat that cannot do what?
A: Retract its claws

Q: Elephants are the only animals that, apart from trunks, have what?
A: Four knees

Q: The otter is the only amphibious member of which animal family?
A: The weasel

Q: Which animals were dachshunds originally bred to hunt?
A: Badgers

Q: Of which creatures are there most species on earth?
A: Beetles

Q: What is unusual about the basenji dog?
A: It can't bark

Q: What is the world's fastest land mammal?
A: The cheetah

Q: What is a dhole?
A: A wild dog

Q: What does a squirrel live in?
A: A drey

Q: What is the world,s largest land animal after the elephant?
A: The white rhinoceros

Q: There are two species of alligator, one in southern U.S.A. where does the other live?
A: China

Q: In which country are Europe's only wild bison found?
A: Poland

Q: What is the name of the wild mountain sheep of North Africa also called an Aoudad?
A: The Barbary sheep

Q: What is the largest cat in the Americas?
A: The jaguar

Q: Which animal causes more deaths in the Americas than any other?
A: The fer de lance

Q: What are the only wild animals that respect their ancestors?
A: Elephants

Q: Which animals kill more humans than any other large animals?
A: Crocodiles and alligators

Q: What are the only animals that from birth instinctively hold their breath when immersed in water?
A: Humans

Q: What are the only animals who will drink alcohol voluntarily?
A: Pigs

Q: Which creature has the greatest field of vision?
A: The woodcock

Q: Which creatures have the most complex colour vision?
A: Birds

Q: Which creature has the best underwater vision?
A: The cormorant

Q: Which creature has the most sophisticated eyesight targeting system in the animal world?
A: The mantis shrimp

Q: What is the fastest moving body part in the animal world?
A: The chameleon's tongue

Q: Which creature is considered to have a better sense of smell than a bloodhound?
A: The salmon

Q: What bodily function can a rat not perform that makes it susceptible to poison?
A: Vomit

Q: What is the world's smallest primate?
A: The mouse lemur

Q: What is Europe's smallest rodent?
A: The harvest mouse

Q: Which is the only species of cat that can hang by its back legs?
A: The South American margay

Q: The capybara is the world's largest rodent. What does capybara mean?
A: Master of the grasses

Q: How do lions hunt?
A: By stalking

Q: Which animal is the largest member of the seal family?
A: The walrus

Q: What is the colour of a polar bears tongue?
A: Black

Q: What is the only marsupial that can move its hind legs one in front of the other?
A: The Australian tree kangaroo

Q: What are believed to have been the first creatures to develop poison to protect themselves?
A: Centipedes

Q: On which creatures will you find a carapace?
A: A tortoise or a turtle

Q: The jaguar is the only big cat that is excellent at swimming, but what can it not do?
A: Dive or swim under water

Q: Which large aquatic rodent builds lodges and dams?
A: The beaver

Q: Which animal is sometimes said to be in velvet?
A: A deer

Q: Which creatures live in a formicary?
A: Ants

Q: What animal derived its name from two Greek words meaning terrible lizard?
A: The dinosaur

Q: What animal takes its name from the Spanish 'el largato' meaning the lizard?
A: The alligator

Q: What name is given to a young mink?
A: A kit

Q: What does the name mink mean in its native Swedish?
A: Stinking animal

Q: Which animal has the best defence against predators?
A: The African hedgehog

Q: There are more of which animals in Australia than humans?
A: Kangaroos

Q: Except for lions all adult cats do what?
A: Hunt alone

Q: What is North America's largest rodent?
A: The beaver

Q: What do you call a male ferret?
A: A hob

Q: What is the fastest killer in the Amazon rainforest?
A: The leaf fish

Q: What are the most powerful animals in North America?
A: The bison

Q: Which animal has the densest coat?
A: The musk ox

Q: What herd animals live furthest north?
A: The musk ox

Q: What are the only two venomous mammals in the world?
A: The duck-billed platypus and the water shrew

Q: What is the most popular pet in the western hemisphere?
A: The cat

Q: What is the largest member of the deer family?
A: The moose

Q: Next to the lion what is Africa's second largest killer?
A: The spotted hyena

Q: What are the only two egg laying mammals in the world?
A: The duckbilled-platypus and the echidna

Q: Which creature is the world's greatest contortionist?
A: The octopus

Q: What is the most prolific creature on the planet?
A: The ant

Q: Where is the only place in the world wild boars kill cattle and sheep?
A: Uruguay

Q: How many species of bears are there in the world?
A: Eight

Q: Apart from humans which are the only animals that know how to make tools?
A: The chimpanzee

Q: After humans what animal has the most facial expressions?
A: The chimpanzee

Q: What is the world's largest big cat?
A: The Siberian tiger

Q: What is the only seal that feeds on penguins?
A: The leopard seal

Q: What are the only known animals able to digest beeswax?
A: Honeyguides

Q: What is the largest land carnivore on earth?
A: The polar bear

Q: Which small carnivore has a winter coat known as ermine?
A: The stoat

Q: What do all polar bears have in common?
A: They are all left handed

Q: How does a cheetah bring down its prey?
A: It trips it up

Q: What is the largest spider in the world?

A: The goliath tarantula

Q: What is Europe's largest spider?
A: The Steppes tarantula

Q: What is the fastest growing tissue in any animal?
A: Reindeer antlers

Q: Which creature has the fastest acting venom on the planet?
A: The cone snail

Q: What is the most venomous creature on the planet?
A: The box jellyfish

Q: Which breed of dog is considered to be closest to the wolf?
A: The sheepdog

Q: Three quarters of all the animals on the planet known to man are of what type?
A: Arthropoda

Q: What were the first animals to develop vocal chords?
A: Frogs

Q: What is the largest toothed mammal?
A: The sperm whale

Q: What is the world's smallest non-flying mammal?
A: The pygmy shrew

Q: What is the only animal source of vitamin C?
A: The narwhal

Q: What is the world's smallest mammal?
A: The bumblebee bat

Q: What is the world's smallest rodent?
A: The Baluchistan pygmy jerboa

Q: What is the fastest land mammal over long distances?
A: The pronghorn antelope

Q: What are the sleepiest mammals on the planet?
A: The three toed sloth

Q: What is the most fearless mammal on the planet?
A: The ratel or honey badger

Q: Which mammal forages at the highest altitude?
A: The large eared pika

Q: What are the only animals that are born as clones of their parents?
A: Armadillo

Q: What are the only animals that have no natural predators?
A: Humans

Q: What human trait is never found in the animal world?
A: Revenge

Q: What are believed to have been the first animals to have developed, a head, eyes and a nervous system?
A: Flatworms

Q: What is the only animal other than a snake that can unhinge its lower jaw to swallow its prey?
A: The monitor lizard

Q: What is unusual about the marmoset monkey?
A: It has claws instead of fingernails

Q: What primate is considered to be a human's closest living relative?
A: The bonobo or pygmy chimpanzee

Q: What is another name for a water tortoise?
A: A terrapin

Q: What is the world's largest marsupial carnivore?
A: The Tasmanian devil

Q: What are the most successful life forms on the planet?
A: Bacteria

Q: What is the largest land predator on earth?
A: The Alaskan brown bear

Q: What is the largest animal in North America?
A: The bison

Q: What is the fastest flying insect in the world?
A: The hawkmoth

Q: Which animal makes the longest migration?
A: The Grey whale

Q: What are the only insects that are wingless and can't hop walk or jump?
A: Head lice

Q: Where in the world is the only place caymen can be found?
A: The Americas

Q: In the scientific world what do all animals produce?
A: A magnetic field

Q: What is the world's largest amphibian?
A: The giant salamander

Q: What is unusual about goat's teeth?
A: The two front teeth are missing

Q: What is the only known animal that can't be photographed with infrared cameras?
A: The polar bear

Q: The mastiff and the greyhound were crossed to produce which breed of dog?
A: The Great Dane

Q: Which continent has most poisonous creatures?
A: Australia

Q: What is the world's smallest marsupial?
A: The Australian planigale

Q: Which group of animals have been on the planet the longest?
A: Lizards

Q: What is the only animal that can starve to death with a full stomach?
A: The three toed sloth

Q: Which animal can be found in every ocean?
A: Killer whales

Q: What is the only marsupial in North America?
A: The possum

Q: What were the most successful group of animals that ever lived?
A: The dinosaurs

Q: What animal has the largest tongue in the world?
A: The blue whale

Q: What is the world's smallest land vertebrate?
A: The Madagascar pygmy chameleon

Q: What is the world's rarest breed of wolf?
A: The Mexican grey wolf

Q: After humans what are the most adaptable primates?
A: Baboons

WILDCAT SPECIES

1 African Golden Cat
2 Andean mountain Cat
3 Asian Golden Cat
4 Black-Footed Cat
5 Bobcat
6 Bornean Bay Cat
7 Canadian Lynx
8 Caracal
9 Cheetah
10 Chinese Mountain Cat
11 Clouded Leopard
12 Cougar
13 Eurasian Lynx
14 Fishing Cat
15 Flat Headed Cat
16 Geoffroys Cat
17 Iberian Lynx
18 Jaguar

19 Jaguarundi
20 Jungle Cat
21 Kodkod
22 Leopard
23 Leopard Cat
24 Lion
25 Marbled Cat
26 Margay
27 Ocelot
28 Oncilla
29 Pallas Cat
30 Pampas Cat
31 Rusty Spotted Cat
32 Sand Cat
33 Serval
34 Snow Leopard
35 Tiger
36 Wildcat

ART

Q. How many paintings did Vincent Van Gogh sell in his lifetime?
A. One (Red Vineyard at Aries)

Q. By what name is La Giocanda better known ?
A. The Mona Lisa

Q. How many people feature in Leonardo Da Vinci's famous painting the Last Supper?
A. Thirteen

Q. In art, Annigoni's portrait of whom caused the Royal Academy to break attendance records in 1995?
A. The Queen

Q. How many of Leonardo da Vinci's paintings still exist?
A. Twelve

BACTERIA and DISEASE

Q. What bacteria can cause typhoid fever and food poisoning?
A. Salmonella

Q. What is the technical name for German measles?
A. Rubella

Q. What is the most dangerous insect in the world?
A. The mosquito

Q. Where can the greatest concentration of bacteria be found?
A. In soil

Q. Which type of mosquito transmits malaria?
A. The Anopheles mosquito

Q. What was the world's most deadly form of bacteria?
A. The plague

BIRDS

Q: What is the most widely spread land bird in the world?
A: The barn owl

Q: What bird has the best eyesight of any animal?
A: The Patagonian white tailed hawk

Q: Which species of U.S. cuckoo can move across the ground at 24km/15mph?
A: The roadrunner

Q: What is the world's only poisonous bird?
A: The pitohui

Q: What is the largest bird in the world which can hover?
A: The osprey

Q: What type of bird is a peewit?
A: A lapwing

Q: What is unique about the beak of the wrybill, a New Zealand plover?
A: It curves sideways

Q: What is considered to be the world's oldest breed of bird?
A: The ostrich

Q: What is unique about the sword-billed hummingbird?
A: It has a beak longer than its body

Q: The canary is a member of which bird family?
A: The finch

Q: What is the largest of all the hummingbirds?
A: The Patagonian giant

Q: What is believed to be the first species of wild birds to be domesticated by humans?
A: The pigeon

Q: What is the only known bird that carries its young with it on flights?
A: The sungrebe

Q: What is the only bird able to walk up and down a tree looking for food?
A: The nuthatch

Q: What is the largest breed of kingfisher?
A: The Australian kookaburra

Q: What are the young of gannets called?
A: Gugas

Q: Which breed of bird has the most powerful beak?
A: The hyacinth macaw

Q: What is a young turkey called?
A: A poult

Q: What is the only bird that can fly backwards?
A: The hummingbird

Q: Where will you find mutton birds?
A: S.E. Australia

Q: Which game bird season runs from 1 October to the 1 February each year?
A: The pheasant

Q: What is the world's largest bird of prey?
A: The Andean condor

Q: What is the largest sea bird in the world?
A: The emperor penguin

Q: What is the smallest species of the partridge family?
A: The quail

Q: What is the most dangerous bird in the world?
A: The cassowary

Q: What is the world's smallest bird?
A: The bee hummingbird

Q: To which bird family does the peacock belong?
A: The pheasant

Q: Which bird has the longest wingspan of any living bird?
A: The wandering albatross

Q: The nightingale is a member of which bird family?
A: The thrush

Q: What is the only bird with its nostrils at the end of its beak?
A: The kiwi

Q: If a bird is ratite what can it not do?
A: Fly

Q: What colour is the trumpeter swan's bill?
A: Black

Q: What does it mean if a bird of prey is diurnal?
A: It's active during the day

Q: What is the northern equivalent to the southern albatross?
A: The fulmar

Q: What is the largest living bird?
A: The ostrich

Q: What name is given to a bird's entire covering of feathers?
A: Plumage

Q: What bird is believed to have the best sense of smell?
A: The fulmar

Q: Egyptian vultures are the only birds in the world to do what?
A: Use stones to open eggs

Q: Which birds build the largest nests in the world?
A: The sociable weaver birds

Q: What name is given to a young hawk taken from its nest for training?
A: An eyas

Q: What bird is sometimes known as the sea parrot?
A: The puffin

Q: As a bird of prey what two things can a vulture not do?
A: Catch and kill its own prey

Q: What is Europe's smallest owl?
A: The pygmy owl

Q: What name is given to a male turkey?
A: A stag

Q: Which breed of bird has the most feathers?
A: The penguin

Q: Guillemots, puffins and razorbills belong to which family of birds?
A: The auks

Q: What is the only bird in the world to have only two toes on each foot?
A: The ostrich

Q: What is considered to be the smartest bird on the planet?
A: The raven

Q: What are the only birds that fly towards a gunshot?
A: Ravens

Q: The name of which seabird spits vile smelling oil at intruders to its nest?
A: The fulmar

Q: What are the only birds of prey that indicate their sex by the colour of their wing feathers?
A: Kestrels

Q: Of what material are birds feathers made?
A: Keratin

Q: Which creature is considered to be the fastest communicator in the world?
A: The woodpecker

Q: What is believed to be the only bird with no sense of smell?

A: The hummingbird

Q: What physical feat can the hummingbird not perform?
A: It can't walk or hop

Q: What is Europe's largest bird of prey?
A: The black vulture

Q: What is the only bird that is totally dependent on other birds for its existence?
A: The cuckoo

Q: Where is the only place flamingos and penguins can be found living in the same environment?
A: The Galapagos Islands

Q: Of which family is the roadrunner a member?
A: The cuckoo

Q: What is the national bird of Panama?
A: The harpy eagle

Q: What is the largest eagle in the world?
A: The harpy eagle

Q: What is considered to be the most primitive bird in the world?
A: The hoatzin

Q: The ostrich lays the largest egg. Which bird lays the smallest?
A: The vervain humming bird

Q: What is the largest pigeon in the world?
A: The crested pigeon (native to Papua New Guinea)

Q: What is the smallest bird of prey?
A: The falconet

Q: What is the world's heaviest flying bird?
A: The bustard

Q: What type of bird is a galah?

A: A cockatoo

Q: What is strange about the frigate bird?
A: It is a seabird with no oil in its feathers and can't land on the sea

Q: What are the only known birds to use bait to catch fish?
A: The green herons

Q: What is the only known breed of bird capable of smashing a snails shell?
A: The song thrush

Q: What is the world's most endangered bird of prey?
A: The caracara (Falkland Islands flying devils)

Q: What is the world's largest owl?
A: The eagle owl

Q: Being a seabird what is strange about the cormorant?
A: It does not have oil in its feathers (it relies on air in its feathers for waterproofing)

Q: Which bird has the largest eyes in relation to its head size?
A: The owl

Q: How many degrees can an owl turn its head?
A: 270

Q: Which are the only birds of prey that live all year round in the Arctic?
A: Snowy owls

Q: What is the world's smallest owl?
A: The elf owl

Q: Which country has the biggest diversity of owls?
A: Africa

Q: The owl is the only bird that can do what?
A: Hunt by hearing alone

Q: What is the largest bird in Australia?
A: The cassowary

Q: Where in the southern hemisphere is the only place ospreys breed?
A: Australia

Q: What is the only bird in the world with a hard bone like crest on its head?
A: The cassowary

Q: What is the only bird of prey that does not kill its prey before eating it?
A: The goshawk

Q: What is the fourth largest eagle in the world?
A: The white-tailed sea eagle

Q: Which type of bird is America's worst bird pest?
A: The starling (Introduced in 1890)

Q: What was the last bird to be made extinct by man?
A: The carrier pigeon (1914)

Q: What is the official bird of Hawaii?
A: The Ne-Ne (Hawaiian Goose)

Q: Which bird has the longest tail in relation to its body size?
A: The long tailed bird of paradise

Q: The ostrich egg is the largest and heaviest in the world. What other record does it hold?
A: It is the smallest in relation to the bird's size

Q: What are the only birds of prey that hunt in groups?
A: The American Harris hawks

Q: Apart from its colour and shape what is different about a puffin's beak compared to other birds?
A: The top and bottom parts remain horizontal when open

Q: All domestic ducks are descended from which breed of duck?
A: The mallard duck

Q: In the bird,s name peregrine falcon, what does perigrine mean?
A: Foreign or pilgrim

Q: How many species of albatross are there in the world?
A: 24

Q: What is the only known seabird that uses previously caught fish as bait
A: The green heron

Q: What is the world's largest owl?
A: The eagle owl

Q: What is Europe's largest game bird?
A: The wood grouse

Q: What is the fastest bird on water?
A: The gentoo penguin

Q: What is the world's heaviest flying bird?
A: The great bustard

Q: What is the only known species of meat eating duck?
A: The South Georgian pintail duck

Q: Which breed of bird is the most prolific on the planet?
A: The domestic chicken

Q: What is the largest species of parakeet?
A: Alexandrines

Q: What are the UK's only naturalised parrots?
A: Ring-necked parakeets

Q: What is the only breed of bird that the young actually play together?
A: The New Zealand kea

Q: What bird is the highest flyer?
A: The Ruppell Vulture

Q: What seabird is the deepest diver?
A: The emperor penguin

Q: Which flying bird can can dive the deepest of any flying bird?
A: The great northern diver or loon

Q: What is the most prolific breed of wild bird in the world?
A: The red-billed quelea (Africa)

Q: What are the only breed of birds that moult their beaks?
A: Puffins

Q: What bird has the widest variety of diet?
A: The North American ruffled grouse

Q: What is the only vegetarian bird of prey
A: The palm nut vulture (West Africa)

Q: What is the only bird that can drop its upper eyelid in order to blink?
A: The owl (all the other birds do it by raising their lower eyelid)

Q: What is the only breed of bird that can sing two tunes at once?
A: The reed warbler

Q: What is the world's only nocturnal fruit eating bird?
A: The oilbird (tropical South America)

Q: Which of the hummingbirds lives at the highest altitude?
A: The Andean hillstar

Q: What is the only woodpecker that lives above the treeline?
A: The Andean flicker

FLIGHTLESS BIRDS

Cassowary

A very large bird related to the emu and is native mainly to New Guinea. It is the world's most dangerous bird

Emu

A large fast running Australian bird resembling the ostrich

Galapagos Cormorant

A diving seabird found only in the Galapagos Islands

Guam Rail

A small flightless bird with brown plumage. It is found only on the island of Guam

Kagu

A flightless crested bird found only on the island of New Caledonia in the western Pacific Ocean, it is the size of a domestic hen with the general shape of a heron

Kakapo

An endangered nocturnal New Zealand parrot with greenish plumage

Kiwi

A tailless New Zealand bird with hair like feathers and a long downcurved bill

Magellanic Steamer Duck

A large flightless duck of the Falkland Islands, it is grey and white with yellow legs

Ostrich

A large fast running bird found in Africa

Penguin

A black and white seabird of the southern hemisphere

Rail

A species of flightless bird found only on the islands of Gough and Tristian Da Cunha in the South Atlantic

Rhea

A large bird of the South American grasslands resembling a small ostrich

Solitaire	A common name applied to various species of American thrush. In the United States, one species, Townsend's Solitaire, is found chiefly in the Rocky Mountains. The bird is largely grey in colour with a white eye-ring and a buff wing patch
Takahe	Found only in the remote valleys of New Zealand,s south island,in an area known as Fiordland. It is a kind of coot related to the moorhen. It has deep blue plumage shading to green on its back and a huge brilliantly scarlet bill
Weka	A large flightless New Zealand rail

THE TOP TEN BIRDS with the LARGEST WINGSPAN

	Inches	Millimetres
Great White Pelican	141	3,581
Wandering Albatross	138	3,505
Andean Condor	126	3,200
Himalayan Griffon	122	3,098
Black Vulture	116	2,946
Maribou Stork	113	2,870
Lammergeier	111	2,819
Sarus Crane	110	2,794
Kori Bustard	106	2,692
Steller's Sea Eagle	104	2,641

BOOKS

Q: Who created the naval character Hornblower?
A: C.S. Forester

Q: The Diamond Soutra was the world's first what?
A: Printed book

Q: Which literary character rode a horse called Rosinante?
A: Don Quixote

Q: What is the most widely read magazine in the world?
A: Reader's Digest

Q: What is uniquely strange about the book Gatsby written by Ernest Vincent Wright?
A: It does not contain the letter E

Q: What is believed to be the earliest printed secular song?
A: Three Blind Mice

Q: What is considered to be the world's oldest story?
A: Noah's Flood or Noah's Ark

Q: Which famous British secret agent was created by Ian Fleming?
A: James Bond

Q: Which British prime minister wrote Vivian Grey?
A: Disraeli

Q: Who wrote the Journey to the Centre of the Earth?
A: Jules Verne

Q: Which leader wrote his thoughts in a little red book?
A: Chairman Mao

Q: What publication was first published in 1700 under the title Voices of the Stars?
A: Old Moore's Almanac

Q: What is the name of the dog in Oliver Twist?
A: Bullseye

Q: What was the first paperback book to be published?
A: Faust (by Johann Von Goethe 1867)

Q: Who wrote the novel Moby Dick?
A: Herman Melville

Q: Under what name did Eric Blair write?
A: George Orwell

Q: What famous adventure story was originally titled the Sea Cook?
A: Treasure Island

Q: In Jules Verne's novel 20,000 Leagues Under the Sea, who captained the submarine Nautilus?
A: Captain Nemo

Q: The name of what type of book comes from two Greek words meaning a circle of Learning?
A: Encyclopaedia

Q: Which fictional character's main opponent was Von Stalhein?
A: Biggles

Q: Which author created Gunga Din?
A: Rudyard Kipling

Q: Which British novelist wrote Bulldog Drummond?
A: Sapper

Q: Who wrote the play The Cherry Orchard?
A: Anton Chekov

Q: Which famous writer's last words were my 'My head - my head'?
A: Robert Louis Stevenson

Q: Whose mother kept the Admiral Benbow inn?
A: Jim Hawkins (in Treasure Island)

Q: In which novel will you encounter Ben Gunn?
A: Treasure Island

Q: What is the children's division of Penguin Books called?
A: Puffin Books

Q: What does ISBN on a book jacket stand for?
A: International standard book number

Q: In the novel Moby Dick what was the name of the ship?
A: The Pequod

Q: Who relentlessly pursued Moby Dick?
A: Captain Ahab

Q: In the Tarzan novels what does Tarzan mean?
A: White skin

Q: In the Tarzan novels who was known as Kora?
A: Tarzan's son

Q: Which Scottish explorer wrote Travels in the Interior Districts of Africa?
A: Mungo Park

Q: In the book Treasure Island what is the name of the ship?
A: Hispaniola

Q: Wackford Squeers appears in which Dickens novel?
A: Nicholas Nickleby

Q: In which Shakespeare play does Sebastian appear?
A: Twelfth Night

Q: Who wrote the stories of Uncle Remus and Brer Rabbit?
A: Joel Chandler Harris

Q: The character Pip appears in which book by Charles Dickens?
A: Great Expectations

Q: What is the Talmud?
A: An encyclopaedia of Jewish Laws

Q: What was the world's first atlas called?
A: Theatrum Orbis Terrarum

Q: In Alice in Wonderland which creature smokes a hookah?
A: The caterpillar

Q: Who in 1924 wrote The Little Grey Men, a story about the last four gnomes in Britain?
A: D. J. Watkins-Pritchard

Q: In literature who were the last four gnomes in Britain?
A: Dodder, Baldmoney, Cloudberry and Sneezewort

Q: Which book is considered to be the world's first modern detective novel?
A: The Murders in the Rue Morgue (Edgar Allan Poe, 1841)

Q: Billy Bones is a character in which book?
A: Treasure Island

Q: Which character in Alice's Adventures In Wonderland remarks 'curiouser and curiouser'?
A: Alice

Q: Call me Ishmael is the opening line of which novel?
A: Moby Dick

Q: What is the name of George Orwell's book about his experience in the Spanish Civil War?
A: Homage to Catalonia

Q: In which book will you find a heffalump?
A: Winnie the Pooh

Q: Who wrote Lucky Jim?
A: Kingsley Amis

Q: Who wrote The Rise and Fall of the Roman Empire?
A: Edward Gibbons

BRIDGES

Q. What is the widest and heaviest arch bridge in the world?
A. The Sydney Harbour Bridge

Q. Clapper, truss and bascule are all types of what?
A. Bridges

Q. What is the real name of the Kew Bridge over the Thames?
A. Edward the VII Bridge

Q. What was the first privately funded bridge built in Britain?
A. The Skye Bridge

Q Where was the world's first box girder bridge built?
A. Across the Menai Strait (The Britannia Bridge)

BUILDINGS

Q: What is the largest building in the world?
A: The Dome of Hagia Sophia

Q: Where is the largest building in the world?
A: Istanbul

Q: Which famous building will you find in the city of Agra?
A: The Taj Mahal

Q: What is the name of the most impressive tower in the Kremlin, Moscow's ruling Centre?
A: The Spassky Tower

Q: The Notre Dame cathedral in France is an example of what type of architecture?
A: Gothic

Q: What is the literal meaning of the word Kremlin?
A: Citadel

Q: What in Italy is a Duomo?
A: A cathedral

Q: What is the world's largest office building?
A: The Pentagon

Q: Where was the first office block in the world built?
A: Portsmouth Dockyard

Q: In which modern country will you locate the world's largest pyramid?
A: Mexico

Q: What sort of religious building derives its name from the Latin for seat?
A: Cathedral

Q: Where is the biggest city centre government building on earth?

A: China (The Great Hall of the People)

Q: Which infamous former American federal prison is sited on an island in San Francisco Bay?
A: Alcatraz

Q: Of what material is the dome of The White House made?
A: Cast iron

Q: What was the first large stone building in the world?
A: The stepped pyramid

Q: What famous hotel was the first important steel framed building in London?
A: The Ritz

Q: Where is the world's largest telephone exchange?
A: The Pentagon

Q: What is considered to have been the world's first skyscraper?
A: The Pharos Lighthouse (at Alexandria)

Q: What building is the U.S. White House based on?
A: Leicester House in Dublin

Q: Prior to being called the White House, by what name was the U.S. President's dwelling known?
A: The Executive Mansion

Q: Until the completion of the White House in1809 which architectural feature had no native born American seen?
A: A building with a dome

Q: Which New York art gallery was designed by Frank Lloyd Wright in the 1960's?
A: Guggenheim

Q: Which prison was demolished after the death of its last inmate Rudolf Hess?
A: Spandau

Q: What is the world's largest occupied castle?

A: Windsor Castle

Q: What aid to the movement of people does the Pentagon not have?
A: Lifts

Q: What is strange about the escalators in the Pentagon?
A: They all travel in the same direction (up in the morning—down in the evening)

Q: Which three buildings are considered to be the most vulnerable in the world?
A: The White House, Capitol Building and the Pentagon

Q: By volume what is the largest building in the world?
A: The Boeing aircraft building hanger (in Seattle)

Q: What was the original name of Alcatraz Prison?
A: The citadel

Q: What is the world's largest residential palace?
A: The Vatican

Q: Where is the largest government building in the world?
A: China (Tiananmen Square Beijing)

Q: Where could you have visited the Dome of Discovery in 1951?
A: The Festival of Britain (near Waterloo, London)

Q: What is the only palace in Britain not in royal hands?
A: Blenheim Palace

Q: Why is America's Empire State Building called the Empire State Building, when America never had an empire?
A: New York's nickname is the Empire State

Q: The Nymphenburg Palace is near which city?
A: Munich

Q: Where is the greatest museum in the world?
A: The National Palace Museum of Taipei (Taiwan)

Q: Which museum contains the most priceless collection of Chinese art and history?
A: The National Palace Museum of Taipei (Taiwan)

Q: In 1950, for what purpose was room 801 on the 9th floor of London's Metropole Building used?
A: The Secret Service to monitor flying saucer sightings

Q: What is the oldest offshore building in the world?
A: The Bell Rock lighthouse

Q: Which modern building is considered to be the last pure example of Gothic architecture in the world?
A: The Washington Cathedral of St Peter and St Paul

Q: What name is given to a domed building?
A: A rotunda

CHRISTMAS

Q: What did my true love give to me on the 11th day of Christmas?
A: Eleven ladies dancing

Q: Who originally recorded Rudolph the Red Nosed Reindeer?
A: Gene Autry

Q: Who in 1958 issued a recorded Christmas message from an orbiting space satellite, 'To all mankind America's wish for peace on earth and goodwill to men everywhere'?
A: President Eisenhower

Q: What did my true love give to me on the 8th day of Christmas?
A: Eight maids a milking

Q: In the Christmas carol, which town is known as Royal David's City?
A: Bethlehem

Q: What is the name given to the period that covers the four Sundays leading up to Christmas?
A: Advent

Q: On what musical instrument was the carol Silent Night first played?
A: A guitar

Q: Good King Wenceslas was king of which country?
A: Bohemia

Q: What was the name of Scrooge's deceased business partner in Charles Dickens' book A Christmas Carol?
A: Jacob Marley

Q: In what country did the real St Nicholas live?
A: Turkey

Q: The day after Christmas Day is known as Boxing Day. The holy day of which saint?

A: St Stephen

Q: When distributing gifts in Holland, St Nicholas is accompanied by whom?
A: His servant Black Peter

Q: What popular Christmas song was actually written for Thanksgiving?
A: Jingle Bells

Q: Complete the title of the John Lennon and Yoko Ono hit Happy Christmas?
A: War is Over

Q: Which crooner originally sang Have Yourself A Merry Christmas and Winter Wonderland?
A: Tony Bennett

Q: What did my true love bring to me on the 7th day of Christmas?
A: Seven swans a swimming

Q: What Christmas song begins Long time ago in Bethlehem, so the Holy Bible Say?
A: Mary's Boy Child

Q: In which country did Jingle Bells originate?
A: America

Q: What group had a massive hit in 1973 with Merry Christmas Everybody?
A: Slade

Q: In what language was the carol Silent Night originally written?
A: German

Q: The biggest selling single of all time is a Christmas song. What is the title and who is the singer?
A: White Christmas—Bing Crosby

Q: Who is Der Weihnachtsmann in Germany?
A: Father Christmas

Q: In China who is Dun Che Lao Ren?
A: Father Christmas

Q: In Mexico who do children send their wish lists to at Christmas time?
A: El Nino Dios (The Holy Child)

Q: In Italy who do children send their wish lists to at Christmas time?
A: Babbo Natale

Q: What ecclesiastic name is given to the 12th day of Christmas?
A: Epiphany

Q: Who wrote the song White Christmas?
A: Irving Berlin

Q: What are the names of Santa's reindeer?
A: Comet, Blitzen, Cupid, Dasher, Dancer, Donner, Prancer and Vixen

Q: How many gold rings are there in the song Twelve Days of Christmas?
A: Five

Q: How many lords a leaping are there in the song Twelve Days of Christmas?
A: Ten

Q: What is frankincense?
A: An aromatic gum resin

Q: What was the occupation of the three wise men?
A: Astrologers

Q: What Wings song was number one at Christmas 1977?
A: The Mull of Kintyre

Q: Who had a Christmas hit with the song All I Want For Christmas Is My Two Front Teeth?
A: Danny Kaye and the Andrew Sisters

Q: In the Christmas story by Dr Seuss who planned to steal Christmas from the Citizens of Whoville?
A: The Grinch

Q: When frankincense is burned what is it known as?
A: Incense

Q: What company in 1931 created Santa Claus as we know him today?
A: Coca Cola

Q: You may come across a furcula in your Christmas dinner. What is it?
A: The wishbone in your turkey

Q: If you arrange Santa's reindeer in alphabetical order, which one comes first and which one comes last?
A: Blitzen and Vixen

Q: What was the name of Tiny Tim's father who worked as a clerk for Scrooge in Dickens' A Christmas Carol?
A: Bob Cratchit

Q: In 1987 Mel Smith and Kim Wilde released which novelty Christmas single?
A: Rockin Around the Christmas Tree

Q: What were the names of the Three Kings?

A: Melchior	King of Arabia	Gold
Casper	King of Tarsus	Frankincense
Balthazar	King of Ethiopia	Myrrh

Q: Christmas pudding should be stirred in a clockwise direction, in whose honour?
A: The Three Kings

Q: Who originally named Santa's reindeer?
A: Clement Moore in 1822

Q: Who created the concept of Santa's workshop and Santa reading letters etc?
A: Thomas Nast in 1863

Q: Which artist created the Santa Claus we know today?
A: Haddon Sunblom in 1931

Q: What festival celebrates the visit of the Magi to the infant Jesus?
A: Epiphany

Q: Christmas pudding should be stirred with a wooden spoon. What does the wooden spoon represent?

A: The manger

Q: If you were born over Christmas, what would your birthstone be?
A: Turquoise

Q: Who told the story of Robin Redbreast who declared I'm going to the king to sing him a sang this fine yule morning?
A: Robert Burns

Q: When is Sowens Night?
A: Christmas Eve

Q: Services of how many lessons and carols are traditional at Christmas?
A: Nine

Q: Which saint is traditionally identified as the model for Father Christmas?
A: Saint Nicholas

Q: What title does Puss assume for his master in the pantomime Puss in Boots?
A: The Marquis of Carabas

Q: Which pre-decimal coin was traditionally included in a Christmas pudding?
A: A silver sixpence

Q: Where in London is the Christmas tree gifted by the people of Norway put up?
A: Trafalgar Square

Q: In Dickens' A Christmas Carol, Scrooge's ghostly ex-partner is called what?
A: Marley

Q: In which pantomime is Dandini a traditional character?
A: Cinderella

Q: Which reindeer is not named in the poem T'was the Night?
A: Rudolph

Q: Which group of comedians sang of Walking Backwards For Christmas?
A: The Goons

Q: Which Roman Emperor's census brought Mary and Joseph to Bethlehem?
A: Augustus Caesar

Q: Which political song is set to the tune of O'Christmas Tree?
A: The Red Flag

Q: Which dish is ceremonially served at Christmas at Queens College Oxford?
A: A boars head

Q: What is the traditional date of Christmas Day in the Russian Orthodox Church?
A: January 7th

Q: Of which country is St Stephen the patron saint?
A: Hungary

Q: Which plant popular at Christmas takes its name from a U.S. ambassador to Mexico?
A: The Poinsettia, from Dr Joel Poinsett in 1882

Q: In which way was the Christmas opera, Amahl and the Night Visitors, a first?
A: It was written for television

Q: Christmas celebrated at Dingley Dell is an episode in which work by Dickens?
A: The Pickwick Papers

Q: Which kind of birds were the four calling birds presented on the 4th day of Christmas?
A: Blackbirds

Q: On which carol did musician Franz Gruber and Priest Joseph Mohr collaborate on Christmas Eve 1818?
A: Silent Night

Q: Where did the domesticated turkey traditionally eaten at Christmas originate?
A: North America

Q: Which saint is honoured in Sweden in December as Queen of Light?

A: St Lucia

Q: Which literary character promised to honour Christmas in his heart and try to keep it all the year?
A: Ebenezer Scrooge

Q: In which Cambridge College has the Festival of Nine Lessons and Carols been held every Christmas Eve since 1918?
A: Kings College

Q: Who had a hit in 1956 with Mary's Boy Child?
A: Harry Belafonte

Q: Candles are lit at Christingle services, but from what are the candle holders made?
A: Oranges

Q: On which Sunday does the Christian season of advent begin?
A: The Sunday nearest November 30th

Q: In 1947 what did Spike Jones and the City Slickers ask for at Christmas in their popular record?
A: Their two front teeth

Q: Wassail derives its name from an old English phrase meaning, what?
A: Good health

Q: According to the hymn, to whom did the angel say the first Nowell (Noel)?
A: The shepherds

Q: Which clown appears in Shakespeare's Twelfth Night?
A: Feste

Q: Which Irving Berlin musical featured a Dream of a White Christmas?
A: Holiday Inn (1942)

Q: What is the date of the Feast of Stephen?
A: 26th December

Q: In which country did the Christmas yule log originate?
A: France

Q: In Portugal at Christmas time what is bacalhau?
A: Dried codfish

Q: Who is the Greek Santa Claus?
A: St Basil

Q: In France at Christmas time what is a buche de Noel?
A: A yule log

Q: On which date is Christmas Day celebrated in Greece?
A: January 1st

Q: Why is plum duff so called?
A: It's a corruption of dough

Q: Why are Christmas hymns called carols?
A: Thought to be adapted from carole, an old word meaning round dance with
   singing

Q: In the Christmas song how many pipers a piping are there?
A: Eleven

Q: Which two animals normally appear in nativity scenes?
A: An ox and an ass

Q: Why do we take our Christmas trees down on the 12th day?
A: The wise men arrived 12 days after Christ's birth

Q: What are the last five words in the song Rudolph the Red Nosed Reindeer?
A: You'll go down in history

Q: Why are they called mince meat pies when they don't contain meat?
A: Originally they contained a mixture of meat and fruit

Q: Why do we wear paper hats at Christmas time?
A: From a Roman custom where masters and slaves swapped
   roles and wore mock crowns for fun

Q: Why was December 25th chosen as the date to celebrate Christmas?
A: It was the date of the winter solstice, a pagan festival

Q: In the Christmas song how many calling birds are there?
A: Four

Q: Who was The Grinch trying to steal Christmas from?
A: The Whos

Q: In which year was Rudolf the Red Nosed Reindeer written?
A: 1939

Q: In which year did Santa's reindeers names first appear in a poem The Night Before Christmas?
A: 1822

Q: What was the occupation of Bob Cratchit?
A: Scrooge's Bookkeeper

Q: How many reindeer did Santa have pulling his sleigh?
A: Eight

Q: Which of the seven dwarfs did not have a beard?
A: Dopey

Q: The song White Christmas comes from which film?
A: Holiday Inn

Q: On which day did the geese lay, in the Twelve Days of Christmas?
A: Sixth

Q: Which three of Santa's reindeers names begin with the letter D?
A: Donner, Dancer and Dasher

Q: Who are Anastasia and Drizella?
A: The ugly sisters

Q: Who was the first singer / actress to fly on stage as Peter Pan ?
A: Anita Harris

Q: Who sang Mary's Boy Child in 1978?
A: Boney M

Q: Which two girls names are contained in the title of a carol?

A: Holly / Ivy

Q: Who wrote the book When the Grinch Stole Christmas?
A: Dr Seuss

Q: Christmas pudding originated as a 14Th century porridge. What was it originally called?
A: Frumenty

Q: In which year was the Christmas carol Silent Night written?
A: 1818

Q: In which year was the Christmas cracker invented?
A: 1847

Q: Why was the Christmas carol Silent Night written to be accompanied by a guitar?
A: The church organ had broken down

Q: What was the original shape of mince pies?
A: Oblong

Q: Why were mince pies originally made oblong?
A: To represent the Baby Jesus's crib

Q: The original mince pies contained three spices, what did they represent?
A: The three gifts given by the three wise men

Q: Who starred in the film Holiday Inn from which we get the song White Christmas?
A: Bing Crosby, Danny Kaye, Rosemary Clooney and Vera Ellen

Q: In the Disney film Snow White and the Seven Dwarfs what were the dwarfs mining fo?r
A: Diamonds

Q: In the film A Muppets Christmas Carol, which home grown actor was the star?
A: Michael Caine (Scrooge)

Q: Which country issued the first Christmas stamp?

A: Austria

Q: At Christmas time why are fairy lights called fairy lights?
A: In the first performance of Gilbert and Sullivan's Iolanthe, the principal fairies had battery operated electric star head-dresses (1882)

Q: In Walt Disney's Pinocchio what was the name of the goldfish?
A: Cleo

Q: In Walt Disney's Pinocchio what was the name of the cat?
A: Figaro

Q: What is unusual about the Cat Who Came for Christmas, a novel by Cleveland Amory?
A: It was named after another animal – the polar bear

Q: In the carol The Twelve Days of Christmas, how many gifts in total did my true love send to me?
A: 364

Q: What was the Christmas song in the James Bond film On Her Majesty's Secret Service?
A: Do you know how Christmas Trees are Grown

Q: In which year did Band Aid's Do They Know It's Christmas first top the charts?
A: 1984

Q: In the Twelve Days of Christmas how many partridges does my true love receive?
A: 12 (because she receives one each day)

Q: Why do we take down our Christmas decorations before the Twelfth Night?
A: It's the eve of the Feast of Epiphany

Q: What is the seasonal significance of meleagris gallopava?
A: It's the scientific name for a turkey

Q: Bing Crosby sang the most famous version of the song White Christmas but who else had a top 30 hit in the UK with the song?
A: Pat Boone

Q: Name four towns or cities beginning with Santa?
A: Santa Cruze, Santa Barbarba, Santa Fe, Santa Monica, Santa Ana, Santa Rosa (etc)

Q: In which collection of stories does the panto character Sinbad the Sailor appear?
A: The Arabian Nights

Q: To where did the Holy Family flee during King Herod's slaughter of the innocents?
A: Egypt

Q: The 1982 Christmas TV animation The Snowman was based on a book by whom?
A: Raymond Briggs

Q: In miles what is the best estimate for the journey from Nazareth to Bethlehem?
A: 70 miles

Q: In which century did the first Christmas card appear?
A: The 19th

Q: Which scientist founded the Royal Christmas Lectures for children ?
A: Michael Faraday

Q: Which Prime Minister appeared in a Morecambe and Wise Christmas special?
A: Harold Wilson

Q: In which city was the first performance of Handel's Messiah heard ?
A: Dublin

Q: What according to tradition was the name of the Virgin Mary's father?
A: Joachim

Q: Erithacus Rubecula is the scientific name for which Christmas symbol?
A: The robin

CHRISTMAS NUMBER 1's

Date	Title	Artist (s)
1950	Rudolph the Red Nosed Rheindeer	Gene Autry
1951	Longing for You	Teresa Brewer
1952	Here in My Heart	Al Martino
1953	Answer Me	Frankie Laine
1954	Lets Have a Party	Winifred Atwell
1955	Christmas Alphabet	Dickie Valentine
1956	Just Walking in the Rain	Johnnie Ray
1957	Mary's Boy Child	Harry Belafonte
1958	It's Only Make Believe	Conway Twitty
1959	What do You Want to Make those Eyes at Me For	Emile Ford
1960	I Love You	Cliff Richard
1961	Moon River	Danny Williams
1962	Return to Sender	Elvis Presley
1963	I Wanna Hold Your Hand	Beatles
1964	I Feel Fine	Beatles
1965	Day Tripper	Beatles
1966	Green Green Grass of Home	Tom Jones
1967	Hello Goodbye	Beatles
1968	Lily the Pink	Scaffold
1969	Two Little Boys	Rolf Harris
1970	I Hear You Knocking	Dave Edmunds
1971	Ernie (The Fastest Milkman in the West)	Benny Hill
1972	Long Haired Lover From Liverpool	Little Jimmy Osmond
1973	Merry Xmas Everybody	Slade
1974	Lonely this Christmas	Mud
1975	Bohemian Rhapsody	Queen
1976	When a Child is Born	Johnny Mathis
1977	Mull of Kintyre	Wings
1978	Mary's Boy Child	Boney M
1979	Another Brick in the Wall	Pink Floyd
1980	There's No-One Quite Like Grandma	St Winifreds School Choir
1981	Don't You Want Me	Human League
1982	Save Your Love	Renee and Renato
1983	Only You	Flying Pickets
Date	Title	Artist (s)
1984	Do They Know it's Christmas	Band Aid

1985	Merry Christmas Everyone	Shaking Stevens
1986	Reet Petite	Jackie Wilson
1987	Always on My Mind	Pet Shop Boys
1988	Mistletoe and Wine	Cliff Richard
1989	Do They Know It's Christmas	Band Aid
1990	Saviours Day	Cliff Richard
1991	Bohemian Rhapsody	Queen
1992	I Will Always Love You	Whitney Houston
1993	Mr Blobby	Mr Blobby
1994	Stay Another Day	East 17
1995	Earth Song	Michael Jackson
1996	2 Become 1	Spice Girls
1997	Too Much	Spice Girls
1998	Good Bye	Spice Girls
1999	I Have a Dream/Seasons in the Sun	Westlife
2000	Can We Fix It	Bob the Builder
2001	Something Stupid	Robbie Williams/ Nicole Kidman
2002	Sound of the Underground	Girls Aloud
2003	Mad World	Gary Jules
2004	Do They Know It's Christmas	Band Aid 20

CITIES and TOWNS

Q: Which is the only city in the world that spans two continents?
A: Istanbul

Q: The name of which South American capital city means good winds?
A: Buenos Aires

Q: Which Italian city lies near the foot of Mount Vesuvius?
A: Naples

Q: What was the former and better known name of the city of Mumbai?
A: Bombay

Q: What was the first town in the world to have a filtered water supply?
A: Paisley

Q: New York is the largest city in America. What is the second largest city?
A: Los Angeles

Q: What is the highest town in Europe?
A: Davos

Q: In which country is the highest town in Europe?
A: Switzerland

Q: What is the oldest still occupied town in the world?
A: Jericho

Q: Apart from Khartoum which other capital city stands on the river Nile?
A: Cairo

Q: What is the capital of Tibet?
A: Lhassa

Q: What town in West Yorkshire shares its name with a major city and port in
   east Canada?
A: Halifax

Q: What is the only capital city to be situated on the equator?
A: Quito

Q: The American city of Las Vegas is Spanish for what?
A: The Meadows

Q: Krung Thep is the capital of which country?
A: Thailand (aka Bangkok)

Q: What is the oldest capital city in the world still occupied?
A: Damascus (In Syria)

Q: Which city is known as La Habana in Spanish?
A: Havana

Q: Which American city is known as the windy city?
A: Chicago

Q: In which city is the only Royal Palace in America?
A: Honolulu

Q: Washington is on the same degree of latitude as which European city?
A: Lisbon

Q: What was the original name of New York?
A: New Amsterdam

Q: In which city was the American constitution signed?
A: Philadelphia

Q: Which ancient city gave its name to a system of weights?
A: Troy

Q: What town was destroyed by Vesuvius?
A: Pompeii

Q: On which river does Washington DC stand?
A: The Potomac

Q: What is the largest city in Africa?
A: Cairo

Q: What European airport is nearest to a city centre?
A: Gibraltar

Q: What is the capital of the state of Tennessee?
A: Nashville

Q: Between which two cities did the first international air service take place in 1919?
A: London and Paris

Q: What is the world's most southerly capital city?
A: Wellington

Q: Which New York street is famous for its theatres?
A: Broadway

Q: In which American city was there a famous tea party in 1773?
A: Boston

Q: Babylon was situated south of which modern day capital city?
A: Baghdad

Q: In which city is the Kremlin?
A: Moscow

Q: What is Europe's most northerly town?
A: Hammerfest

Q: In which city is the Wailing Wall?
A: Jerusalem

Q: What is the capital of the Philippines?
A: Manila

Q: Which capital city's name means meeting of waters?
A: Kuala Lumpur

Q: Which Asian capital city lies on the Red River?
A: Hanoi

Q: Which capital city's name means blackpool?

A: Dublin

Q: What is the capital of Tasmania?
A: Hobart

Q: What is the highest capital city in Europe?
A: Madrid

Q: What is the ancient capital of the Incas?
A: Cuzco

Q: What is the capital of Tanzania?
A: Dodma

Q: Which city is served by Dum-Dum airport?
A: Calcutta

Q: In which city is the United Nations Building?
A: New York

Q: What famous town is virtually dead centre of Australia?
A: Alice Springs

Q: What city is the most heavily populated in Africa?
A: Cairo

Q: What is the largest city in Canada?
A: Toronto

Q: In which city is the world's largest store of uncut diamonds?
A: London

Q: What is the state capital of Alask?a
A: Juneau

Q: In which capital city can you travel on klongs and visit wats?
A: Bangkok

Q: Ragusa was the original name for which modern day European city ?
A: Dubrovnic

Q: Suez lies at one end of the Suez canal. What is the city at the other end?
A: Port Said

Q: What letter do more capital cities start with than any other?
A: B

Q: What is the highest capital city in the world?
A: La Paz

Q: In which European capital city will you find the Vasco da Gamma Bridge?
A: Lisbon

Q: Which city has the widest avenue in the world?
A: Buenos Aires

Q: In which European city does the Red Cross have its headquarters?
A: Geneva

Q: What does the name Singapore mean?
A: City of Lions

Q: In which city is the Trevi Fountain?
A: Rome

Q: In which city is the Moorish Palace of the Alhambra?
A: Granada

Q: What is the capital of the Maldives?
A: Male

Q: What was the first capital city in the world to have its sewage pumped into the sea?
A: London

Q: Which city is furthest from any sea or ocean?
A: Urumqi (China)

Q: In which country is the wettest town on the earth?
A: India (Mawsynram)

Q: What Chinese city is home to the Terracotta Army?

A: Xian

Q: Piraeus is the port of which European city?
A: Athens

Q: What is the most northerly capital city on the European continent?
A: Helsinki

Q: In which city was the first modern skyscraper built?
A: Chicago

Q: What major world capital city lies on the same line of latitude as Edinburgh?
A: Moscow

Q: By what name is the city of Baile Atha Cliath better known?
A: Dublin

Q: Which city is further south, Buenos Aires or Brisbane?
A: Buenos Aires

Q: Where is the coldest town in the world?
A: Siberia

Q: What the coldest town in the world called?
A: Oimyakon

Q: What is the capital of Tenerife?
A: Santa Cruz

Q: In what capital city was Leon Trotsky assassinated?
A: Mexico City

Q: Which European city was almost totally destroyed by an earthquake in 1755?
A: Lisbon

Q: What city is the capital of Brazil?
A: Brasilia

Q: Which Spanish city has a famous art museum that looks like an alien spacecraft?
A: Bilbao

Q: What is the hottest continually inhabited town on the planet?
A: Dallol (Ethiopia)

Q: What is the coldest city in the world?
A: Winnipeg (Canada)

Q: In which country is the driest town on the earth?
A: Chile

Q: What is the driest town on the earth?
A: Arica (Atacama Desert)

Q: In which city in India will you find the Taj Mahal?
A: Agra

Q: Queenstown, the Irish port the Titanic sailed from on her last voyage, is now called what?
A: Cobh

Q: What is the oldest walled city on earth?
A: Jerico

Q: What is Europe's most southerly capital city?
A: Athens

Q: What is Europe's smallest capital city?
A: Valletta

Q: Why is the Bolivian capital of La Paz unique?
A: It is virtually fireproof (because it is so high there is not enough oxygen)

Q: The nearest capitals of two neighbouring countries are what?
A: The Vatican City and Rome

Q: What is the oldest city in America?
A: St Augustine

Q: To what was Saigon renamed in 1976?
A: Ho Chi Min City

Q: What is the second largest city in Austria called?
A: Gaz

Q: Between which two towns in India did the first official airmail service operate?
A: Allahabad and Naini Junction

Q: Which countries' capital cities share the name of their countries?
A: Djibouti, Guatemala, Kuwait and the Vatican

Q: What is the southernmost city in continental America?
A: Key West

Q: What is the largest city in the southern hemisphere?
A: Jakarta

Q: In which city is William Shakespeare's play Measure for Measure set?
A: Vienna

Q: The Arbat is a famous street in which ciy's old quarter?
A: Moscow

Q: What is Bombay in India now called?
A: Mumbai

Q: What is Madras in India now called?
A: Chennai

Q: In 2004 which was the world's largest city?
A: Mexico City

Q: What is the furthest south town in the world?
A: Ushuaia (Near Cape Horn)

Q: The Penny Bridge is a feature in which city?
A: Dublin

Q: What is the most northerly ice-free port in the western hemisphere?

A: Valdez (Alaska)

Q: What is the most northerly city on the planet?
A: Tromso (Norway)

Q: What is the highest village in Europe called?
A: St Vernan (France)

Q: What does the name Shanghai mean?
A: City beside the sea

COLLECTIVE NOUNS

ANIMALS

Animals	Array, Diversity, Menagerie
Antelope	Herd, Cluster, Tribe, Troop
Apes	Shrewdness, Troop
Asses	Pace, Herd, Coffle, Drove, Passel
Baboons	Congress, Troop
Badgers	Cete, Colony
Bats	Colony Roost
Bears	Sloth
Beavers	Colony, Lodge, Family
Bees	Swarm, Cluster
Bison	Herd
Bloodhounds	Sute
Boars	Singular, Sounder
Bucks	Herd, Clash, Brace
Buffalo	Herd, Obstinacy, Gang, Mob
Bullocks	Drove
Camels	Flock, Caravan, Train, Herd
Capybara	Group, Herd
Caribou	Herd
Carnivores	Consolidation
Cats	Clowder, Cluster, Clutter, Glaring, Destruction (Feral or Wild)
Cattle	Herd, Kine, Drove, Drift
Chamois	Herd
Cheetahs (male)	Coalition
Chimpanzees	Group, Troop, Community
Colts	Rag, Rake
Coneys	Bury, Bery, Game
Coral (live)	Colony
Cows	Flink, Herd
Coyotes	Pack, Band, Rout
Crocodiles	Bask, Nest, Float, Congregation
Cubs	Litter
Curs	Cowardice

Deer	Herd, Leash, Parcel, Bevy (Roe Deer)
Dingos	Pack
Dogs	Pack, Kennel
Dolphins	School, Squadron
Donkeys	Herd, Drove, Pace
Eland	Herd
Elephants	Herd, Parade
Elk	Gang, Herd
Ferrets	Business
Flies	Business
Foxes	Leash, Skulk
Frogs	Colony, Army, Knot
Gerbils	Horde
Giraffes	Tower, Herd, Corps
Gnats	Horde, Cloud
Gnu	Herd, Implausibility
Goats	Tribe, Trip, Flock
Gorillas	Band, Woop
Greyhounds	Leash
Guinea Pigs	Group
Hamsters	Horde
Hares	Down, Husk, Leap, Trace and Trip
Harts	Herd
Hedgehogs	Prickle, Array
Hinds	Parcel
Hippopotami	Crash, Bloat, Pod
Hogs	Parcel, Passel, Drove, Sounder
Horses	Harass, Stable, Herd, Remuda, String, Stud
Hounds	Pack, Cry
Hyenas	Clan, Mob
Ibex	Herd
Iguana	Mess
Jackrabbits	Husk
Kangaroo	Mob, Troop, Herd
Killer Whales	Pod, Group, Community
Kittens	Kindle, Intrigue
Lambs	Fall
Lemurs	Clan, Group, Community
Leopards	Leap
Leverets	Kindle
Lions	Pride

Lions	Coalition (of adolescent males)
Lizards	Lounge
Llamas	Herd
Mares	Stud
Meerkats	Family, Clan, Gang, Troop, Team
Mice	Nest, Mischief, Swarm
Moles	Labour, Company, Movement
Mole Rats	Colony
Mongooses	Band, Train (European Mongooses), Gang, Clan
Monkeys	Mission, Tribe, Wilderness, Troop
Mules	Barren, Rake
Otters	Bevy
Piglets	Farrow, Litter
Pigs	Drove, Herd, Sounder
Plankton	Community
Polar Bears	Aurora, Pack
Polecats	Chine
Ponies	String, Herd
Porcupines	Group, Prickle
Possum	Passel
Prairie Dogs	Coterie, Group, Colony, Clan
Rabbits	Bury, Colony, Nest, Infestation
Racehorses	String, Field
Racoons	Gaze
Rats	Colony, Pack, Rabble, Swarm
Rhinoceros	Crash, Herd
Roe Deer	Bevy
Seals	Colony, Raft
Sharks	Shiver
Sheep	Flock, Herd, Drove
Skunks	Surfeit
Squirrels	Colony, Scurry
Stoats	Pack, Trip
Swine	Drift, Sounder, Drove, Herd
Tigers	Ambush, Streak
Voles	Plague, Colony, Complex
Wallabies	Mob, Colony
Wallaroo	Clan
Walrus	Herd
Weasels	Sneak, Pack, Gang
Whales	School, Pod

Wildebeest	Herd
Wild Boar	Sounder
Wild Cats	Dout, Destruction
Wolves	Pack, Rout
Wombats	Mob, Warren
Yaks	Herd
Zebra	Herd, Zeal, Band, Dazzle

BACTERIA, FUNGI, INSECTS, MICROBES

Ants	Colony, Swarm, Army
Bacteria	Culture, Colony
Bees	Girst, Swarm, Hive
Butterflies	Rainbow, Rabble, Kaleidoscope
Caterpillars	Army, Clutch
Cockroaches	Intrusion
Flies	Business, Swarm, Cloud, Grist
Glow Worms	Colony
Gnats	Cloud, Horde, Clout
Grasshoppers	Cloud, Cluster, Swarm, Rabble
Insects	Myriad, Flight, Horde, Plague, Swarm, Proliferation
Lice	Colony, Infestation
Locusts	Plague, Swarm, Cloud
Maggots	Swarm
Microbes	Colony
Midges	Bite
Mites	Acari
Mosquitoes	Scourge
Mushrooms	Troop
Plankton	Community
Social Spiders	Colony
Spiders	Cluster, Clutter, Colony
Termites	Colony
Ticks	Acari
Viruses	Host
Wasps	Nest, Byke
Worms	Squirm

BIRDS

Auks	Colony (on land), Flock (on water), Raft (on water)
Avocet	Colony
Babblers	Colony
Bee Eaters	Colony
Birds	Volery, Flock, Flight
Birds of Paradise	Perch
Bitterns	Sedge
Black Grouse	Lek
Bobolinks	Chain
Budgerigars	Chatter
Bullfinches	Bellowing
Bustards	Flock
Buzzards	Wake
Capercaillies	Tok
Capons	Mews
Caracara	Gang
Chickens	Peep, Brood, Clutch
Choughs	Chattering
Coots	Cover, Raft
Cormorants	Gang, Flight
Cranes	Sedge, Siege, Herd
Crows	Murder, Hover, Storytelling
Curlews	Herd
Dotterel	Trip
Doves	Dole, Flight, Pitying, Prettying
Ducks	Dopping, (Diving) Plump, (Flying) Paddling, (on water) Flush, Raft, Team
Ducks (Eider)	Colony
Dunbirds	Flight, Rush
Dunlin	Fling
Eagles	Convocation
Emus	Mob
Falcons	Cast
Finches	Charm, Trembling, Trimming
Flamingos	Stand, Colony
Flamingo (chicks)	Creche
Gannets	Colony, Company
Geese	Gaggle, Skein (Flying) Flock

Goldfinches	Troubling, Charm, Drum
Goshawks	Flight
Grouse	Covey, Pack, Brood
Guillemots	Bazaar, Colony
Gulls	Colony, Screech, Affliction, Flock
Harrison Hawks	Conglomeration
Hawks	Cast, Kettle
Hens	Brood
Herons	Siege, Flight, Sedge
Hummingbirds	Charm, Chattering, Troubling
Jays	Band, Party, Scold
Keas	Circus, Conspiracy, Gang
Kingfishers	Concentration
Kittiwakes	Colony
Lapwings	Deceit, Desert
Larks	Exaltation, Ascension
Linnets	Parcel
Magpies	Tiding, Charm, Murder, Tribe, Congregation
Mallards	Sord, Lute, Flush
Martins	Richness
Moorhen	Plump
Mudhens	Fleet
Nightingales	Watch
Orioles	Pitch
Ostriches	Herd, Pride, Flock
Owls	Parliament, Stare, Parcel
Oxpeckers	Fling, Flock
Parrots	Company, Pandemonium
Partridges	Covey
Peacocks	Muster, Pride, Ostentation
Pelicans	Pod, Colony, Flock
Penguins	Colony, Creche, Huddle, Raft (swimming), Parcel
Peregrines	Cadge
Pheasants	Bouquet, Covey, Nide, Muster
Pigeons	Loft, Flight
Pigeons (Racing)	Team
Pintail	Knob
Plovers	Congregation, Leash, Wing, Band, Stand
Poultry	Run
Pochard	Rush, Flight, Knob
Ptarmigan	Covey

Puffins	Colony
Quail	Bevy, Covey, Drift
Ravens	Conspiracy, Unkindness, Flock
Ravens	Brood, Roost (adolescents)
Redwing	Crowd
Rheas	Herd
Rooks	Parliament, Building, Clamour
Ruffs	Hill
Sandpipers	Fling
Sea Fowl	Cloud
Seagulls	Flock
Sheldrakes	Doping
Snipe	Walk, Wisp
Sparrows	Host, Quarrel, Ubiquity, Tribe, Colony
Starlings	Murmuration
Storks	Muster, Flight, Colony, Phalanx, (when migrating)
Swallows	Flight
Swans	Bank, Bevy, Whiteness, Wedge (when flying)
Swifts	Flock
Teal	Diving, Spring, Raft
Thrushes	Mutation
Tropicbirds	Flotilla
Turkeys	Raffle, Rafter, Army
Turtledoves	Pitying, Bale, Dule
Vultures	Wake, Colony, Flock, Posse
Waterfowl	Knob, Plump, Raft, Bunch
Weaver Birds	Colony
Widgeon	Coil, Company, Flight
Wildfowl	Trip, Plump
Woodcock	Fall, Covey, Plump, Flight
Woodpeckers	Descent
Wrens	Herd, Flock

FISH AND MOLLUSCS

Angel Fish	Host
Archer Fish	Company, Pack
Barbels	Shoal
Barnacles	Band
Barracuda	Battery, School

Bass	Shoal, Fleet
Blackfish	Grind
Butterfly Fish	School
Clams	Bed
Cockles	Bed
Cod	Shoal, Lap
Coral	Colony of live Coral
Crabs	Horde
Dogfish	Troop
Dolphins	Group
Dragonet Fish	Swarm
Eels	Congregation, Swarm, Cluster
Fish	Shoal, School, Constellation, Drift, Run
Herrings	Glean, Shoal
Invertebrates	Phylum
Jellyfish	Smack, Fluther, Colony
Krill	Swarm
Mackerel	Shoal
Mussels	Bed, Colony
Orca Whales	Team
Perch	Pack
Pilchards	School, Shoal
Plankton	Mass, Wealth, Rain
Porcupine Fish	Cluster
Rainbow Fish	Party
Rays	Pencil, Pod, Group, Squadron
Remora	Squadron, Company
Roach	Shoal
Ruffs	Hill
Salmon	Bind, Run, Leap, Draft
Sardines	Family
Sea Horses	Herd
Sea Urchin	Herd
Shad	Shoal
Sharks	Shiver, School, Shoal, Pack, Gang
Signal Crayfish	Colony
Smelts	Quantity
Starfish	Garden
Sticklebacks	Shoal, Spread
Swordfish	Flotilla
Tadpoles	Mass, Swarm

Trout	Hover, Shoal
Tuna	School
Zander	Shoal, Pack

OBJECTS

Accessories	Range
Accidents	Spate
Actions	Sequence
Activities	Host
Acts	Host
Aerial masts	Outcrop, Plantation
Agreements	Succession
Aircraft	Wing, Squadron, Fleet, Flight
Anecdotes	Anecdotage
Antiques	Wealth, Assemblage
Anti-Aircraft Fire	Curtain
Arrows	Quiver, Hail, Flight, Clouds, Sheaf
Artefacts	Array, Wealth
Artillery	Park
Asteroids	Belt
Attachments	Range
Attractions	Host
Bait (Fishing)	Array, Carpet, Bed
Beads	String
Beakers	Nest
Bells	Peal
Blood Cells	Plethora, Army
Blossom	Riot, Mass
Boats	Cluster
Books	Library
Briefings	Series
Bubbles	Froth, Maelstrom, Cascade, Cauldron, Raft, Cluster
Buildings	Collection
Bullets	Torrent, Storm, Fusillade
Cameras	Battery
Canals	Network
Cards	Pack, Deck, Hand
Cars	Fleet, Convoy, Park

Casinos	Slew
Castles	Network
Catastrophes	String
Cells	Network, Cluster
Changes	Raft
Cheeses	Array
Clouds	Band
Clues	Trail
Coconut Palms	Army
Coins	Rouleau, Roll
Colours	Rainbow, Spectrum, Range, Array
Computers	Network, Arsenal, Array
Concessions	String
Cooperages	Plethora
Costs	Range
Countries	Bloc
Criteria	Range
Curves	Family
Debris	Field
Defences	Arsenal
Delays	Backlog
Demons	Collection
Devastation	Trail
Dispatches	Wealth
Drawers	Chest
Droplets	Spats
Eggs	Clutch, Cluster
E-Mails	Flurry
Equipment	Host, Welter, Cargo
Events	Host, Train
Evidence	Portfolio, Swathe
Excesses	Plethora
Excitement	Frisson
Experiences	Variety
Facts	Flurry
Faults	Catalogue
Fauna	Wealth
Film Clips	Montage
Fingerprints	File
Fires	Series
Floods	Series

Flora	Wealth
Floral Tributes	Carpet
Flowers	Bed, Bunch
Foam	Curtain, Welter, Field
Food	Range
Frauds	String
Frequencies	Range
Froth	Billows
Gadgets	Array
Galleons	Parcel
Gas	Fountain, Sea
Gear	Welter
Goods	Range
Grapes	Bunch
Gunboats	Swarm
Guns	Battery
Habitats	Host
Helicopters	Armada
History	Wealth
Huts	Hutment
Hydrophones	Array
Ideas	Range
Images	Series
Incidents	Spate
Information	Wealth
Initiatives	Parcel
Inventions	Stream
Items	Variety
Jewels	Cache
Kelp	Masses
Keys	Ring, Bunch
Knowledge	Store
Laboratories	System
Landmarks	Series
Leaks	Accumulation
Letters	Wealth
Light	Band
Lights	Array
Lightening	Blitzkrieg
Lorries	Fleet, Convoy
Masts	Forest trees fallen fruits

Measures	Raft
Medals	Raft
Medicines	Armamentaria
Memoranda	Wealth
Messages	Screeds
Missiles	Phalanx
Modifications	Raft
Monitors	Array, Bank
Money	Pile, Wad
Monitors	Bank
Mortars	Phalanx
Mountains	Range, Massif
Musical Notes	Melismata
Mythology	Wealth
Names	Bank
Nations	Galaxy
Negotiators	Teams
Newspaper clippings	Wadge
Objections	Barrage, Wave
Obstacles	Host
Offices	Network
Oil Cans	Compliment
Opportunities	Mass
Patterns	Array
Pearls	String, Rope
Plants	Drifts
Predators	Hordes
Presents	Host
Problems	String, Range
Property	Portfolio
Postponements	Welter
Protests	Storm
Rags	Bundle
Railway Carriages (coupled together)	Rake
Rain Showers	Scattering
Rain	Band, Sheets, Swathe
Reasons	Multiplicity
Reeds	Clump
Reefs	Tangle
Remembrance	Catalogue

Replicas	Host
Reports	Series, String
Resources	Armamentaria
Restaurants	Plethora
Riches	Embarrassment
Ropes	Web
Rosaries	Murmuring
Sailing Cutters	Flutter
Sails	Suite
Salmon fisheries	Plethora
Satellites	Constellation, System
Scaffolding	Swathe
Scents	Melee
Sea Ice	Sheets
Seaweed	Raft
Sensations	Series
Sensors	Banks, Network
Sheets of Paper	Fascicle
Shifts	Variety
Ships	Fleet, Armada, Flotilla
Shops	Arcade
Sightings	Rash
Shops	Arcade, Array, Complex
Sloops	Flutter
Small Ships	Assemblage, Shoal
Smokehouses	Plethora
Sonar Buoys	Field
Sonar Hits	Cluster
Sorrow	Catalogue
Species	Host, Group
Speed Bumps	Rash
Stars	Galaxy, Constellation, Nursery
Statues	Confusion
Steam Engines	Diversity
Steps	Flight
Stores	Array, Complex
Streets	Maze
Subjects	Diversity
Suggestions	Abundance
Surfaces	Family
Talents	Multitude

Targets	Range
Tasks	Multitude
Techniques	Barrage
Tentacles	Ancillary
Tents	Tentage
Tests	Battery
Thoughts	Cascade
Tomatoes	Plantation
Tragedies	Spate
Transgressions	Catalogue
Trees	Forest, Grove, Stand, Clump
Tunes	Medley
Umbrellas	Sea
Uniforms	Flock
Vaults	Network
Views	Range
Warships	Cluster, Fleet, Armada, Squadron
Warplanes	Wave, Squadron, Flight, Fleet
Water Holes	Chain
Water Lilies	Carpet
Waves	Wake
Weapons	Arsenal
Wildlife	Wealth
Wine	Selection, Cellar
Wreckage	Field

PEOPLE

Academics	Faculty
Accountants	Balance
Activists	Cadre
Actors	Cast, Company
Agents	Network
Aides	Cluster, Team
Ambassadors	Host
Ancestors	Legacy
Anglers	Gang
Architects	Team
Armed Forces	Coalition
Arsonists	Conflagration

Artists	Circle
Assassins	Band
Assistants	Army
Athletes	Team, Host
Attorneys	Coven
Authors	Team
Barons	Thought
Bellringers	Gang
Bishops	Bench
Bookkeepers	Audit
Boarders (pirates etc.)	Swarm, Party
Bridegrooms	Gaggle
Brilliant Persons	Galaxy
Bureaucrats	Shuffle, Posse
Candidates	Slate
Cardinals	Conclave, Consistory
Celebrities	Host, Posse
Chefs	Brigade
Climbers	Team
Cobblers	Drunkship
Colleagues	String, Throng
Commentators	Collection
Conquerors	Hordes
Conservationists	Community
Consultants	Cadre
Contributors	Fellowship
Courtiers	Threatening
Craftsmen	Army, Team
Criminals	Body
Critics	Chorus
Dancers	Troupe
Directors	Board
Doctors	Doctrine
Dodgers	Assortment
Drivers	Army
Employees	Staff
Enthusiasts	Gathering
Experts	Panel, Pool
Fans	Legion
Friars	Scull
Ghosts	Collection

Grandparents	Wisdom
Guards	Army, Squadron
Harpists	Melody
Hoodlums	Gang
Horsemen	Cavalcade, Troop
Humanity	Flood
Husbands	Multiply
Immigrants	Band
Instrumentalists	Orchestra
Insurgents	Ranks
Intellectuals	Intelligentsia
Invaders	Wave
Investigators	Army
Journalists	Passel
Judges	Bench
Jugglers	Neverthriving
Jurors	Array
Knights	Banner, Rout, Troop
Lawyers	Huddle
Lepers	Colony
Listeners	Audience
Maharajas	Multiplicity
Magicians	Circle, Host
Magistrates	Bench
Marines	File, Cordon, Team
Mathematicians	Number, Set
Members	Gathering
Men	Band, Cluster
Miners	Colony
Minstrels	Troupe
Models (Human)	Tableau
Mothers	Gaggle
Motionless Figures	Tableau
Mourners	Cortege
Musicians	Group, Army, Band, Orchestra
Natives	Tribe
Negotiators	Team
News Media	Swarm
Nuns	Superfluity
Objectors	Raft
Officers	Parcel, Host, Audience, Suit

Onlookers	Crowd
Painters	Illusion
Passengers	Flow, Droves, Group
Patients	Wave, Waiting List
People	Crowd, Race, Pool, Press, Coterie, Knot, Mass, Multitude
People with shared interests	Coterie
Performers	Troupe
Philosophers	Ponder
Photographers	Posse
Pilgrims	Group
Pipers	Circle, Parade
Police	Posse
Politicians	String
Porters	Flock
Preachers	Converting
Priests	Pontification
Princes	State
Prisoners	Hall, House
Privateers	Swarm
Pundits	Collection
Refugees	String
Reinforcements	Army
Reporters	Passel, Hive, Horde
Rescuers	Armada
Researchers	Group, Team
Rogues	Assortment
Runners	Field
Sailors	Crew, Company (on a warship), Troop
Savages	Horde
Scoutmasters	Pack
Scribes	Flock
Senators	House
Servants	Obesiance, Staff
Singers	Chorus
Slaves (Shackled)	Coffle
Soldiers	Division, Brigade, Battalion, Company, Platoon, Troop
Spectators	Audience
Spies	Ring

Spiritual Gurus	Team
Staff	Host, Team
Students	Class
Supporters	Raft, Crowd, Network
Survivors	Stream, Horde
Suspects	Cast
Tailors	Disguising
Taverners	Glozing
Teachers	Cadre
Technicians	Team
Terrorists	Cell
Thieves	Den, Gang
Tourists	Flock, Influx, Cluster
Traders	Variety
Trainers (racehorses)	Family
Troops	Parel
Vendors	Army
Vicars	Prudence
Victims	List, Army
Viewers	Hordes
Visitors	Droves, Influx
Volunteers	Group, Army
Widows	Ambush
Witches	Coven, Sabbath
Women	Plague
Worshippers	Congregation
Workers	Army, Wealth, Team, Force
Writers	Circle
Yeomen	Fellowship

MISCELLANEOUS

Accents	Melange
Actions	Series
Activity	Flurry, Maelstrom
Adventures	String
Ailments	Host
Alerts	Series
Anecdotes	Anecdotage
Anger	Torrent

Angles	Range
Anomalies	String
Antics	String
Apparatus	Maze
Areas	Raft
Arguments	Assembly
Atrocities	Litany
Attacks	Series, String
Attractions	String
Auditions	String
Bangs	Crescendo
Beehives	Apiary
Bets	Flurry
Blows	Avalanche
Blunders	String, Catalogue
Books	Procession
Bubbles	Train
Buildings	Nest
Challenges	Set, Variety
Changes	Raft, Tide, Series
Choices	Embarrassment
Chromosomes	Genome
Circumstances	Series
Clicks	Series
Clues	Abundance
Cold cooked meats	Charcuterie
Collective Nouns	Catch
Colours	Array, Combination, Range
Commands	Series
Companies	Web
Complaints	Raft, Catalogue, Flood, Spate
Complications	Succession
Computer Folders	Hierarchy
Conditions	Range
Conflicts	Spectrum
Convictions	String
Countries	Coalition
Cries	Host
Crimes	Catalogue
Criticism	Chorus
Customs	Wealth

Dangers	Raft
Data	Wealth, Stream, Accumulation
Deals	String, Range
Debris	Scatter, Spray
Decisions	Spectrum
Delays	Series
Descriptions	Variety
Destructive Forces	Rain
Details	Myriad
Diets	Rash
Disappointments	Series
Duties	Breadth
Electrons	Flow
Entertainment	Pabulum
Errors	Catalogue
Events	Sequence
Evidence	Mountain
Excursions	Series
Experiences	Corporation
Expletives	String
Explosions	Series, Succession
Expressions	Mixture
Facts	Accumulation
Failures	Cascade, Avalanche, Catalogue
Firms	Host
Flames	Stream, Welter
Flavours	Complexity
Garden Plants	Profusion
Gathering	Assemblage
Gears	Train
Gestures	Range
Grapes	Cluster
Guesses	Variation
Gunfire	Cacophony
Historical documents	Archives
History	Wealth
Homework	Slew
Hotel rooms	Blur
Household linen	Napery
Humorous remarks	Facetiae
Ideas	Spectrum, Wealth

Impediments	Vagary
Impressions	Blur
Incidents	String
Influences	Mixture
Information	Wealth, Mass, Harvest, Mine, Avalanche
Injuries	Litany
Innovations	Series
Intellectual matter	Pabulum
Intelligence	Wealth
Interest	Flood
Islands	Chain, Archipelago
Issues	Range, Host, Floodgate, Spectrum
Items	Variety
Joints	Articulation
Jokes	Diversion
Knowledge	Arena, Bank, Storehouse, Repository
Landmarks	Progression
Languages	Phylum
Lawsuits	Avalanche
Measures	Series, Raft, Range, Package
Missiles	Battery
Mistakes	Litany
Movement	Blur, Flurry
Muscle fibres	Fasciculus (also of nerves)
Museums	Cluster
Musical notes	Gamut, Melismata
Names	Passel
Nations	Comity
Naval charts	Folio
Nerve cells	Network
Noise	Tumult, Cacophony
Nostalgia	Feast
Numbers	Sequence
Objections	Raft, Wave
Occasions	Scores
Offences	String
Opinions	Spectrum, Hue
Opportunities	Variety
Opposition	Wave
Orders	Hubbub
Outrage	Storm

Panic	Wave
Passages	Labyrinth
Performances	String
Poems	Anthology
Policies	Range, Issue, Raft
Possibilities	Range
Power	Pool
Priorities	Raft
Prizes	Host
Problems	Catalogue, Complex, Collection
Proposals	Range
Prose	Anthology
Protests	Wave, Storm
Proverbs	Paroemiography
Quantity	Slew
Questions	Variety, Sea
Quizzes	Run, Range
Rebuttals	Quiver
Reefs	Tangle
Revelations	Series
Resources	Abundance, Range
Responses	Array
Rubbish	Dump, Heap, Tip
Sacrifices	Hecatomb
Sanctions	Range
Sayings	Ana
Scandals	List, Spate
Scents	Library
Seaweed	Tangle (of brown seaweed)
Secrecy	Culture
Securities	Slew
Senses	Repertoire
Sequences	Kaleidoscope
Services	Range
Setbacks	Sequence, Series
Shadows	Toss
Shot from guns	Storm
Shootings	Spate
Shouts	Hue
Situations	Host
Skills	Abundance

Smells	Waft
Smoke	Plumes
Sounds	Repertoire, Melee, Cacophony
Sources	Variety
Sparks	Stream, Shower, Welter
Species	Diversity, Multitude
Speeches	Array
Standards	Criteria
Stars	Host
Stores	Burden
Stories	Barrage
Strikes	Series
Styles	Variety
Subjects	Diversity
Successes	Range
Symptoms	Range, Manifestation
Talents	Alchemy, Combination, Pabulum
Tasks	Agenda, Series
Techniques	Batter
Territories	Swathe
Tests	Battery
Thefts	String, Spate
Theme Nights	Array
Things	Bunch, Mixture, Combination
Thoughts	Collection, Series
Tongues	Melange
Traffic Lights	Forest
Uncertainties	Cauldron
Vandalism	Wave
Vegetation	Bounty
Verbs	Mood
Views	Diversity
Wagers	Book
Waves	Wake
Weapons	Cache
Weather Conditions	Range
Weather Zones	Diversity
Whistles	Crescendo
Wit	Stream
Work	Backlog
Wreckage	Raffle

COMPANIES

Q: Which shipping company owned the Titanic?
A: The White Star Line

Q: Which company was founded as Fabrica Italania Automobilein Torina in 1935?
A: Fiat

Q: Which company originally launched the Jaguar car in 1935?
A: The Swallow Sidecar Company

Q: Which European car manufacturer's name is Latin for let it be done?
A: Fiat

Q: Which Italian motor manufacturer specialised in tractors before building cars?
A: Lamborghini

Q: What does M F I stand for?
A: Mullard Furniture Industries

Q: What do the letters B&Q stand for in the name of the D I Y store?
A: Richard Block and David Quale

Q: Which Japanese company did Thomas Blake Glover, a Scotsman from Fraserburgh and founder of the modern Japanese navy and shipbuilding company owner found?
A: Mitsubishi

Q: Which Italian company began making typewriters 1908?
A: Olivetti

Q: The name of which car manufacturer comes from two words meaning Japan Industry?
A: Nissan (From Nihon Sangyo)

Q: The name of which motor car manufacturing company is derived from the

Latin for I Roll?
A: Volvo

Q: Which car manufacturer gets its name from Japanese words meaning three diamonds?
A: Mitsubishi

Q: In modern Korean what does Hyundai mean?
A: Modern

Q: What do the three M's stand for in the company's name that make Scotch sticky tap?e
A: Minnesota Mining and Manufacturing

Q: From where does the name Nike come from in the company who make the sports shoes?
A: The Greek Goddess of Victory

Q: In the oil and petrol company Texaco what does Texaco stand for?
A: Texas Oil Company

Q: In the company Black and Decker who were Black and Decker?
A: Its founders Duncan Black and Onzo Decker

Q: Which company made the Univac 1, the world's first commercially available computer?
A: Remington Rand

Q: Which company introduced cable television ?
A: The Zenith Radio Corporation

Q: Which company was the first to make Seagull outboard engines?
A: The Sunbeam Motorcycle Company

Q: Which company employed the world,s first door to door salesmen?
A: Wedgwood and Bentley (pottery makers)

Q: What company manufactured the tyres for the first car to break the 100kph (62mph) barrier in 1899?
A: Michelin

Q: What is the largest commercial airfreight company in the world?
A: FedEx

Q: What was the name of the world's first commercial airline?
A: DeLag (Using Count Zepplin's airships)

Q: Which is the worlds longest surviving goldmine?
A: The homestead goldmine (Dakota USA)

Q: Which company was the parent company of Saab aircraft?
A: Bofors

Q: What does Esso stand for?
A: Eastern Seaboard Standard Oil

Q: What do the initials of the IBM company stand for?
A: International Business Machines

Q: Which company assembled and serviced Sir Clive Sinclair's C5 electric car?
A: Hoover

Q: Which electronics company's name means sound?
A: Sony

Q: Which company made the 4360 the largest piston engine ever made for an aircraft ?
A: Pratt and Whitney

Q: How did the company Tesco get its name?
A: Tes from the first tea supplier T.E. Stockwell and Co from the founder's first name Jack Cohen

Q: What do the initials of the courier delivery company TNT stand for?
A: Thomas Nationwide Transport

COMPOSERS

Q: Who wrote the opera from which the melody known as Here Comes the Bride comes?
A: Wagner

Q: Who composed the Bolero?
A: Maurice Ravel

Q: Who composed the Four Seasons?
A: Antonio Lucio Vivaldi

Q: Who composed Happy Birthday To You?
A: Clayton F. Summy

Q: Who composed the Trumpet Voluntary ?
A: Purcell

Q: Who composed the tango Jealousy?
A: Jacob Gade

Q: Who composed the tango La Cumparsita?
A: G. M. Rodriguez

Q: Who composed the Moonlight Sonata?
A: Beethoven

Q: When Irish Eyes are Smiling, was written by George Gaffe. What nationality was he?
A: German

Q: Who wrote La Boheme?
A: Puccini

Q: What does Gustave Holst call The Bringer of Old Age?
A: Saturn

Q: Mozart composed the opera The Marriage of Figaro. What opera featuring the same character was composed by Rossini?
A: The Barber of Seville

Q: Who composed Twinkle Twinkle Little Star?
A: Mozart

Q: Which Italian composed the William Tell Overture?
A: Rossini

Q: Who composed the opera Finlandia?
A: Jean Sibelius

Q: What geographical feature is immortalised in music by Mendelssohn?
A: Fingal's Cave

Q: Who wrote the words for Ave Maria?
A: Sir Walter Scott

Q: Who composed the opera Tosca?
A: Giacomo Puccini

Q: What was Giacomo Puccini's last opera?
A: Turandot

Q: Who was the most recorded conductor in musical history ?
A: Herbert von Karajan

Q: Who composed the opera Die Fledermaus?
A: Strauss

Q: Who composed the Enigma Variations?
A: Elgar

Q: Who wrote Nobody's Child?
A: Cy Coben (1969)

Q: Which opera was composed by Verdi to commemorate the opening of the Suez Canal?
A: Aida

Q: Which is the most famous piece of music in the opera The Tale of the Tsar?
Sultan
A: The Flight of the Bumble Bee?

Q: From which opera do we get the Bridal Chorus?
A: Wagner's Lohengrin

Q: Which Gilbert and Sullivan operetta has the subtitle The King of Barataria?
A: The Gondoliers

Q: Which famous piece of music was composed in 1717 to be used as an
accompaniment to a river procession?
A: Handel's Water Music

Q: Which 1878 opera was alternatively entitled The Lass Who Loved A Sailor?
A: HMS Pinafore

Q: What was the alternative title of the Gilbert and Sullivan operetta The
Pirates of Penzance?
A: A Slave of Duty

Q: What is the text of an opera or operetta called?
A: The Libretto

Q: Who composed the Warsaw Concerto?
A: Richard Addingsell

Q: Who composed Rule Britannia?
A: James Thomson

Q: Who composed the opera Fandango?
A: Hans Werner Henze

Q: Who composed the opera Bonducain in 1695 from which we get Rule
Britannia?
A: Purcell

Q: Who composed the opera Rigoletto?
A: Verdi

Q: Which 1951 opera by Benjamin Britten is set on the warship HMS

Indomitable during the Nepoleonic Wars?
A: Billy Budd

Q: Which German composer wrote the opera Parsifal?
A: Richard Wagner

Q: Which Russian composer wrote the unfinished opera Prince Igor?
A: Aleksander Borodin

Q: Which German composer wrote Italian and Scottish symphonies?
A: Felix Mendelssohn

Q: Which German composer wrote the opera The Flying Dutchman?
A: Richard Wagner

Q: Which German composer wrote the Mass in D' Missa Solemnis?
A: Ludwig van Beethoven

Q: Which Puccini opera was unfinished at his death?
A: Turandot

Q: What is the British name for Wagner's opera Der Fliegende Hollander?
A: The Flying Dutchman

Q: Which U.S. composer wrote the music for the ballets Billy the Kid and Rodeo?
A: Aaron Copeland

Q: Who wrote the music for the Threepenny Opera?
A: Kurt Weill

Q: Which Italian composer wrote Stabat Mater?
A: Giovanni Pergolesi

Q: Which French composer wrote the Symphonie Fantastique?
A: Hector Berlioz

Q: Which French composer wrote Harold in Italy?
A: Giacomo Meyerbeer

Q: Who composed the French National Anthem La Marseillaise?

A: Claude Joseph Rouget de Lisle

Q: Which French composer wrote The Sorcerer's Apprentice?
A: Paul Dukas

Q: Which Russian composer wrote Scherherazade?
A: Nikolai Rimsky-Korsakov

Q: Who wrote the orchestral suite The Planets?
A: Gustav Holst

Q: Which German composer wrote the opera Salome?
A: Richard Strauss

Q: Who composed Orpheus in the Underworld?
A: Jacques Offenbach

Q: Which German composer wrote the opera Der Rosenkavalier?
A: Richard Strauss

Q: Which of Tchaikovsky's ballets features the Waltz of the Flowers?
A: The Nutcracker

Q: Who composed the Tales of Hoffman?
A: Jacques Offenbach

Q: Who composed the opera the Merry Widow?
A: Franz Lehar

Q: Who composed the opera Don Giovanni?
A: Mozart

Q: Who composed the music for the Nutcracker Suite?
A: Tchaikovsky

Q: Who composed the music for the Sleeping Beauty?
A: Tchaikovsky

Q: Who composed the music for Serenade?
A: Tchaikovsky?

Q: From 1948 when Israel was established as a country, whose music has been banned?
A: Richard Wagner

Q: Who composed the Magic Flute?
A: Mozart

COUNTRIES

Q: What is the highest country in the world?
A: Nepal

Q: What do the Egyptians call Egypt?
A: Misr

Q: What does the name Canada mean?
A: A settlement

Q: What is the largest country in the world?
A: Russia

Q: What is the second largest country in the world?
A: Canada

Q: Which three countries comprise Scandinavia?
A: Denmark, Norway and Sweden

Q: Which Sovereign State came into being in 1929 as copies of the Lateran Treaty were being exchanged in Rome?
A: The Vatican City

Q: Where is the longest underground cave system in the world?
A: Nohoch Nah Chich (Mexico-Yucatan)

Q: In which country will you find the world's highest railway station ?
A: Bolivia (Condor 4,787mtrs)

Q: What country, which forms part of Lapland, contains the greatest number of Lapps?
A: Norway

Q: Give the modern names for the countries formerly, Abyssinia, Siam and Burma?
A: Ethiopia, Thailand and Myanmar

Q: Bharat is the ancient Hindi name for which former British Colony?
A: India

Q: Where was the first Hydrogen bomb exploded?
A: Eniwetok Atoll (in the Pacific Ocean)

Q: Of which country is Fiordland the largest national park?
A: New Zealand

Q: In which country is the source of the Amazon?
A: Peru

Q: What is the largest natural harbour in the world ?
A: Pearl Harbour

Q: Where is the world's biggest seaport?
A: Rotterdam

Q: If you sailed west from Lands End and followed the same line of latitude, which country will you reach first?
A: Canada

Q: Where is the world's deepest natural harbour?
A: Mahon (Menorca)

Q: If you fly due east from New York, which European country will you fly across first?
A: Portugal

Q: Where does the skeleton of Pizzaro lie?
A: Lima

Q: Yellowish brown raw cane sugar is called Demerara sugar after the region where it is produced. Where is Demerara?
A: Guyana (South America)

Q: Bad Water is the western hemisphere's lowest point. Where can it be found?
A: Death Valley (California)

Q: Where can the largest collection of snakes in the world be found?

A: Chapell Island (SE Australia)

Q: Gebel-al-Tarik is now known as which British possession?
A: Gibraltar

Q: Name two European countries which have both a Mediterranean and Atlantic coastline?
A: France and Spain

Q: Between which two points on a map or globe does a meridian run?
A: The North and South Poles

Q: High latitudes are regions near the poles, but where will you find low latitudes ?
A: Regions near the equator

Q: Geographically where in the world are the four corners of the earth?
A: Ireland, south east of the cape of Good Hope, west of the Peruvian coast and between New Guinea and Japan

Q: Where is the worlds largest sand mass?
A: Fraser Island (SE Australia)

Q: What country lies between Algeria and Libya?
A: Tunisia

Q: What country's name means Land of Silver?
A: Argentina

Q: What country has the highest rate of animal extinction?
A: Australia

Q: In which country does the river Danube rise?
A: Germany (In the Black Forest)

Q: From which country did Panama declare its independence in 1903?
A: Colombia

Q: Of which country is a Candiot a native?
A: Crete

Q: In what country was bingo first played?
A: Italy

Q: What country has the oldest parliament?
A: Iceland

Q: What country suffers more lightening strikes than any other?
A: America

Q: In which country can you visit the ruins of the Aztec civilisation?
A: Mexico

Q: In which country did the thuggee operate, from which we derive the word thug?
A: India

Q: What country has no railways or army?
A: Iceland

Q: What was the first country to use number plates on cars?
A: France

Q: What was the first country to place a man made object on the moon?
A: Russia (USSR)

Q: Which republic lies between Poland and Hungry?
A: Slovakia

Q: What country has as its joint heads of state a Spaniard and a Frenchman?
A: Andorra

Q: In what country did polo originate?
A: Iran

Q: In which country did stamp collecting originat?e
A: France

Q: What is the only French speaking republic in the Americas?
A: Haiti

Q: In which European country is the port of Malmo?

A: Sweden

Q: What country will lose its independence once there is no heir to the throne?
A: Monaco

Q: What country is the only Grand Duchy in the world?
A: Luxembourg

Q: In which country was the world's first oil refinery built
A: Scotland (Pumpherston)

Q: What Scandinavian country extends farthest north?
A: Norway

Q: White Russia is an alternative name for which country in Eastern Europe?
A: Belarus

Q: Cape Trafalgar, where the famous battle of 1805 took place, is off the coast of which country?
A: Spain

Q: What was the first country to abolish capital punishment ?
A: Austria (1787)

Q: In which country will you find the Sutherland Falls?
A: New Zealand

Q: What is the only country in the world to have every climate?
A: New Zealand

Q: What country has no rivers?
A: Saudi Arabia

Q: What country has 845 languages, more than any other country in the world?
A: India

Q: What country has taken its name from a line of latitude?
A: Ecuador

Q: What two countries contain continental Europe's only active volcanoes?
A: Italy and Iceland

Q: What country has the longest coastline?
A: Canada

Q: What country has the shortest coastline?
A: Monaco

Q: What African country is closest to Italy?
A: Tunisia

Q: In which country can you visit the Great Slave Lake?
A: Canada

Q: What country's name means The Saviour?
A: El Salvador

Q: In which modern country will you locate the source of the river Rhine?
A: Switzerland

Q: What country lies immediately to the south of Egypt?
A: The Sudan

A: What land locked republic lies between Russia and China?
A: Mongolia

Q: In which country is the port of Archangel?
A: Russia

Q: In which country does the Amazon reach the sea?
A: Brazil

DESERTS

Q: The Takala desert, the place from which there is no return, is found where?
A: China

Q: The Negev desert is located where in the Middle East?
A: Israel

Q: In which country is the Atacama desert?
A: Chile

Q: What is the largest true sand desert in the world?
A: The Rub al Khali (Saudi Arabia)   (the empty quarter)

Q: What is the world's most northerly desert?
A: The Gobi

Q: Where is the world's largest sand ridged desert?
A: Australia

Q: What is the name of the worlds largest sand ridged desert?
A: The Simpson (Australia)

Q: The Kalahari desert is the worlds largest what?
A: Unbroken sand mass

Q: What large desert is situated in Botswana?
A: The Kalahari

Q: Where are the oldest desert sands in the world?
A: Namibia's Skeleton Coast

Q: Where is the driest sand desert in the world?
A: Namibia's Skeleton Coast

Q: What is the driest desert in the world?
A: The Atacama (In Chile)

Q: What is the largest desert in the world?
A: Antarctica

Q: Where can the smallest desert in the world be found?
A: Canada (in Alaska along the Kobuk river)

DRINK

Q: In which country was gin first produced?
A: Holland

Q: What drink is stored in a bodega?
A: Sherry

Q: What liqueur can be yellow, green or clear and was created by Carthusian Monks?
A: Chartreuse

Q: What evergreen tree's berries are used to flavour gin?
A: The Juniper

Q: How many types of grapes can be used to make champagne?
A: Three (Chardonny, Pinot Meunier and Pinot Noir)

Q: Grenadine is a syrup made from which fruit?
A: Pomegranates

Q: How old is brandy or port marked V S O P?
A: 25 years

Q: What staple foodstuff is the main ingredient of the Japanese drink sake?
A: Rice

Q: What is the name of the grape of Beaujolais?
A: The Gamay

Q: What drink does pear juice make?
A: Perry

Q: What type of drink is pisco?
A: A white brandy made in Peru from Muscat grapes

Q: What is pekoe?
A: A high quality black tea

Q: What is added to mineral water to make tonic water?
A: Quinine

Q: What name is given to the study of wines?
A: Oenology

Q: What well known drink was originally called Usquebaugh?
A: Whisky

Q: Which French liqueur has a strong anise taste?
A: Absinthe

Q: From what fruit is the spirit kirsch made?
A: Cherries

Q: Translated from the Gaelic what does Drambuie mean?
A: The drink which satisfies

Q: Which blended whisky features all seven of Islay's malts?
A: Black Bottle

Q: If whisky is matured in a cask, what is port matured in?
A: A pipe

Q: If whisky is matured in a cask, what is sherry matured in?
A: A butt

Q: If whisky is matured in a cask, what is madeira matured in?
A: A drum

Q: In whisky distilling, what does the term wood finish mean?
A: Re-filling casks that previously held other wines and spirits

Q: What does the Scotch whisky name Auchentoshan mean in Gaelic?
A: Corner of the field

Q: It means Aunt Mary in our language but by what name do we know this drink?
A: Tia Maria

Q: What flavour is Grand Marnier liqueur ?
A: Orange

Q: What flavour is the liqueur triple sec?
A: Orange

EXPLORATION and NAVIGATION

Q: What do you call the disturbance to a ship's compass at the poles where the earth's diameter is smallest?
A: The Coriolis Effect

Q: Shackleton used three lifeboats as sledges after his ship the Endurance was crushed in the ice in 1915. What were their names?
A: Dudley Docker, Janet Stancombe Willis and James Caird

Q: Shackleton's ship the Endurance was trapped in the ice in January 1915. What was her original name?
A: The Polaris

Q: In August 1916 Shackleton returned to Elephant Island on a Chilean steam tug to rescue his crew. What was the name of the tug?
A: The Yelcho

Q: Who was the first explorer to cross the Antarctic Circle?
A: Captain James Cook

Q: What was crossed on foot for the first time in 1968-69?
A: The North Pole

Q: Who reached the magnetic South Pole first in 1909?
A: Alistair Forbes MacKay

Q: Whose expedition was Alistair Forbes MacKay a member of when he reached the Magnetic South Pole in 1909?
A: Ernest Shackleton

Q: In what year did Amundsen and Scott reach the South Pole?
A: 1912

Q: What navigational instrument is shaped in an arc of the sixth part of a circle?
A: A sextant

Q: What was the first expedition to Antarctica to make extensive use of a radio?
A: The Byrd Expedition of 1929 (to fly to the South Pole)

POINTS OF A COMPASS

Moving Clockwise

North 0 Degrees

Direction	Degrees	Direction	Degrees
N by E	11°	S by W	191°
N N E	22°	S S W	202°
N E by N	33°	S W by S	213°
N E	45°	S W	225°
N E by E	56°	S W by W	236°
E N E	67°	W S W	247°
E by N	78°	W by S	258°
E 90	W		270°
E by S	101°	W by N	281°
E S E	112°	W N W	292°
S E by E	123°	N W by W	303°
S E	135°	N W	315°
S E by S	146°	N W by N	326°
S S E	157°	N N W	337°
S by E	168°	N by W	348°
S	180°	N by W	360°

A compass is diveded into 32 points each of 11° degrees

Cardinal points   N S E W

Half cardinal points   N E   S E   S W   N W

The remaining twenty-four divisions being full points

FESTIVALS

Q: What is Rosh Hashana?
A: The Jewish new year

Q: The name of which Jewish holiday means Day of Atonement?
A: Yom Kippur

Q: What does Mardi Gras mean?
A: Fat Tuesday

Q: Which annual Festival of Drama and Art was founded in 1947 by Rudolf Bing?
A: The Edinburgh Festival

Q: What does a native of India celebrate at Burra Din?
A: Christmas

Q: What is the Jewish celebration A Festival of Lights called?
A: Hanukkah (also Chanukkah)

Q: What name is given to the Jewish spring festival commemorating the liberation of the Israelites from Egyptian bondage?
A: The Passover

Q: What name is given to the Jewish festival held fifty days after the second day of the Passover, originally a harvest festival, but now also commemorating the giving of the Torah?
A: Shavuot (Also Shavuoth)

Q: What name is given to the Jewish new year?
A: Rosh Hashana (Also Rosh Hashanah)

Q: In which month is Rosh Hashana celebrated by Jewish people?
A: The First Day of Tishri in September (Sometimes the second day)

Q: What in the Jewish calendar is Tishri?
A: The first month of the civil and seventh of the religious year

Q: The most solemn Religious Fast of the Jewish Year and the last ten days of penitence that began with Rosh Hashana is known as what?
A: Yom Kippur (Day of Atonement)

Q: Which Jewish festival commemorates the sheltering of the Israelites in the wilderness?
A: Succoth (Also Tabernacles)

Q: What do the Vietnamese people celebrate at Tet?
A: The new year

Q: In India what does the festival of Saka celebrate?
A: The new year

FICTIONAL and CARTOON CHARACTERS

Q: Alexander Selkirk was the inspiration for which fictional character?
A: Robinson Crusoe

Q: Whose nephews were Huey, Dewey and Louie?
A: Donald Duck

Q: Which hobby was taken up by Sherlock Holmes in his retirement?
A: Bee keeping

Q: What was the name of Dick Turpin's horse?
A: Black Bess

Q: Who was the minstrel in Robin Hood's band of merry men?
A: Alan A'Dale

Q: The name Pinocchio derives from the Italian for what?
A: Pine Seed

Q: Which of Disney's seven dwarfs does not have a beard?
A: Dopey

Q: Can you name Batman's three male arch rivals?
A: The Penguin, The Riddler and the Joker

Q: Who was Bugs Bunny's old enemy?
A: Yosemite Sam

Q: Which of Disney's seven dwarfs wears glasses?
A: Doc

Q: Which character,s chief opponent was Carl Peterson?
A: Bulldog Drummond

Q: Who was Dan Dare's arch rival?
A: The Mekon

Q: Which fictional hero was born on Krypton?
A: Superman

Q: What was the name of the dog in Peter Pan?
A: Nana

Q: What school did Billy Bunter attend?
A: Greyfriars

Q: Who was Flash Gordon's arch rival?
A: Ming the Merciless

Q: Which great bird carried off Sinbad the Sailor?
A: A Roc

Q: What was Superman's secret identity ?
A: Clark Kent

Q: Which cartoon character has a cat called Jess?
A: Postman Pat

Q: Which cartoon character has Bluto as his arch rival?
A: Popeye

Q: In which town do the Flintstones live?
A: Bedrock

Q: In the nursery rhyme Cock a Doodle Doo, what has my master lost?
A: His fiddling stick

Q: Which comic character was known as The Pilot of the Future?
A: Dan Dare

Q: Which fictional hero was accompanied by Algy and Ginger?
A: Biggles

Q: What was the name of the Cisco Kid's horse?
A: Diablo

Q: Which film cowboy rode a horse called Tony?
A: Tom Mix

Q: In fiction which hero died at Fort Zinderneuf?
A: Beau Geste

Q: Which part of Peter Pan was kept in a drawer in the Darling household?
A: His shadow

Q: Who could only play one tune, Over the Hill and Far Away?
A: Tom the piper's son

Q: What is the occupation of a Leprechaun?
A: A cobbler

Q: Who was the best friend of Yogi Bear?
A: Boo Boo

Q: What are the names of the seven dwarfs in Disney's cartoon, Snow White and the Seven Dwarfs?
A: Doc, Sneezy, Grumpy, Happy, Sleepy, Dopey and Bashful

Q: What is the name of the dog in the Punch and Judy show?
A: Toby

Q: Who was known as Lord Greystoke?
A: Tarzan

Q: What was Hopalong Cassidy's horse called?
A: Topper

Q: Who lodges at 32, Windsor Gardens with Mr and Mrs Brown?
A: Paddington Bear

Q: Which fictional character lived in the Emerald City?
A: The Wizard of Oz

Q: Which phrase, from his attire, is sometimes used to describe Batman?
A: The Caped Crusader

Q: What is the name of the cow in the Magic Roundabout?
A: Ermintrude

Q: What was the name of Tonto's horse?
A: Scout

Q: What is Donald Duck's middle name?
A: Fauntleroy

Q: Who narrated the Wombles?
A: Bernard Cribbens

Q: What are the first words of Winnie-the-Pooh after he wakes up in the morning?
A: What's for breakfast

Q: What was Paddington Bear's country of origin?
A: Peru

Q: What character in Disney's Pinocchio has the same name as an Italian volcano?
A: Stromboli (the puppet master)

Q: Who is the cartoon adversary of the roadrunner?
A: Wile E Coyote

Q: What is the name of the park where Yogi Bear lives?
A: Jellystone Park

Q: What was the name of Gene Autry's horse?
A: Champion

Q: What is the name of the dog in the Wizard of Oz?
A: Toby

Q: What was the name of the country where Gulliver met the little people?
A: Lilliput

Q. What kind of creature was Rikki-Tikki-Tavi?
A. A mongoose

Q: What was the name of King Arthur's wizard?
A: Merlin

Q: Which fictional detective was created by Sir Arthur Conon Doyle?
A: Sherlock Homes

Q: What was hung round the Ancient Mariner's neck?
A: An albatross

Q: Who was the leading character of the story that had a fairy called Tinkerbell?
A: Peter Pan

Q: What was Long John Silver's parrot called?
A: Captain Flint

Q: Who does the Beast fall in love with?
A: Beauty

Q: What did the rat do in the house that Jack built?
A: Ate the malt

Q: What war did Rip-Van-Winkle sleep through?
A: The American War of Independence

Q: Who owned the Spyglass Inn in Treasure Island?
A: Long John Silver

Q: In the cartoon strip the Peanuts, what is the name of the bird?
A: Woodstock

Q: Wimpy is a hamburger eating character in which cartoon series?
A: Popeye

Q: Who does Alice follow down a hole into wonderland?
A: The White Rabbit

Q: What was the favourite food of Paddington Bear?
A: Marmalade sandwiches

Q: What is the shape of the tattoo on Popeye's arm?
A: An anchor

Q: On which common would you find the Wombles?
A: Wimbledon

Q: In the nursery rhyme what did Tom, Tom the piper's son steal?
A: A pig

Q: Which cartoon character has a dog called Gnasher?
A: Dennis the Menace

Q: What breed of dog was Rin-Tin-Tin?
A: An Alsatian

Q: What breed of dog was Scooby Doo?
A: A Great Dane

Q: Which animated character made his debut in the 1928 cartoon Steamboat Willie?
A: Mickey Mouse

Q: What was Mickey Mouse's original name?
A: Mortimer Mouse

Q: What colour is Pudsey Bear's eye bandage?
A: White with red spots

Q: In Alice's Adventures in Wonderland, what game did the Red Queen invite Alice to play when they first met?
A: Croquet

Q: According to the nursery rhyme, who saw Cock Robin die?
A: The fly

Q: What was Tex Ritter's horse called?
A: White Flash

Q: How did the cartoon dog Scooby Doo get its name?
A: After the refrain from Frank Sinatra's Strangers in the Night (Scooby Doo Doo)

Q: In the original version of what is now Snow White and the Seven Dwarfs, how many dwarfs were there?
A: 11

Q: What were the names of the dwarfs deleted from the original eleven, in the

Disney film Snow White?
A: Deafy, Dirty, Awful and Biggo Ego

Q: Can you name the policeman in the Top Cat cartoon?
A: Officer Dibble

Q: What are the names of Popeye's four nephews?
A: Pipeye, Peepeye, Pupeye and Poopeye

Q: Which marvellous land was created by Frank Braum in 1904?
A: Oz

Q: What were the names of the characters on the TV programme the Magic Roundabout?
A: Florence, Dylan, Dougal, Ermintrude, Mr Rusty and Brian

Q: What is the name of the bulldog in the Tom and Jerry cartoons?
A: Butch

FILMS

Q: There are only two Disney films based on real events. Can you name them?
A: The Aristocats and Pocahontas

Q: In the film industry what does the best boy do?
A: Right hand man to the gaffer

Q: In the film industry what does the gaffer do?
A: Supervises the lighting crew

Q: In the film industry what does the foley artist do?
A: Creates sounds that cannot be recorded during the shoot

Q: In the film industry what does the key grip do?
A: In charge of the staff who assist camera crew

Q: What was the name of the only western film where there was not one single gunshot fired?
A: Four Faces West aka They Passed this Way

Q: What was the first film to be made in cinemascope?
A: The Robe

Q: From which Walt Disney cartoon film does the Oscar winning song When You Wish Upon A Star come?
A: Pinocchio

Q: What was the first live action Disney feature film?
A: Treasure Island

Q: What was Disney's first feature length animated film?
A: Snow White and the Seven Dwarfs

Q: What was Disney's second feature length animated film?
A: Pjnocchio

Q: Which screen cowboy had a horse called Bullet?

A: Roy Rodgers

Q: What was the title of Robert Flaherty's 1922 documentry film about Eskimos?
A: Nanook of the North

Q: Who in 1925 was the first film detective?
A: Harry Houdini (dressed as a robot)

Q: What was Walt Disney's first colour cartoon?
A: Flowers and Trees

Q: What was the first cartoon film to include synchronised sound?
A: Steamboat Willie

Q: What was the name of the first entirely computer generated feature film?
A: Toy Story

Q: In 1925 the first in flight movie was shown on aa Imperial Airways flight from London to Paris. What was the name of the film?
A: The Lost World

Q: Which Bing Crosby film is also a chain of hotels?
A: Holiday Inn

Q: In the Wizard of Oz which character is seeking courage?
A: The Cowardly Lion

Q: In which film did Donald Duck make his debut?
A: The Wise Little Hen (1934)

Q:What was the name of the toy cowboy in the Disney film Toy Story?
A: Woody

Q: Which Walt Disney film was the first to combine live action and animation?
A: The 1944 Three Caballeros

Q: Who starred in the film Singing in the Rain?
A: Donald O'Connor, Gene Kelly, and Debbie Reynolds

Q: What was the name of the first film made in Hollywood?

A: In Old California

Q: What was the name of Laurel and Hardy's theme tune?
A: Dance of the Cuckoo

Q: What is the only Walt Disney film in which the main character does not speak?
A: Dumbo

FISH

Q: To which family does the minnow belong?
A: The carp

Q: What is the largest European fresh water fish?
A: The catfish

Q: To which fish family does the anchovy belong?
A: The herring

Q: What is an adult elver called ?
A: An eel

Q: What is the largest known fish?
A: The whale shark

Q: What is the largest species of flat fish?
A: The halibut

Q: What type of flat fish has both eyes on its left side?
A: The turbot

Q: What is the fastest fish in the sea?
A: The Atlantic sail fish

Q: Kelts, alvins and grilse are all forms of what ?
A: Salmon

Q: What is the most poisonous fish in the world?
A: The death puffer

Q: What is the worlds largest freshwater fish?
A: The Amazonian pirarucu

Q: What is the largest creature to inhabit the Arctic Ocean?
A: The bowhead whale

Q: Which type of fish has the largest population?
A: The herring

Q: Is a shark a hot or cold blooded creature?
A: Hot

Q: What is the second largest creature to inhabit the seas?
A: The basking shark

Q: What is the largest dolphin in the world?
A: The killer whale or (orca)

Q: To which family do pilchards and sardines belong?
A: The herring

Q: What is the fastest and fiercest killer found on a coral reef ?
A: The barracuda

Q: What is the worlds most widely eaten fish?
A: The herring

Q: What is the deadliest predator found in the sea?
A: The killer whale

Q: What is the fastest sea mammal?
A: The killer whale

Q: What is a coelacanth?
A: A primitive fish

Q: What is the most venomous fish in the sea?
A: The stone fish

Q: What is the second most venomous fish in the sea?
A: The scorpion fish

Q: How many species of fresh water fish are found in the British Isles?
A: 37

Q: There are two types of recreational fishing in Britain, what are they ?
A: Game fishing and course fishing

Q: What name is given to a sardine up to one year old?
A: A pilchard

Q: What is the UK's largest fresh water fish?
A: The catfish

Q: How many species of sharks are there in the world?
A: 405

Q: What on a salmon or a trout is a kype?
A: The hook on it's lower jaw

Q: From what substance are fish bones made?
A: Cartilage

Q: What considered to be the oldest type of fish in the northern hemisphere?
A: The chimaera

Q: What fish has the fastest strike rate in the world?
A: The frogfish

Q: What is the worlds most ferocious fresh water fish?
A: The piranha

Q: What is the largest of all the rays?
A: The giant manta

Q: What is the slowest fish in the sea?
A: The sea horse

Q: Which of the shark family is the most ranging?
A: The blue shark

Q: What is the smallest fish found in British waters?
A: The Guillets Goby

Q: What are the most widespread fish in the world?
A: Bristlemouths

Q: What is the rarest fish in the world?

A: The devils hole pupfish (Nevada-USA)

Q: What is the worlds second largest fish
A: The basking shark

Q: Goldfish are the only creatures able to see, what
A: Both infra-red and ultraviolet light

FRESHWATER FISH FOUND in the BRITISH ISLES

1	Arctic Char	20	Minnow
2	Barbel	21	Orfe
3	Bittering ‡	22	Perch
4	Bleak	23	Pike
5	Bream	24	Powan *
6	Brown Trout	25	Rainbow Trout
7	Bulhead	26	Roach
8	Catfish	27	Rudd
9	Chub	28	Ruffe
10	Common Carp	29	Salmon
11	Crucian Carp	30	Sea Trout
12	Dace	31	Silver Bream ‡
13	Eel	32	Stickleback
14	Ghost Carp	33	Stone Loach
15	Grass Carp	34	Tench
16	Grayling	35	Vendace *
17	Gudgeon	36	Wild Carp
18	Koi Carp	37	Zander
19	Mirror Carp		

* Powan and Vendace are protected species
‡ Bittering and Silver Bream are not easily identifiable and their locations are
  difficult to pinpoint

FLAGS

Q: The first Union Flag of 1606 was a combination of the crosses of which two patron saints?
A: St Andrew and St George

Q: What do the stars on the Australian flag represent?
A: The Southern Cross

Q: What is the oldest national flag in Britain and Europe?
A: The Saltire

Q: Which colours are behind the red dragon on the Welsh flag?
A: Green and white

Q: How many stars are there on the Australian flag?
A: Six

Q: What is the background colour of the Union flag?
A: Blue

Q: What do the stars on the New Zealand flag represent?
A: The Southern Cross

Q: How many white stripes are on the American flag?
A: Six

Q: How many red stripes are there on the American flag?
A: Seven

Q: What do the stripes on the American flag represent?
A: The original 13 colonies

Q: The United Nations flag shows a map of the world. What is on the other side of the map?
A: An olive branch

Q: What are the colours of the five rings on the Olympic flag?

A: Blue, yellow, black, green and red

Q: There are 13 stars on the Confederate flag. What states do they represent?
A: South Carolina, Mississippi, Alabama, Florida, Georgia, Lousiana, Texas, Arkansas, North Carolina, Tennessee, Virginia, Missouri and Kentucky

Q: Which three saints crosses make up the British Union flag?
A: St Andrew, St Patrick and St George

Q: What name is given to the wheel on the Indian flag?
A: An asoka

Q: How many stars are there on the New Zealand flag?
A: Four

Q: Where was the American flag flown for the first time?
A: Cambridge USA

Q: The original pirate flag was known as what?
A: The jolie rougere (pretty red)

Q: The original pirate flag was a red pennant. When it was hoisted, what did it indicate?
A: No prisoners would be taken alive

Q: When the pirate flag with the skull and crossbones was hoisted, what did it indicate?
A: That prisoners would be taken alive

FOOD

Q: Petit Fours means literally little ovens. What are they?
A: Small French cakes or biscuits

Q: You often see the French phrase hors d'oeuvres on a menu meaning appetiser, but what is the literal translation?
A: Outside the work

Q: What is the main ingredient of taramasalata?
A: Cod roe

Q: In culinary terms what is stellini?
A: Star shaped pasta

Q: If a dish on a menu in a restaurant reads a la du barry, what should it be garnished with?
A: Cauliflower

Q: If you are eating nibs, what are you eating?
A: The bumps of the ends of fresh peanuts

Q: If you are eating salmagundi in a restaurant, what would you be eating?
A: Chopped meat, anchovies, eggs and onions

Q: From what foodstuff is tofu made?
A: Soya bean curd

Q: In cooking what is crème du barry?
A: Cauliflower soup

Q: What kind of drink is lapsang souchong?
A: A unique blend of China tea

Q: What tangy spread is named after a French earthenware pot?
A: Marmite

Q: What common edible object's name literally means cooked twice?

A: A biscuit

Q: What is the only food that does not go bad?
A: Honey

Q: What type of drink would you make in a samovar?
A: Tea

Q: The name of which chocolate covered cream cake means lightening in French?
A: The eclair

Q: Which type of pasta translates from the Italian meaning large tubes?
A: Cannelloni

Q: What gives Earl Grey tea its distinctive flavour?
A: Bergamot oil

Q: Which popular food dish was first mentioned in a report of 1876?
A: Fish and chips

Q: Which type of milk is used to make Roquefort cheese?
A: Ewe's

Q: The protein casein is present in what common foodstuff?
A: Milk

Q: What is the oldest known vegetable?
A: The pea

Q: Can you name the most nutritious and the least nutritious fruits in the world?
A: Most kiwi; least cucumber

Q: Vol-au-vents are a popular snack, but what does it mean?
A: Flight on the wind

Q: What was the first frozen food to go on sale Britain?
A: Asparagus

Q: In cookery what is a framboise?
A: A raspberry

Q: What does the phrase foie gras mean as in the food pate de fois gras?
A: Fat liver

Q: The bummalo fish is the main ingredient of which dish?
A: Bombay Duck

Q: In cookery what is a fraise?
A: A strawberry

Q: Which French word meaning froth is a dish of flavoured cream, whipped and frozen?
A: Mousse

Q: If you ordered calamares in a restaurant, what would you be eating?
A: Squid

Q: In culinary terms what does al dente mean?
A: Firm to the bite

Q: If you are eating sashimi in a Japanese restaurant, What would you be eating?
A: Thinly cut strips of raw fish

Q: In culinary terms what are charcuteries?
A: Cold cooked meats collectively

Q: What was the worlds first substitute food?
A: Margarine

Q: In which country did chilli con carne originate?
A: America

Q: Which vegetable is in the egg dish florentine?
A: Spinach

Q: Which culinary word describes vegetables cut into very thin pieces?
A: Julienne

Q: What is the more common name for grape sugar?
A: Glucose

Q: Which fish is the traditional ingredient of the Scandinavian dish gravad lax?
A: Salmon

Q: What is the culinary name for a bunch of herbs used in flavourings?
A: A bouquet garni

Q: In Italy if you are served pesce martello. What would you be about to eat ?
A: Shark

Q: Which French term meaning blue ribbon is used to describe food that achieves a degree of excellence?
A: Gordon Bleu

Q: In a restaurant if you are eating brandon rost what are you eating?
A: Smoked salmon

Q: In Middle Eastern cookery what is meze?
A: A selection of hot and cold hors d'oeuvres

Q: In a restaurant if you are eating a Sergeant Baker, what are you eating?
A: A brightly coloured Australian fish

Q: In culinary terms what is alfredo?
A: A sauce for pasta

Q: In culinary terms what are mange tout?
A: A variety of pea with an edible pod

Q: In culinary terms what is tahini?
A: A sesame seed paste

Q: In culinary terms what is tzatziki?
A: A yoghurt, cucumber and mint dip

Q: In culinary terms what is arugula?
A: The salad vegetable rocket

Q: In culinary terms what is bearnaise?
A: A rich sauce thickened with egg yolks and flavoured with tarragon

Q: In culinary terms how is napped food served?

A: In a sauce or other liquid

Q: In culinary terms what is a croque-monsieur?
A: A fried or grilled cheese and ham sandwich

Q: If you are eating a romaine sandwich what is the filling?
A: Cos lettuce

Q: What does the HP in HP sauces stand for?
A: Houses of Parliament

Q: In a restaurant, if you are eating angels on horseback what are you eating?
A: Oysters wrapped in bacon served on toast

Q: In a restaurant, if you are eating angel hair what are you eating?
A: Pasta consisting of very fine long strands

Q: In culinary terms what is an andouille?
A: A French pork sausage

Q: Which fruit did Christopher Columbus discover on Guadeloupe in 1493?
A: The pineapple

Q: What name is given to the fruit of the blackthorn tree?
A: The sloe

Q: What name is given to the citrus fruit that is a cross between an orange, tangerine and a grapefruit?
A: The ugli fruit

Q: In which fruit would you be taking an interest in if you studied ampelography?
A: Grapes

Q: Which fruit's other name is the Chinese gooseberry?
A: The kiwi fruit

Q: Which fruit shares its name with a form of transport?
A: A pear (Concord)

Q: Which fruit shares its name with a meeting?

A: A pear (Conference)

Q: In culinary terms what does en croute mean?
A: In a pastry crust

Q: In culinary terms if something is served a la maitre d'hotel, how is it prepared?
A: Served plain with parsley garnish

Q: What is tartare sauce?
A: A mayonnaise dressing with chopped pickles, olives, capers etc

Q: What kind of food product is aioli?
A: Garlic mayonnaise

Q: In culinary terms what is a chateaubriand ?
A: A thick grilled fillet steak

Q: In a restaurant if you are eating bouillabaisse, what are you eating?
A: A thick soup made of different kinds of fish

Q: What are crepes suzettes?
A: Thin, hot pancakes with lemons or oranges

Q: Which vegetable is known as a rutabaga in the USA?
A: A swede

Q: What name is given to the fruit which is a cross between a plum and a peach?
A: A nectarine

Q: What grain is used to make semolina?
A: Wheat

Q: What is the most consumed fruit in the world?
A: The banana

Q: Which is the only vegetable not sold frozen, bottled, processed or pre-cooked?
A: Lettuce

Q: In culinary terms what is paupiette?
A: A long thin slice of fish or meat rolled and stuffed with a filling

Q: In culinary terms what is court bouillon?
A: A stock made from wine and vegetables, typically in fish dishes

Q: In culinary terms what is a coulis?
A: A thin fruit or vegetable puree used as a sauce

Q: In culinary terms what are crudites?
A: An appetiser of vegetables cut into strips, usually served with a dip

Q: In culinary terms what are alliaceous vegetables?
A: Vegetables belonging to the onion family (garlic, chives, shallots, leeks etc.)

Q: If you finish a meal in Turkey with sweet coffee and loucoumi, what would you be eating?
A: Turkish Delight

Q: What do you call the Greek starter of rolls of savoury rice wrapped in vine leaves?
A: Dolmades

Q: What would you expect to find in abundance in an Indian dish described as dopiaza?
A: Onions

Q: What is the main ingredient of the dressing on the Indonesian vegetable salad dish gado-gado?
A: Peanuts

Q: What sort of vegetable is a kohlrabi?
A: A cabbage

Q: In culinary terms if food is said to be picante, what does it taste of ?
A: Spices

Q: In culinary terms if food is served en papillote, how is it served?
A: Cooked and served in a paper wrapper

Q: What is the main ingredient of the Chinese dish foo yong?

A: Egg

Q: In culinary terms what is baclava?
A: Pastry filled with nuts and honey

Q: If something is cooked a la king, what does it mean?
A: In mushrooms with a cream sauce and pimentos

Q: What is saltimbocca?
A: An Italian dish of veal, ham and cheese

Q: What sort of wheat is used to make pasta?
A: Durim wheat

Q: If an item on a menu has veronique after it, with what will it be served?
A: White grapes

Q: What name is given to a small fireproof dish used for cooking small portions of food?
A: A cocotte

Q: In culinary terms what name is given to a garnish of spinach?
A: Florentine

Q: If you were eating fish a la Normande, how would the fish be cooked?
A: Braised in white wine

Q: What is the most widely used vegetable in the world?
A: The onion

Q: With which meat would you use alboni sauce?
A: Venison

Q: What is the world's most plentiful food source?
A: Plankton

Q: What sugar is found in fruit and honey?
A: Fructose

Q: What is the original fast food?
A: A piece of fruit

Q: In culinary terms what is mirepoix?
A: A mixture of sauteed chopped vegetables used in sauces

Q: What is crowdie on a restaurant menu?
A: A soft Scottish cheese

Q: In culinary terms what is a morel?
A: A mushroom

Q: Which fruit makes up a belle helene?
A: A pear

Q: What was the only take away food not rationed in WW2?
A: Fish and chips

Q: What is the most expensive food in the world?
A: Caviar

Q: What is the world's most eaten meat?
A: Pork

Q: Which were the only type of sweets not rationed in WW2?
A: Cough sweets

Q: In culinary terms what is bisque?
A: A rich lobster or other shellfish soup

Q: Which product was the first known to use a sell-by date?
A: A carton of Lyons coffee

Q: What is soya cheese called?
A: Tofu

Q: On a restaurant menu what is abaisee?
A: A very thinly rolled puff pastry used in desserts

Q: On a restaurant menu what is au gratin?
A: A dish topped with breadcrumbs and/or cheese then baked

Q: On a restaurant menu what is beurre noisette?
A: To heat butter until it turns a golden brown colour giving it a nutty flavour

Q: On a restaurant menu if something is cooked broche how is it cooked ?
A: On a skewer over a flame

Q: On a restaurant menu how is dauphinoise prepared ?
A: With garlic and cream and slowly baked

Q: On a restaurant menu how has food been prepared if it is emince?
A: Cut or thinly sliced

Q: On a restaurant menu what is ganache?
A: A smooth rich blend of chocolate and cream. By changing the proportions this combination can be used either as a glaze or a base or filling for a wide range of desserts

Q: On a restaurant menu what is a gaufrette?
A: A fan shaped honeycomb wafer used to garnish ice cream

Q: On a restaurant menu what is genoise?
A: A light fine-crumbled sponge cake with French origins made with warm whole eggs, sugar, flour and occasionally melted butter

Q: On a restaurant menu what is an olive a twist?
A: A tomato, garlic, olive oil, capers, anchovies and a black olive salad, otherwise a salade nicoise

Q: How is granita prepared?
A: A mixture of water and sugar often flavoured with fruit juice, alcohol or coffee that is stirred while frozen to give a granular texture

Q: How is gratin prepared?
A: Any sweet or savoury dish served with a golden crust

Q: How is julien prepared ?
A: Cut into very thin matchstick like strips

Q: What does jus mean?
A: A French word meaning juice

Q: On a restaurant menu what are lyonnaise potatoes?
A: Sliced potatoes sauteed in a pan with onion

144

Q: What is mascarpone cheese?
A: An Italian cream cheese that can be used in both savoury and sweet dishes. The name derives from the Spanish term masque bono

Q: On a restaurant menu what is picode gallo?
A: A chunky tomato salsa. Picode gallo the name is Spanish for rooster's beak

Q: On a restaurant menu what is provencale?
A: A dish using garlic, parsley and olive oil

Q: On a restaurant menu what is marinier?
A: Seafood cooked in white wine often with onions

Q: On a restaurant menu what is millefeuille?
A: A type of very thin puff pastry, the term is French for a thousand layers

Q: On a restaurant menu what is papillote?
A: A dish cooked (and sometimes served) in a protective parcel of greaseproof paper to help it retain its flavour and aroma

Q: On a restaurant menu what is quenelle?
A: A dumpling shaped out of seafood or meat – often salmon or chicken poached in stock

Q: On a restaurant menu what is ragout?
A: A thick poultry, game, fish or vegetable stew. It can be white or brown depending on how it is prepared

Q: On a restaurant menu what is vichyssoise?
A: A soup made from potatoes, cream and vegetables – usually leek – served cold

Q: On a restaurant menu what is wasabi?
A: Sometimes called Japanese horse-radish this is a pungent green paste served as an accompaniment with Sushi

Q: On a restaurant menu what is zabaglione?
A: Italian custard style frothy dessert consisting of egg yolk, sugar and wine

Q: What name is given to the American dish of fresh corn and Lima beans boiled together?

A: Succotash

Q: On a restaurant menu what is carbonara?
A: A pasta sauce made with bacon or ham, egg and cream

Q: What was the world's first preserved convenience meat food?
A: The sausage

Q: From which country does the purple coloured potato come?
A: Peru

Q: What was the original colour of a carrot ?
A: Purple

Q: What is believed to have been a Roman gladiator's staple diet ?
A: Barley, beans and bread

Q: What is the main ingredient of the Irish dish champ?
A: Potatoes

Q: What delicacy is made from the liver of specially fattened geese?
A: Foie gras

Q: What is the principal ingredient in a guacamole dip?
A: Avocado pear

Q: Which is the world's largest herb?
A: The banana plant (the banana is a plant not a tree)

Q: In the food paste pate what does pate mean?
A: A pie of seasoned meat

Q: What is the only British fresh product to have EU Protection of Designation of origin?
A: Jersey Royals (potatoes)

Q: Which is the only pastry that can be frozen again after de-frosting?
A: Filo (owing to its low fat content)

Q: By which name is the fruit granadilla more commonly known?
A: Passion fruit

Q: The tree citrus paradisi bears which fruit?
A: Grapefruit

Q: Do peanuts grow above or under the ground?
A: Under

Q: What colour are pistachio nuts?
A: Green

Q: What type of edible nut is produced by a variety of hickory tree?
A: The pecan

Q: If you did not pick a courgette, what would it become?
A: A marrow

Q: The poisonous plant deadly nightshade belongs to the same family as which vegetable?
A: The potato

Q: The onion is a member of which family?
A: The lily

Q: Which spice is made from the outer covering of the nutmeg?
A: Mace

Q: The capital of French Guina gave its name to which spice?
A: Cayenne pepper

Q: Which two fruits are anagrams of each other?
A: Lemons and melons

Q: Which dish is said to have been named after a summer month in the French Revolutionary calendar because that was the month in which Napoleon first tasted it?
A: Lobster thermidor (mid July to mid August)

Q: What is considered to be the worlds most addictive food?
A: Chocolate

Q: What is the most consumed fruit in the world?
A: The banana

Q: What spice is extremely poisonous if injected intravenously ?
A: Nutmeg

Q: Which are the only vegetables that are not annuals?
A: Asparagus and rhubarb

FROM WHAT

Q: From what do we get the expression private eye for a detective?
A: The Pinkerton's logo of an all seeing eye

Q: From what plant is linseed oil derived?
A: Flax

Q: From what language does the word ombudsman come?
A: Swedish

Q: From what language does Yiddish derive?
A: German

Q: From what language do we get the word police?
A: French

Q: From what modern language do the words embargo and flotilla derive?
A: Spanish

Q: From what language do we get the word paprika?
A: Hungarian

Q: From what language do we get the word ketchup?
A: Chinese

Q: From what language does the word shampoo originate?
A: Hindi

Q: From what language do we get the word admira?l
A: Arabic

Q: From what creature do we get ambergris from?
A: The whale

Q: From what language do the words, kiosk, tulip and coffee com?e
A: Turkish

Q: From what language do we get the word Mayday?
A: French (m'aider – come and help me)

GEMS and PRECIOUS METALS

Q: What is the only known gem to come from outer space?
A: Moldavite

Q: What is the only gem that is of animal origin?
A: The pearl

Q: When rubies are heated they change colour. What colour do they change to?
A: Green

Q: The finding of what started the Kimberly gold rush?
A: The Eureka Stone

Q: What is the most valuable cut diamond in the world?
A: The Hope Diamond

Q: In which city is the largest store of uncut diamonds kept?
A: London

Q: What is the largest diamond on record?
A: The Cullinan

Q: What is the largest cut and set diamond in the world?
A: The Golden Jubilee Diamond

Q: What are the only gems that will dissolve in vinegar?
A: Pearls

HISTORY

Q: In the 16th century which was the first country to have an empire where the sun never set?
A: Spain

Q: Which historical event is known in France as Jour-J?
A: D-Day

Q: 'Eileen is married to Joe. It is hot in Suez' was the start of the coded message indicating what?
A: The D-Day Invasion

Q: What is the historical significance of the bonfires on the 5th November?
A: The deliverance of King James VI of Scotland and 1st of England

Q: What momentous event occured off the Falkland Islands in 1914?
A: The German battleship fleet was sunk

HUMAN BODY

Q: The adjective glossal refers to what part of the human body?
A: The tongue

Q: What is the only moveable bone in the skull?
A: The jawbone (mandible)

Q: How many bones are there in the human face?
A: 14

Q: What name is given to the chisel-edged tooth at the front of the mouth?
A: Incisor

Q: Where in the human body will you find the pisiform bone?
A: The wrist

Q: What is the average breathing rate of a human adult?
A: 16 times a minute

Q: Of what substance are finger and toe nails composed?
A: Keratin

Q: What is the only organ in the body that does not use calories?
A: The brain

Q: Which bone in the human body is most frequently broken?
A: The collar bone

Q: What is the only one hormone in the human body that makes fat?
A: Insulin

Q: What is the human body's largest organ?
A: The skin

Q: Apart from hair, skin and nails which two parts of your body keep growing all your life?
A: Your ears and nose

Q: Where in the body is the labyrinth?
A: In the inner ear

Q: What is the most common human eye colour?
A: Brown

Q: What part of the body consumes 40% of the blood's oxygen?
A: The brain

Q: By what name is the femur more commonly known?
A: The thighbone

Q: What is the human body's natural defence against extreme cold?
A: Shivering

Q: What is the only part of the human body that can't repair itself?
A: The teeth

Q: Your timpanic membrane is more commonly called what?
A: The eardrum

Q: What is the most common disease in the world?
A: Tooth decay

Q: Relative to size what is the strongest muscle in the human body?
A: The tongue

Q: What is the third largest artery in the human body?
A: The jugular vein

Q: What is the largest gland in the human body?
A: The liver

Q: How many ventricles are there in the human heart?
A: Two

Q: In the human body in which organ is the pineal gland?
A: The brain

Q: Which of the five senses develops first?
A: Smell

Q: What name is given to the study of the human body ?
A: Anatomy

Q: What in the human body is your hallux?
A: Your big toe (halluces)

Q: What is the longest bone in the human body ?
A: The femur or thigh bone

Q: What is the most common human blood group?
A: O

Q: Where in the human body is your talus
A: It's part of your ankle joint

Q: What is the most mobile joint in the human body ?
A: The shoulder joint

Q: The human tongue can only taste four sensations. What are they?
A: Sweet, sour, salt and bitter

Q: In which part of the human body is the parietal bone?
A: The skull

Q: In which part of the human body is your scapula?
A: The shoulder

Q: In which part of the human body is your patella?
A: The knee cap

Q: In which part of the human body are your tarsals?
A: Your feet

Q: Where in the human body are the islets of langerhans?
A: The pancreas

Q: What, in the human body, is the coronal bone?
A: The frontal bone of the skull

Q: What, in the human body, is strange about cartilage?
A: It does not show on an x-ray

Q: Where in the human body are cells known as rods and cones?
A: The eye retina

Q: The number of what in the eye gives good night vision?
A: Rods

Q: The number of what in the eye gives good daylight vision?
A: Cones

Q: How many bones make up the human skeleton?
A: 200

Q: How many grams of salt are in a litre of perspiration?
A: 3

Q: Where in the human body is your philtrum?
A: On your face (it's the channel above your top lip)

Q: What is the white part of the fingernail called?
A: The lunula

Q: On average how many steps does the human body take in a day?
A: 10,000

Q: On average how many thoughts does the human brain process in a day?
A: 40,000

Q: How many litres of blood are pumped round the human body per day?
A: 36,000

Q: In humans which is the most highly developed sense?
A: Sight

Q: What is the largest internal organ in the human body?
A: The liver

Q: What are the four colours of the human eye?
A: Blue, brown, green and hazel

Q: On what part of the human body is the skin the thinnest?
A: The eyelids

Q: What is the lowest register of the human voice in singing or speaking?
A: Chest voice

Q: What condition is the most common neurological in the world?
A: Headache

Q: What condition is the second most neurological in the world?
A: Epilepsy

Q: Which fibrous tissue takes its name from the Latin for mouse?
A: Muscle

Q: What is the biggest cause of human deaths in the western world?
A: The aids virus

Q: What was the worlds most deadly disease to humans?
A: The plague

Q: Of which ailment is strabismus the medical name?
A: An eye squint

Q: Which organ enables humans and some animals to distinguish colours?
A: The brain

Q: What does the eye only see?
A: Light

Q: Eye rods are how many times more sensitive to light than eye cones?
A: 500

Q: What angle of sight do humans have?
A: 140 degrees

Q: What is the fastest moving muscle in the human body ?
A: The one that opens and closes the eyelid

Q: What organ in the human body has only one function?
A: The eye

Q: Which human body function is also known as sternutation?
A: Sneezing

Q: What is the only vitamin that the human body can produce?
A: Vitamin D

IN WHICH YEAR

Q: Which year is considered as the start of Islam?
A: 622

Q: In which year did Muhammad die?
A: 632

Q: In which year was the first zoo in Britain opened?
A: 1235

Q: In which year were spectacles invented?
A: 1281

Q: In which year was the first recorded mention of European playing cards?
A: 1377

Q: In which year was the first recorded use of gunpowder in Europe?
A: 1380 (Germany)

Q: In which year did storks last breed in Britain?
A: 1416 (Edinburgh)

Q: In which year was Bartholomew Diaz the first European to land on southern African soil?
A: 1488

Q: In which year did Pedro Alvarez Cabral discover Brazil and claim it for Portugal?
A: 1500

Q: In which year was the first complete printed Bible in English published?
A: 1535

Q: In which year was the first Naval Dock in Britain built at Portsmouth?
A: 1540

Q: In which year was the Bible first divided into chapters?

A: 1540

Q: In which year did the Mary Rose sink?
A: 1545

Q: In which year were newspapers first printed?
A: 1556

Q: In which year was tea first drunk in Britain?
A: 1557

Q: In which year was the world's first atlas published?
A: 1570

Q: In which year was the Gregorian Calendar adopted?
A: 1582

Q: In which year was the water closet invented?
A: 1596

Q: In which year did the Mayflower land the first pioneer settlers in America?
A: 1620

Q: In which year were horse drawn taxis first used in London?
A: 1630

Q: In which year was the banana first available in Britain?
A: 1633

Q: In which year was the rack last used in the Tower of London?
A: 1640

Q: In which year was the first record of communication between ship to ship in the British Royal Navy other than by word of mouth or message sent by boat, but sent by flags?
A: 1653

Q: In which year was the first practical slide rule produced?
A: 1654

Q: In which year were stagecoaches first used in Britain?

A: 1657

Q: In which year were cheques introduced?
A: 1659

Q: In which year was the microscope invented?
A: 1665

Q: In which year was the pressure cooker or digester as it was originally?
known invented
A: 1682

Q: In which year was cappuccino coffee first drunk?
A: 1683

Q: In which year was the world's first diving bell with a renewable air supply
first available?
A: 1691

Q: In which year was coke used for the first time to smelt iron?
A: 1709

Q: In which year did the Copyright Act come into effect?
A: 1710

Q: In which year was the world's first steam engine in use?
A: 1712 (A vacuum engine) (Thomas Newcommen)

Q: In which year was the first machine gun patented?
A: 1718

Q: In which year was Rule Britannia written?
A: 1740

Q: In which year did the Battle of Culloden take place?
A: 1746

Q: In which year was sugar cane first cultivated in America?
A: 1751

Q: In which year was the lightning conductor invented?

A: 1752

Q: In which year was the human blood pressure measured for the first time?
A: 1754

Q: In which year was the world's first steam reciprocating engine in use?
A: 1755

Q: In which year was the first sugar mill opened?
A: 1758

Q: In which year was the first true steam condensing engine available?
A: 1760 (James Watt)

Q: In which year were outside signs on shops banned forcing owners for the first time to paint their name on the shop front?
A: 1762

Q: In which year was the worlds first post office established?
A: 1763

Q: In which year was HMS Victory launched?
A: 1765

Q: In which year was nitrogen discovered?
A: 1772

Q: In which year was the first machine available to bore out the barrels of cannons?
A: 1774

Q: In which year was the speed of light first calculated?
A: 1776

Q: In which year was the American flag first flown?
A: 1776

Q: In which year did the American Turtle carry out the first underwater attack on a ship?
A: 1776

Q: In which year was the American flag legally established by congress?
A: 1777

Q: In which year was the principle of the compounding steam engine first patented?
A: 1781

Q: In which year did man first ascend in a balloon?
A: 1783 (At Lyons, France)

Q: In which year did the first British person leave the ground in a machine made for flying, a hot air balloon?
A: 1784

Q: In which year did Robert Burns write his address to the haggis?
A: 1786

Q: In which year was the first immunisation against smallpox?
A: 1786

Q: In which year did the first convicts sail from England to Australia?
A: 1787

Q: In which year did the first convicts arrive in Australia?
A: 1788

Q: In which year did the French Revolution begin?
A: 1789

Q: In which year did the Mutiny on the Bounty take place?
A: 1789

Q: In which year was the prefix HMS on Royal Naval Warships first recorded?
A: 1789

Q: In which year did Fletcher Christian and eight other mutineers land on Pitcairn Island?
A: 1790

Q: In which year was the guillotine first used?
A: 1792

Q: In which year was the corner stone of the U.S. White House laid?
A: 1792

Q: In which year was the American mint established, striking its first silver dollars?
A: 1792

Q: In which year was the French national anthem composed?
A: 1792

Q: In which year was the optical telescope invented in France?
A: 1792

Q: In which year did the Bank of England issue the £5 pound note?
A: 1793

Q: In which year was the United States Navy formed ?
A: 1794

Q: In which year was the world's first successful hydraulic jack available?
A: 1795

Q: In which year did the naval mutiny at Spithead take place?
A: 1797

Q: In which year was the Nore Mutiny ?
A: 1797

Q: In which year were synthetic dyes first used?
A: 1797

Q: In which year were £1 banknotes first issued by the Bank of England?
A: 1797

Q: In which year did Richard Trevithick demonstrate the first moving steam engine?
A: 1801

Q: In which year was the world's first automatic weaving loom introduced?
A: 1801

Q: In which year was the world's first mass production line introduced, to make ships' pulleys?
A: 1802

Q: In which year did the first steam powered vehicle run?
A: 1802

Q: In which year did the first prisoners land in Tasmania?
A: 1803

Q: In which year was the first gun with a rifled barrel available?
A: 1804

Q: In which year did Richard Trevithick's first steam locomotive run?
A: 1804

Q: In which year was morphine invented?
A: 1805

Q: In which year was the gun sight first available?
A: 1806

Q: In which year was the Clermont the first ship to be fitted with a steam engine?
A: 1807

Q: In which year was the word Viking first used?
A: 1808

Q: In which year did the Crinan Canal open?
A: 1809

Q: In which year was the world's first commercial canning factory opened?
A: 1812

Q: In which year did George Stephenson run his first locomotive?
A: 1814

Q: In which year was the world's first steam driven printing press introduced?
A: 1814

Q: In which year was the worlds first steam powered warship available?
A: 1815

Q: In which year were cast iron water-carrying pipes introduced?
A: 1817

Q: In which year was the first iron ship to be built in Scotland launched?
A: 1818

Q: In which year did America buy Florida from Spain?
A: 1819

Q: In which year did the first British settlers arrive in Cape Province South Africa?
A: 1820

Q: In which year was Britain's last sailing ship of the line built?
A: 1821

Q: In which year did Napoleon Bonaparte die?
A: 1821

Q: In which year did the Caledonian Canal open?
A: 1822

Q: In which year did the world's first iron built steamship make her first voyage?
A: 1822

Q: In which year was the world's first iron built steamship launched ?
A: 1822

Q: In which year was Portland Cement invented ?
A: 1824

Q: In which year did the Stockton to Darlington railway open for passengers?
A: 1825

Q: In which year did the Royal Bank of Scotland issue banknotes printed on both sides – the world's first?
A: 1826

Q: In which year did Robert Stephenson's Rocket first run?
A: 1829

Q: In which year were slow sand filters used for water filtration for the first time?
A: 1829

Q: In which year was the dynamo first demonstrated?
A: 1831

Q: In which year was the French Foreign Legion founded?
A: 1831

Q: In which year did the first iron ship make an ocean voyage?
A: 1832

Q: In which year did the Palace of Westminster burn down?
A: 1834

Q: In which year did the Tower of London zoo close?
A: 1835

Q: In which year was the first patent for a ship's propeller taken out?
A: 1836

Q: In which year did the Tower of London open as a tourist attraction?
A: 1837

Q: In which year did the Royal Mail's travelling post office start?
A: 1838

Q: In which year was the first regular Atlantic steamship service started?
A: 1838

Q: In which year did the first steamship cross the Atlantic?
A: 1838

Q: In which year was the Grand National first run?
A: 1839

Q: In which year did the 237 ton Archimedes become the first ship to be

driven by screw propeller?
A: 1839

Q: In which year was the first Sherlock Homes novel published?
A: 1840

Q: In which year was the first adhesive postage stamp, the Penny Black, produced?
A: 1840

Q: In which year was the first propeller driven ship, the sloop HMS Rattler, ordered by the British Royal Navy?
A: 1841

Q: In which year was the Act of Parliament passed compelling rail companies to abolish roofless passenger carriages?
A: 1841

Q: In which year was lager first brewed?
A: 1842

Q: In which year was the gas meter invented ?
A: 1843

Q: In which year was the Morse code invented?
A: 1844

Q: In which year did the first Co-op open?
A: 1844

Q: In which year was standard time introduced in Britain?
A: 1845

Q: In which year was the Irish potato famine?
A: 1845

Q: In which year was the anaesthetic ether first used?
A: 1846

Q: In which year was the alarm clock invented?
A: 1847

Q: In which year was the anaesthetic chloroform first used?
A: 1847

Q: In which year was spiritualism founded in America?
A: 1848

Q: In which year was chewing gum first commercially available?
A: 1848

Q: In which year was the modern seismograph invented?
A: 1848

Q: In which year was the safety pin patented?
A: 1849

Q: In which year was the world's first box girder bridge built?
A: 1849

Q: In which year did the Manchester-Liverpool railway service begin?
A: 1850

Q: In which year did the first immigrant ship arrive in New Zealand?
A: 1850

Q: In which year did the New Houses of Parliament open?
A: 1851

Q: In which year was the world's first public toilet opened at London's Crystal Palace Great Exhibition?
A: 1851

Q: In which year did Henry Wells and William Fargo found Wells Fargo?
A: 1852

Q: In which year was the House of Commons completed?
A: 1852

Q: In which year was the first ship specifically designed as a single screw battleship launched?
A: 1852

Q: In which year were what we now call Jeans first available?
A: 1853

Q: In which year were potato crisps invented?
A: 1853

Q: In which year was the first Steinway piano produced?
A: 1853

Q: In which year did the Crimean War start?
A: 1854

Q: In which year was the red ensign allotted to the British Merchant Navy?
A: 1855

Q: In which year was the white ensign allotted to the British Royal Navy?
A: 1855

Q: In which year was the blue ensign allotted to the Royal Navy Reserve?
A: 1855

Q: In which year did the British Government order every city to have its own police force?
A: 1856

Q: In which year was the Big Ben tower completed ?
A: 1858

Q: In which year was the first electric burglar alarm installed in America?
A: 1858

Q: In which year did the Miracle of Lourdes take place?
A: 1858

Q: In which year was the can opener invented?
A: 1858

Q: In which year did work start on building the Suez Canal?
A: 1859

Q: In which year was the first successful oil well drilled?

A: 1859

Q: In which year did Charles Darwin publish his Origin of the Species?
A: 1859

Q: In which year did the American Pony Express start running?
A: 1860

Q: In which year did the first weather forecast appear in the Times?
A: 1860

Q: In which year was HMS Warrior, the world's first iron-clad warship, launched?
A: 1860

Q: In which year was the first British mass produced steel available?
A: 1860

Q: In which year was the postcard introduced?
A: 1861

Q: In which year was the first package holiday?
A: 1861

Q: In which year did Richard Jordan Gatling patent his Gatling Gun?
A: 1862

Q: In which year was the US Monitor, the world's first ship to be fitted with a rotating gun turret and armour plating, launched?
A: 1862

Q: In which year did the Battle of Hampton Roads, the first battle between Ironclads, take place?
A: 1862

Q: In which year did London's underground open?
A: 1863

Q: In which year was the world's first mass produced product available?
A: 1863

Q: In which year were the first Pullman railway carriages available?
A: 1864

Q: In which year were squadronal colours abolished in the Royal Navy?
A: 1864

Q: In which year was the first warship sunk by a submarine?
A: 1864

Q: In which year were the first exploding safety detonators used on British railway lines?
A: 1865

Q: In which year did the British Government make the fitting of safety valves on steam boilers compulsory?
A: 1865

Q: In which year was the Ku Klux Klan founded in America?
A: 1866

Q: In which year was Nestle condensed milk first available?
A: 1866

Q: In which year was barbed wire invented?
A: 1867

Q: In which year was cellulose invented?
A: 1869

Q: In which year did the world's first torpedo research centre open in America?
A: 1869

Q: In which year did the Suez Canal open?
A: 1869

Q: In which year was Alcatraz Prison completed ?
A: 1869

Q: In which year was Heinz tomato ketchup first made available?
A: 1869

Q: In which year was margarine invented?
A: 1869

Q: In which year was the Americas Cup yacht race first held ?
A: 1870

Q: In which year was the first steam driven triple expansion engine available?
A: 1870

Q: In which year were the first multi-cylinder hand pumps available for fighting fires?
A: 1870

Q: In which year was electricity first used to restart a human heart?
A: 1871

Q: In which year did London's Royal Albert Hall open?
A: 1871

Q: In which year was HMS Devastation, the world's first practical battleship, launched?
A: 1871

Q: In which year was the first ship launched from the Clydebank shipyards?
A: 1872

Q: In which year were British trains fitted with toilets – but only in sleeping carriages?
A: 1873

Q: In which year was lawn tennis first played?
A: 1874

Q: In which year was the grey squirrel introduced into Britain?
A: 1876

Q: In which year did the Battle at the Little Bighorn take place?
A: 1876

Q: In which year was the Plimsoll line on ships introduced?
A: 1876

Q: In which year was the torpedo first used in action?
A: 1877

Q: In which year was the first human cannonball act performed at London's Amphitheatre?
A: 1877

Q: In which year did the first submarine torpedo attack take place?
A: 1877

Q: In which year was the first weekly weather report published by the Meteorological Office?
A: 1878

Q: In which year did the first Tay railway bridge collapse?
A: 1879

Q: In which year did the first imported frozen meat from Australia arrive in Britain?
A: 1880

Q: In which year was the first telephone directory published by the London Telephone Company?
A: 1880

Q: In which year was the electric iron invented?
A: 1880

Q: In which year was the bullet invented?
A: 1881

Q: In which year did the first imported frozen meat from New Zealand arrive in Britain?
A: 1882

Q: In which year was Jesse James shot and killed?
A: 1882

Q: In which year was the drink Horlicks first available?
A: 1883

Q: In which year did the first American bank robbery take place?
A: 1883

Q: In which year did work begin on the building of the Forth railway bridge?
A: 1883

Q: In which year did the Orient Express make its first journey from Paris to Constantinople?
A: 1883

Q: In which year was powdered milk patented?
A: 1884

Q: In which year was the Co-op started in Rochdale?
A: 1884

Q: In which year was the steam turbine invented?
A: 1884

Q: In which year was Tate and Lyle golden syrup first made?
A: 1885

Q: In which year did the world's first cafeteria open in New York?
A: 1885

Q: In which year was the first American skyscraper completed?
A: 1885

Q: In which year was the gas mantle invented?
A: 1885

Q: In which year was the complete revised version of the Bible published?
A: 1885

Q: In which year was Coca Cola first available in America?
A: 1886

Q: In which year did the last British convict ship sail to Australia?
A: 1886

Q: In which year did the Times become the first newspaper to institute a

classified personal column?
A: 1886

Q: In which year was the Statue of Liberty inaugurated?
A: 1886

Q: In which year was a sword last used in the Royal Navy in a battle afloat?
A: 1887

Q: In which year did Paris and Brussels become the first cities to be linked by telephone?
A: 1887

Q: In which year did the world's first motor race take place?
A: 1887

Q: In which year was the first recorded sale of a manufactured motor car to Emile Roger of Paris who bought a petrol driven Benz?
A: 1888

Q: In which year did the Eiffel Tower open?
A: 1889

Q: In which year was the world's first guided torpedo introduced ?
A: 1890

Q: In which year was the Forth railway bridge opened?
A: 1890

Q: In which year was the Battle of Wounded Knee?
A: 1890

Q: In which year did the first oil tanker have its engines in its stern?
A: 1890

Q: In which year was London's underground electrified?
A: 1890

Q: In which year were goal nets first used?
A: 1891

Q: In which year were travellers' cheques introduced?
A: 1891

Q: In which year was the detachable pneumatic tyre for bicycles first available?
A: 1891

Q: In which year was the Manchester Ship Canal opened?
A: 1893

Q: In which year was the world's first speedboat built in America?
A: 1893 (speed 9mph)

Q: In which year was London's Tower Bridge opened?
A: 1894

Q: In which year was the first disposable razor blade available?
A: 1895

Q: In which year were electric Christmas tree lights first used?
A: 1895

Q: In which year was the detachable pneumatic tyre for cars first available?
A: 1895

Q: In which year was the zip fastener patented?
A: 1896

Q: In which year did Pathe start making newsreels?
A: 1896

Q: In which year did the Glasgow underground open?
A: 1896

Q: In which year was the first steam driven quadruple expansion engine available?
A: 1897

Q: In which year was heroin invented?
A: 1898

Q: In which year did America go to war by sea for the first time?
A: 1898

Q: In which year was H P sauce first available?
A: 1899

Q: In which year was Paxo stuffing first availabl?
A: 1900

Q: In which year was the world's first tape recorder, the Telegraphone, invented?
A: 1900

Q: In which year was the escalator first demonstrated?
A: 1900

Q: In which year was the paper clip invented ?
A: 1900

Q: In which year was Coca Cola first available in Britain?
A: 1900

Q: In which year was the word brunch first used?
A: 1900

Q: In which year was aspirin first made available?
A: 1900

Q: In which year did the first issue of the Daily Express appear?
A: 1900

Q: In which year did Marconi demonstrate wireless communication?
A: 1901

Q: In which year was oil first discovered in Texas?
A: 1901

Q: In which year was instant coffee first available?
A: 1901

Q: In which year was Britain's first submarine commissioned?

A: 1901

Q: In which year were blood groups first classified?
A: 1901

Q: In which year was oil discovered in Texas?
A: 1901

Q: In which year was the world's first finger print file installed at New Scotland Yard?
A: 1901

Q: In which year were gramophone records first available?
A: 1901

Q: In which year was Iron Brew invented?
A: 1901

Q: In which year was the safety razor patented?
A: 1901

Q: In which year was the first transatlantic wireless message sent?
A: 1901

Q: In which year was air conditioning first demonstrated?
A: 1902

Q: In which year was the term curriculum vitae first used?
A: 1902

Q: In which year was the word electronic first used?
A: 1902

Q: In which year was the first parcel mail sent from Britain to America?
A: 1902

Q: In which year was the first direct commercial shipment of bananas into Britain?
A: 1902

Q: In which year was Marmite first made available?

A: 1902

Q: In which year was a diesel engine first fitted in a ship?
A: 1902

Q: In which year did the first small internal combustion engined ship cross the Atlantic?
A: 1902

Q: In which year did the Tour de France first take place?
A: 1903

Q: In which year was the first western film shown?
A: 1903

Q: In which year were the first motion pictures available?
A: 1903

Q: In which year was the first successful cataract operation?
A: 1903

Q: In which year were cars first required to be registered?
A: 1903

Q: In which year was cocaine taken out of Coca Cola?
A: 1903

Q: In which year were experiments with radar carried out?
A: 1903

Q: In which year was radar invented?
A: 1904

Q: In which year were teabags invented?
A: 1904

Q: In which year was the wrist watch invented?
A: 1904

Q: In which year was the first book of postage stamps available?
A: 1904

Q: In which year did the first main-line electric train in the UK run between Liverpool and Southport?
A: 1904

Q: In which year were intelligence tests invented?
A: 1905

Q: In which year was Rolls Royce founded?
A: 1906

Q: In which year was the S O S signal established?
A: 1906

Q: In which year were turbines first fitted in a ship?
A: 1906

Q: In which year did the submarine U1 enter the German Navy?
A: 1906

Q: In which year was the first Boy Scout camp held?
A: 1907

Q: In which year was the photocopier first marketed?
A: 1907

Q: In which year did taxi cab meters first appear in London's taxis?
A: 1907

Q: In which year was chemotherapy invented?
A: 1907

Q: In which year did the world's first helicopter flight take place?
A: 1907

Q: In which year was the Territorial Army founded?
A: 1908

Q: In which year was cellophane invented?
A: 1908

Q: In which year was the first payment of old age pensions in Britain made?
A: 1909

Q: In which year did Ernest Shackleton discover the magnetic South Pole?
A: 1909

Q: In which year was plastic invented?
A: 1909

Q: In which year was the North Pole first reached?
A: 1909

Q: In which year was the SOS distress signal first used at sea?
A: 1909

Q: In which year was work started on building the Titanic?
A: 1909

Q: In which year was drambuie first produced?
A: 1909

Q: In which year were x-rays first used?
A: 1910

Q: In which year were the first British pilots licences granted?
A: 1910

Q: In which year did a seaplane first fly?
A: 1910

Q: In which year was the first film made in Hollywood?
A: 1910

Q: In which year were the first steam powered fire fighting pumps available?
A: 1910

Q: In which year was a car driven on Antarctica for the first time?
A: 1911

Q: In which year were tungsten light bulbs invented ?
A: 1911

Q: In which year was the Titanic launched?
A: 1911

Q: In which year was the word vitamin first used?
A: 1911

Q: In which year was the first air mail carried?
A: 1911

Q: In which year were escalators first used on London's underground?
A: 1911

Q: In which year was the first parachute jump from an aeroplane?
A: 1912

Q: In which year was sickness benefit introduced in Britain?
A: 1912

Q: In what year was unemployment benefit introduced in Britain?
A: 1912

Q: In which year did the Titanic sink?
A: 1912

Q: In which year was a heart attack in a living person first diagnosed?
A: 1912

Q: In which year was the electric cooker invented?
A: 1912

Q: In which year was the first neon advertising sign?
A: 1912

Q: In which year did the first person loop the loop in an aeroplane?
A: 1913

Q: In which year did the Panama canal open?
A: 1914

Q: In which year was the first ever Victoria Cross awarded?
A: 1914

Q: In which year was the first ship sunk by a U-Boat?
A: 1914

Q: In which year did the first all metal aeroplane fly?
A: 1915

Q: In which year were passports invented?
A: 1915

Q: In which year was poison gas used for the first time?
A: 1915

Q: In which year was a machine gun first able to fire through a spinning propeller on an aeroplane?
A: 1915

Q: In which year did tanks go into battle for the first time?
A: 1916

Q: In which year was the Boeing Aircraft Company founded?
A: 1916

Q: In which year did the Russian Revolution start ?
A: 1917

Q: In which year was the Tower of London first bombed from the air?
A: 1917

Q: In which year was Moscow declared the new capital of Russia?
A: 1918

Q: In which year did the Royal Naval Air Service and the Royal Flying Corps merge to become the Royal Air Force?
A: 1918

Q: In which year did Britain get its first purpose built aircraft carrier?
A: 1918

Q: In which year did the R34 airship make the first air return crossing of the Atlantic Ocean?
A: 1919

Q: In which year did KLM establish the world's first airline?
A: 1919

Q: In which year was the Nazi Party founded?
A: 1919

Q: In which year was prohibition introduced in America?
A: 1920

Q: In which year was the original music sythesiser invented?
A: 1920

Q: In which year did the first police motor cycle patrols go on duty in London?
A: 1921

Q: In which year did America get its first aircraft carrier?
A: 1922

Q: In which year were the first radio commercials broadcast?
A: 1922

Q: In which year was the tomb of Tutankhamun discovered?
A: 1922

Q: In which year did the BBC start transmitting?
A: 1922

Q: In which year was television invented?
A: 1923

Q: In which year was the automotive diesel engine first available?
A: 1923

Q: In which year did the Flying Scotsman locomotive begin a service between Scotland and England?
A: 1923

Q: In which year was the first book of crosswords published?
A: 1924

Q: In which year was Happy Birthday to You first published by Clayton F. Summy?
A: 1924

Q: In which year did frozen food first become available?
A: 1924

Q: In which year were the pips or time signals from Greenwich Observatory first heard?
A: 1924

Q: In which year was the gas chamber used for the first time as a form of execution?
A: 1924

Q: In which year was the gramophone with the ability to change records automatically first available in Britain?
A: 1924

Q: In which year did the name Tesco first appear?
A: 1924

Q: In which year were quantum mechanics established?
A: 1925

Q: In which year was the first in-flight movie shown?
A: 1925

Q: In which year was Scotch sticky tape first available?
A: 1925

Q: In which year was the condensing microphone invented which improved recorded music?
A: 1925

Q: In which year was the first commercially successful 35mm camera, the Leica 1A available?
A: 1925

Q: In which year was the first liquid fuelled rocket launched?
A: 1926

Q: In which year was Britain's first set of traffic lights installed at Piccadilly Circus?
A: 1926

Q: In which year was the first flight over the North Pole?
A: 1926

Q: In which year were waxed paper bags invented?
A: 1926

Q: In which year was the dial thermostat invented?
A: 1926

Q: In which year was the first parachute jump from a Swedish aeroplane?
A: 1926

Q: In which year was the petrol driven chain saw first available?
A: 1926

Q: In which year was the first trans-Atlantic telephone call made?
A: 1927

Q: In which year did electricity pylons first appear in the countryside?
A: 1927

Q: In which year did the lance cease to be an official weapon in the British Army?
A: 1927

Q: In which year was cannabis declared illegal in Britain?
A: 1928

Q: In which year were antibiotics first developed?
A: 1928

Q: In which year was Alcatraz prison converted to a military prison?
A: 1928

Q: In which year was the first cartoon film shown with synchronised sound?
A: 1928

Q: In which year did the Red Ensign last fly on a square rigged ship?
A: 1929

Q: In which year was the first flight over the South Pole?

A: 1929

Q: In which year did the R101 airship make its maiden voyage?
A: 1929

Q: In which year was the Scammel Scarb, Britain"s first and only three wheeled lorry. first mad?e
A: 1929

Q: In which year did (Sir) Frank Whittle poineer the jet aircraft engine?
A: 1929

Q: In which year was the analog computer or differential analyser invented?
A: 1930

Q: In which year did Radio Luxembourg start broadcasting?
A: 1930

Q: In which year was wrapped sliced bread first available?
A: 1930

Q: In which year was the Star Spangled Banner adopted as the American national anthem?
A: 1931

Q: In which year were Seagull outboard engines first manufactured?
A: 1931

Q: In which year was the highway code introduced ?
A: 1931

Q: In which year was Santa Claus first portrayed as we know him today?
A: 1931

Q: In which year did a speedboat first travel at 100 mph on water?
A: 1931

Q: In which year was the first colour cartoon shown?
A: 1932

Q: In which year did Malcolm Campbell set a new world land speed record of

254 mph?
A: 1932

Q: In which year did book tokens first go on sale?
A: 1932

Q: In which year was prohibition abolished in America?
A: 1932

Q: In which year was Saudi Arabia established?
A: 1932

Q: In which year was the atom first split?
A: 1932

Q: In which year was Alcatraz prison opened for civil prisoners?
A: 1933

Q: In which year did the Catalina flying boat first fly?
A: 1935

Q: In which year was the driving test made compulsory in Britain?
A: 1935

Q: In which year was the Glasgow underground electrified?
A: 1935

Q: In which year did canned beer go on sale for the first time?
A: 1935

Q: In which year was the iron lung introduced for polio suffers?
A: 1935

Q: In which year was the 30 mph speed limit introduced in built up areas in Britain?
A: 1935

Q: In which year did the Swallow Sidecar Company launch the Jaguar car?
A: 1935

Q: In which year was the first Penguin paperback book published?

A: 1935

Q: In which year did the Hawker Hurricane first fly?
A: 1935

Q: In which year was Nestles Milky Bar introduced?
A: 1936

Q: In which year did the Spitfire first fly ?
A: 1936

Q: In which year did the Spanish Civil War start?
A: 1936

Q: In which year did the world's first successful helicopter fly?
A: 1936

Q: In which year was Spam launched by the Hormel Company ?
A: 1937

Q: In which year was Snow White and the Seven Dwarfs first shown?
A: 1937

Q: In which year was the world's first purpose built aircraft carrier built?
A: 1937

Q: In which year did the BBC make its first television outside broadcast?
A: 1937

Q: In which year was the 999 emergency number launched?
A: 1937

Q: In which year did the old threepenny bit come into circulation?
A: 1937

Q: In which year was the first Christmas stamp issued?
A: 1937

Q: In which year did the first nylon toothbrush go on sale?
A: 1938

Q: In which year was the tumble dryer patented in America?
A: 1938

Q: In which year was the first commercially successful instant coffee produced?
A: 1938

Q: In which year did Ivor Sikorsky make his first successful tethered flight in his helicopter prototype?
A: 1939

Q: In which year did the last public guillotining take place in France?
A: 1939

Q: In which year did Germany fly its first jet engined combat fighter?
A: 1939

Q: In which year was Pinocchio premiered?
A: 1940

Q: In which year did the Heikel HE 176, the world's first rocket powered aircraft, first fly?
A: 1939

Q: In which year was penicillin first available?
A: 1940

Q: In which year were metal strips introduced into the Bank of England's £1 notes?
A: 1940

Q: In which year did the Queen Elizabeth make her maiden voyage to New York?
A: 1940

Q: In which year did work start on building the Pentagon?
A: 1941

Q: In which year did Britain's first jet propelled aircraft fly for the first time?
A: 1941

Q: In which year was the first national fire service set up in Britain?
A: 1941

Q: In which year was radar first used in naval gunnery action?
A: 1941

Q: In which year was radar first able to detect a submarine on the surface?
A: 1942

Q: In which year was the world's first standard designed oil tanker C10?
available
A: 1942

Q: In which year were searchlights first fitted on the underside of an aircraft?
A: 1942
0
Q: In which year did the rationing of sweets begin in Britain?
A: 1942

Q: In which year was the first known sell-by date used on a food product?
A: 1942

Q: In which year was the world's first nuclear reaction?
A: 1942

Q: In which year did the famous Dambuster's raid take place?
A: 1943

Q: In which year was LSD first synthesized?
A: 1943

Q: In which year was the first electric driven torpedo introduced into the
American Navy?
A: 1943

Q: In which year was the Pentagon completed?
A: 1943

Q: In which year was the aqualung successfully tested?
A: 1943

Q: In which year did the world's first jet fighter, the Meteor, enter service with the RAF?
A: 1944

Q: In which year did the world's first working computer go on line?
A: 1944

Q: In which year did the first V2 rockets land on London?
A: 1944

Q: In which year did the pre-fab, the world's first prefabricated home, go on show?
A: 1944

Q: In which year did the first rescue by helicopter take place?
A: 1944

Q: In which year was the M52 the first British powered jet aircraft to fly?
A: 1945

Q: In what year was the first atom bomb tested?
A: 1945

Q: In which year was the International Monetary fund (IFM) established?
A: 1945

Q: In which year was the world's greatest maritime disaster?
A: 1945

Q: In which year did Saab make their first car?
A: 1945

Q: In which year was the Royal Military Academy at Sandhurst founded?
A: 1946

Q: In which year did London's Heathrow airport open for passengers?
A: 1946

Q: In which year was the expression Ground Zero first seen in print?
A: 1946

Q: In which year was the first airborne ejection seat tested?
A: 1946

Q: In which year did the world's first swept-back wing aircraft fly?
A: 1946

Q: In which year was the first television soap opera broadcast on American television?
A: 1947

Q: In which year did Iron Brew change its name to Iron Bru?
A: 1947

Q: In which year was the first missile launched from a submarine?
A: 1947

Q: In which year did New Zealand become independent?
A: 1947

Q: In which year did an aircraft first break the sound barrier?
A: 1947

Q: In which year was the first Presidential Address by an American President on television?
A: 1947

Q: In which year was the photocopier as is known now invented?
A: 1948

Q: In which year was the transistor invented?
A: 1948

Q: In which year did jam come off the rationing list of WW2?
A: 1948

Q: In which year did bread come off the rationing list of WW2?
A: 1948

Q: In which year did the DeHavilland Comet, the world's first jet powered airliner, make its maiden flight?
A: 1949

Q: In which year was the world's first commercially available computer invented?
A: 1951

Q: In which year were the first fare paying passengers carried on the world's first jet airliner the Comet?
A: 1952

Q: In which year was the video recorder first demonstrated?
A: 1952

Q: In which year was the world's first experimental nuclear powered aircraft ordered?
A: 1952

Q: In which year was the first hydrogen bomb exploded?
A: 1952

Q: In which year were identity cards abolished in Britain?
A: 1952

Q: In which year was the first British hit parade published?
A: 1952

Q: In which year was the first nuclear guided missile fired from a submarine?
A: 1952

Q: In which year were the first external pacemakers fitted?
A: 1952

Q: In which year was the first double crossing of the Atlantic Ocean in the same day?
A: 1952

Q: What year did the rationing of sweets end in Britain?
A: 1953

Q: In which year was cinemascope first available?
A: 1953

Q: In which year was the Royal Yacht Britannia launched?

A: 1953

Q: In which year was Britain's first soap opera transmitted?
A: 1954

Q: In which year was the TV dinner first available?
A: 1954

Q: In which year did rationing end in Britain?
A: 1954

Q: In which year were the first non-stick cooking utensils first available?
A: 1955

Q: In which year did ITV start broadcasting?
A: 1955

Q: In which year did the first McDonald's hamburger store open?
A: 1955

Q: In which year did Russia officially end its war with Germany?
A: 1955

Q: In which year was the USS(N) Nautilus the world's first nuclear submarine launched?
A: 1955

Q: In which year did the Massey Harris company build in Scotland the first combine harvester in Britain?
A: 1955

Q: In which year was a diamond first artificially produced?
A: 1955

Q: In which year did the (N) B36 Corsair fly with a working, though not connected, nuclear reactor aboard?
A: 1955

Q: In which year was the television remote control first available?
A: 1956

Q: In which year did tramcars stop running in Edinburgh?
A: 1956

Q: In which year were Premium Bonds introduced?
A: 1956

Q: In which year did British Rail abolish its third class carriages?
A: 1956

Q: In which year was the European song contest first staged?
A: 1956

Q: In which year was the first underwater ballistic missile fired?
A: 1956

Q: In which year were the white £5 pound notes replaced by the smaller blue ones?
A: 1957

Q: In which year did the British SR53, the world's first rocket-jet powered fighter, first fly?
A: 1957

Q: In which year did the USSR launch Sputnik One and Two, the first earth satellites?
A: 1957

Q: In which year was the first living creature launched into space?
A: 1957

Q: In which year did K3, Russia's first nuclear submarine, enter service?
A: 1957

Q: In which year was the last flight of the (N) B36 nuclear bomber?
A: 1957

Q: In which year was the Treaty of Rome set out establishing the six member states of the original 'Ecconomic Community'?
A: 1957

Q: In which year was the first American satellite, the Explorer, launched?

A: 1958

Q: In which year was the first internal pacemaker fitted?
A: 1958

Q: In which year was the last steam locomotive made at Crewe?
A: 1958

Q: In which year was the tumble dryer first available in Britain?
A: 1958

Q: In which year did the first transatlantic jet passenger service begin?
A: 1958

Q: In which year did the SR53, the world's first rocket-jet powered fighter, go supersonic for the first time?
A: 1958

Q: In which year was the silicon chip invented?
A: 1958

Q: In which year were post codes introduced into Britain?
A: 1959

Q: In which year did the first Mini roll off the production line?
A: 1959

Q: In which year did Alaska become the 49th State of America?
A: 1959

Q: In which year was the first Polaris Missile carrying submarine?
commissioned
A: 1959

Q: In which year did the first section of the M1, Britain's first motorway, open between London and Birmingham?
A: 1959

Q: In which year was the world's first nuclear powered submarine launched?
A: 1960

Q: In which year did national service end in Britain?
A: 1960

Q: In which year was the first implanted pacemaker fitted?
A: 1960

Q: In which year did Rio de Janeiro cease to be the capital of Brazil?
A: 1960

Q: In which year was Britain's first nuclear submarine launched?
A: 1960

Q: In which year was the word Jeans used in advertising for the first time?
A: 1960

Q: In which year did the farthing cease to be legal tender in Britain?
A: 1960

Q: In which year did the USS(N) George Washington launch the first polaris missile from under the water?
A: 1960

Q: In which year was the first man in space?
A: 1961

Q: In which year was the Berlin Wall built between East and West Germany?
A: 1961

Q: In which year was the first rocket powered aircraft ejection seat tested?
A: 1961

Q: In which year was the first suspected criminal identified using an identi-kit picture?
A: 1961

Q: In which year was the nuclear aircraft programme abandoned?
A: 1961

Q: In which year did Yuri Gagarin become the first man in space?
A: 1961

Q: In which year did the last steam train run on the London underground?
A: 1961 (central line)

Q: In which year were the first TV pictures relayed by satellite?
A: 1962

Q: In which year was the football coupons pool panel introduced?
A: 1963

Q: In which year was the cassette tape first available, creating the world's first portable music machine?
A: 1963

Q: In which year did Alcatraz prison in San Francisco Bay close?
A: 1963

Q: In which year was the first television instant re-replay?
A: 1963

Q: In which year was the first American aircraft fitted with both rocket and jet engines?
A: 1963

Q: In which year was home kidney dialysis first available?
A: 1964

Q: In which year were the polaris carrying submarines introduced in Britain?
A: 1964

Q: In which year was the Moog music synthesiser invented?
A: 1964

Q: In which year was the £10 note reintroduced for the first time since the war?
A: 1964

Q: In which year did the first space walk take place?
A: 1965

Q: In which year was the 70mph speed limit on British roads introduced?
A: 1965

Q: In which year was cigarette advertising banned in Britain?
A: 1965

Q: In which year was packet switching, essential for the internet, first available?
A: 1965

Q: In which year was the first whole earth viewing weather satellite put into orbit?
A: 1966

Q: In which year were Christmas stamps first issued in Britain?
A: 1966

Q: In which year was the breathalyser used on motorists for the first time?
A: 1967

Q: In which year was North Sea gas first piped ashore near Durham?
A: 1967

Q: In which year were decimal coins first issued in Britain?
A: 1968

Q: In which year did the world's first supersonic jet airliner, the Soviet T-144, first fly?
A: 1968

Q: In which year did the Trades Description Act come into force?
A: 1968

Q: In which year were steam locomotives withdrawn from service?
A: 1968

Q: In which year did man first land on the moon?
A: 1969

Q: In which year did Concorde fly for the first time?
A: 1969

Q: In which year was the first decimal coin circulated in Britain?
A: 1969

Q: In which year did Britain abolish the death penalty ?
A: 1969

Q: In which year were global communications first established?
A: 1969

Q: In which year did the 50p coin go into circulation?
A: 1969

Q: In which year were watches with LCD displays first available?
A: 1970

Q: In which year were the World Trade Centre Towers completed?
A: 1970

Q: In which year was the £20 note reintroduced for the first time since the war?
A: 1970

Q: In which year were decimal postage stamps first issued for sale in Britain?
A: 1970

Q: In which year was a computer floppy disc first available?
A: 1970

Q: In which year were compact discs invented?
A: 1970

Q: In which year did Pathe stop making newsreels?
A: 1970

Q: In which year was the CAT scan first available?
A: 1971

Q: In which year was decimal currency introduced into Britain?
A: 1971

Q: In which year did Rolls Royce become bankrupt?
A: 1971

Q: In which year was the first E mail sent?
A: 1971

Q: In which year was the microprocessor invented?
A: 1971

Q: In which year were pit ponies last used down mines?
A: 1972

Q: In which year was the pocket calculator first available in Britain?
A: 1972

Q: In which year did Britain join the EEC?
A: 1972

Q: In which year did the last manned flights to the moon take place?
A: 1972

Q: In which year were cars fitted with air bags first available in Britain?
A: 1973

Q: In which year were polar bears declared an endangered species?
A: 1973

Q: In which year did the Royal Navy lose its rum ration?
A: 1973

Q: In which year did Britain formally enter the common market?
A: 1973

Q: In which year did the Royal Navy stop using hammocks?
A: 1973

Q: In which year was the mobile phone first available?
A: 1973

Q: In which year was value added tax (vat) introduced in Britain?
A: 1973

Q: In which year was the first colour photocopier available?
A: 1973

Q: In which year did bar codes first appear on food products?
A: 1974

Q: In which year did the BBC's Ceefax teletext service begin?
A: 1974

Q: In which year were plastic disposable razors introduced in Britain?
A: 1974

Q: In which year was the world's first video game available?
A: 1974

Q: In which year was the home computer first available in Britain?
A: 1975

Q: In which year did the first commercial North Sea oil flow ashore?
A: 1975

Q: In which year did the last recorded case of smallpox in the world occur?
A: 1975

Q: In which year were VHS and BETAMAX video recorders first available in Britain?
A: 1976

Q: In which year did Concorde fly for the first time commercially?
A: 1976

Q: In which year was the Ebola or Green Monkey virus first identified?
A: 1976

Q: In which year did the maiden flight of the prototype space shuttle take place?
A: 1977

Q: In which year was the Apple11, the first mass produced personal computer, launched?
A: 1977

Q: In which year was the guillotine last used?
A: 1977

Q: In which year was the European Monetary System established as the start of the road to the Euro?
A: 1979

Q: In which year did Xerox researchers demonstrate the first point and click mouse to Apple engineers?
A: 1979

Q: In which year did the Jersey Flower Post start?
A: 1980

Q: In which year were the Sony Walkman and the ghetto blaster first available in Britain?
A: 1980

Q: In which year did the sixpence cease to be legal tender?
A: 1980

Q: In which year did Radio Caroline sink?
A: 1980

Q: In which year did France abolish the guillotine?
A: 1981

Q: In which year was the £50 note introduced?
A: 1981

Q: In which year did garages start selling petrol by the litre rather than the gallon?
A: 1981

Q: In which year did the U. S. Columbia space shuttle make its first mission?
A: 1981

Q: In which year was the London marathon first run?
A: 1981

Q: In which year did the space shuttle make its first flight?
A: 1981

Q: In which year did the Falklands war start?
A: 1982

Q: In which year was video keyhole surgery first available in Britain?
A: 1982

Q: In which year was Channel 4 launched?
A: 1982

Q: In which year were £1 coins introduced into Britain?
A: 1983

Q: In which year did Chatham Dockyard close?
A: 1983

Q: In which year was the wearing of front seat belts made compulsory in Britain?
A: 1983

Q: In which year was synthetic insulin for use in humans made available in Britain?
A: 1983

Q: In which year was the first televised maximum snooker break?
A: 1983 (Cliff Thorborn)

Q: In which year was the first cordless telephone capable of operating up to 600feet from its base introduced?
A: 1983

Q: In which year was the Data Protection Act introduced?
A: 1984

Q: In which year was the BMX bicycle first available?
A: 1984

Q: In which year was the aids virus first discovered?
A: 1984

Q: In which year was Sir Clive Sinclair's C5 electric car launched?
A: 1985

Q: In which year was the wreckage of the Titanic found?
A: 1985

Q: In which year was the first registered dot com?
A: 1985

Q: In which year was the first UK conviction using DNA as evidene?
A: 1986

Q: In which year was the lap top computer first available in Britain?
A: 1986

Q: In which year did the Mir space station first go into orbit round the earth?
A: 1986

Q: In which year was the first attempt to reach the Titanic by submarine mad?e
A: 1986

Q: In which year did the Bank of England £1 pound note cease to be legal tender?
A: 1988

Q: In which year were the World's Superbike Championships first held?
A: 1988

Q: In which year did a toaster become the first machine to be controlled over the internet?
A: 1989

Q: In which year was the internet started?
A: 1989

Q: In which year was the Berlin wall built between East and West Germany demolished?
A: 1989

Q: In which year did the internet become established?
A: 1989

Q: In which year was the Exxon Valdez oil tanker spillage?
A: 1989

Q: In which year was the widget first introduced?
A: 1989

Q: In which year was the Hubble space telescope launched?
A: 1990

Q: In which year did the Desert Storm war against Iraq begin?
A: 1990

Q: In which year was the first internet browser established?
A: 1991

Q: In which year was British Rail privatised?
A: 1991

Q: In which year did Yugoslavia cease to be one nation?
A: 1992

Q: In which year was the £2 pound coin first issued?
A: 1992

Q: In which year was the poll tax abolished?
A: 1992

Q: In which year was the first mobile phone text message?
A: 1992

Q: In which year was Hurricane Andrew the most expensive in damage ever recorded?
A: 1992

Q: In which year did the Ravenscraig steel plant near Glasgow shut down?
A: 1992

Q: In which year were global positioning satellites first put into service?
A: 1993

Q: In which year were the first satellite-linked cellular phones available?
A: 1993

Q: In which year did the oil tanker Braer run aground in the Shetland Isles?
A: 1993

Q: In which year did the Treaty of Maastricht come into force creating the European Union with a common social policy?
A: 1993

Q: In which year were the first genetically modified tomatoes available?
A: 1994

Q: In which year did the channel tunnel open?
A: 1994

Q: In which year was the UK lottery launched?
A: 1994

Q: In which year was the first entirely computer-generated feature film?
A: 1995

Q: In which year did the Skye Bridge open?
A: 1995

Q: In which year were the first deep field photographs of our universe?
A: 1996

Q: In which year was Dolly the sheep, the first cloned mammal, born?
A: 1996

Q: In which year was the Tory wipe out in Scotland?
A: 1997

Q: In which year was the Treaty of Amsterdam which allowed for the enlargement of the EU?
A: 1997

Q: In which year was the Royal Yacht Britannia de-commissioned?
A: 1997

Q: In which year were the Petrona Towers completed?
A: 1997

Q: In which year was Hong Kong handed back to the Chinese?
A: 1997

Q: In which year was the former Royal Yacht Britannia opened as a tourist attraction?
A: 1998

Q: In which year was Scotland's Parliament reconvened after adjournment on March 25 1707?
A: 1999

Q: In which year was the world's first satellite launch from a ship at sea?
A: 1999

Q: In which year did the Euro become the currency of the eleven member states of the EU?
A: 1999

Q: In which year did the Terrorism Act become law in Britain?
A: 2000

Q: In which year was the Treaty of Nice which was the start of the road to a EU constitution?
A: 2000

Q: In which year were the new style car index number plates introduced in Britain?
A: 2001

Q: In which year was the Euro introduced?
A: 2002

Q: In which year did the Falkirk Wheel open?
A: 2002

Q: In which year did the British Raleigh bicycle company cease UK production?
A: 2002

Q: In which year did BBC3 start?
A: 2003

Q: In which year did the Challenger Space Shuttle explode on re-entry?
A: 2003

Q: In which year did the old style Volkswagen Beetle cease production?
A: 2003

Q: In which year were mobile phones with cameras first available?
A: 2003

Q: In which year did the Royal Mail,s travelling post office stop running between Glasgow and Cardiff?
A: 2003

Q: In which year was the mobile phone push to talk (P2T) first available in Britain?
A: 2003

Q: In which year was the channel first crossed by unpowered flight?
A: 2003

Q: In which year did Concorde fly commercially for the last time?
A: 2003

Q: In which year did China first put a man in space?
A: 2003

Q: In which year did the British space probe Beagle2 land on Mars?
A: 2003

Q: In which year did the temperature exceed 100 degrees F for the first time in recorded history in Britain?
A: 2003

Q: In which year did Pioneer10 become the first spacecraft to leave the solar system?
A: 2003

Q: In which year was the QE 2 floated out of the drydock for the first time?
A: 2003

Q: In which year did the American Spirit Rover land on Mars?
A: 2004

Q: In which year did the railway travelling post offices stop?
A: 2004

Q: In which year did the Queen Mary 2 enter service?
A: 2004

Q: In which year did the American space probe Pioneer land on Mars?
A: 2004

Q: In which year did the Royal Navy stop using swords at a court martial?
A: 2004

Q: In which year was the first known hurricane in the South Atlantic Ocean recorded?
A: 2004

Q: In which year was the Brussels Summit to finalise the EU constitution?
A: 2004

Q: In which year did the QE2 make its final Atlantic crossing as Cunard's flagship?
A: 2004

Q: In which year was the telephone pager service discontinued?
A: 2004